Ready For Absolutely Nothing

SUSANNAH CONSTANTINE

PENGUIN BOOKS

PENGUIN BOOKS

UK | USA | Canada | Ireland | Australia
India | New Zealand | South Africa

Penguin Books is part of the Penguin Random House group of companies
whose addresses can be found at global.penguinrandomhouse.com

First published by Penguin Michael Joseph 2022
Published in Penguin Books 2023

001

Typeset by Jouve (UK), Milton Keynes
Printed and bound in Great Britain by Clays Ltd, Elcograf S.p.A.

The authorized representative in the EEA is Penguin Random House Ireland,
Morrison Chambers, 32 Nassau Street, Dublin D02 YH68

A CIP catalogue record for this book is available from the British Library

ISBN: 978–0–241–55521–7

To Smell

Lazy Susan.

Act One

A Matter of Chance

November 3rd 1991, it turns out, was a pivotal moment. Unbeknown to me I was about to meet the man who would go on to become my husband, but, on the night in question, I was forty days and forty nights into a prolonged period of humiliation. I was in no mood for small talk.

El Tel's shoot in what appears to be the Linton Travel Tavern function room.

I'd been happily bonking Dolph Lundgren for a couple of months, but he'd now ghosted me and was refusing to return my calls. It was incredibly annoying, particularly since I didn't even like him. I'd now have to get drunk in order to walk into Alan Aldridge's book party alone.

As an episode, this is a fairly good snapshot of my life. An anecdote about a rather ordinary woman who threw herself at the feet of a man in whose opinions she had absolutely no interest. Who never once thought to question the patriarchy that raised her or what it did to her self-respect; who drank her way through both a wide range of social events and self-esteem issues, collected and lovingly cared for over the previous thirty years.

It's an extraordinary story about some pretty ordinary truths.

All in all it was a night of highs and lows, but ultimately one that taught me never to give a Swede a blow-job if you don't think he'll recognise you with your clothes on ten years later in the queue for drinks at the premiere of *Miss Congeniality*. We live and learn.

The journey to the night in question was one I regarded as fairly mundane. I considered myself the archetypal girl-next-door. A lot happened *to* me but I was never the person at the centre of things. I was always someone else's plus-one. I know I brought something to the table that people liked, and I knew I could hold my own, but I was only ever along for the ride, never the one driving the bus. The great thing was, from where I was sitting at the back, I could see everything, and the view was incredible.

Meeting my husband that night and getting married was a watershed moment for a girl like me who'd been prepared other country person did between September and March: hunt and shoot. Anything we did in town, we did during the week. Even Wednesday late-night shopping in Knightsbridge allowed rich people to spend their money off-peak rather than with all the riff-raff on a Saturday.

When my parents were first married my mother kept house herself but by the time I was born, we'd acquired a Cockney to tidy up after us. Like Nelson, Peggy was blind in one eye, though much less heavily decorated. Her overall appearance was that of a dusty old doll in the window of a long-abandoned high-street shop. As she was only inclined to tidy what was instantly visible from her good eye, her performance as a cleaner was rather patchy. Whilst the left side of the house was reasonably presentable, the right did not bear close inspection by anyone who did not need glasses. Nevertheless, she was a key member of the small team of staff who ran Pelham Place – tidying bedrooms and washing up after our beans on toast. There was never a conversation about who would feed the proverbial cat or whether the milk would turn sour while we were away. There was always somebody watching over things while we were busy doing something 'more important'. How these people took care of their own lives was an issue I was not to consider until much later in life. Money gave my parents the luxury of being accountable for absolutely nothing and to absolutely no one, including me and my sister.

Annette was six years older and, as such, a source of pleasure and pain in equal measure. If she offered to brush my hair I'd eagerly accept, even though I knew it meant she'd begin just under my chin before dragging the bristles over my face – more often than not with a filthy dog brush. I was so devoted to her that when she was fitted with braces on her teeth, I wrapped picture wire around my own. Given our six-year age difference, Annette had a head start on me and our paths diverged completely. I may as well have been an only child. While she was off at school, I was left to sleep in my Silver Cross pram, unattended on the Yorkstone paving of our front garden. There were no fears about my being snatched as I had Kimmy, our Yorkshire terrier, to sit in the carriage with me *in loco parentis*. As I grew up I often found an animal to be a more reliable, readable source of loyalty and affection than the adults in my life. Kimmy was just the prototype.

There were no single mothers or abandoned shopping trolleys on our street. No dusty net curtains or dirty windows. Why would there be? Every home had staff to take care of those sorts of inconveniences. These unpalatable truths were simply swept away by hard-working men and women paid to maintain a comfortable distance between my parents and the realities of life beyond their immediate purview.

The elderly gentleman who lived next door would appear daily like a figurine on an Alpine weather house and doff his fedora as I played on my blanket. His emergence always meant the sun was out and he was ready for his morning stroll. He would be beautifully dressed in waistcoat, houndstooth trousers, jacket and pocket square, with lacquered cane and always some sort of scarf – paisley Kashmiri in the winter and patterned silk in the summer. Whatever the tweaks in his outfit, he always, always wore a hat, jauntily positioned a little bit forward and slightly to the left. To the untrained eye he looked exactly like a dapper Cecil Beaton. The fact that he was Cecil Beaton didn't become clear until I was apparently

The lovely man from number 8.

introduced to him in our drawing room at the age of five. The significance of his identity was still entirely lost on me – I just knew our lovely old neighbour had come to ask if he could take my mother's photograph. I watched her twirl in front of the bedroom mirror as she considered whether to wear her Gina Fratini or the Zandra Rhodes.

In my teens I became obsessed with one of Beaton's sitters – Mick Jagger – and the penny finally dropped. It was the nice man from number 8. The magnitude of Beaton's request came into sharp focus. He'd photographed many of the decade's greatest beauties but sadly not my mother. In the event, my father had refused to grant him permission. I never knew why but as I've come to understand the dynamics of their marriage better, I believe it was to do with control. My father was a collector and my mother his greatest and most valued acquisition, always carefully positioned in the best light so he could bathe in her reflected glory. He made sure she was never out of sight or handled by anyone who might truly covet her. So there is no Cecil Beaton portrait of my late mother hanging in my hall but, knowing her husband as she did, I doubt she would have ever seriously believed there would be.

Linda

Although my parents had two children, they had very little intention of handling either of us. Had we been aristocrats, my mother would have kept going until she'd produced a boy. With no title to consider, they were content to stop at two girls. Whilst I never doubted my parents loved me, theirs was a hands-off approach to child-rearing. Much of it was carried out by a third party and the first significant one of these was Linda.

Linda began as a 'just in case'; someone who gave my parents the freedom to do whatever they liked at the drop of a hat. A last-minute dinner invitation or tickets to *La Traviata* would never be turned down on account of the children, and the notion that we might accompany them anywhere socially during the week was utterly preposterous. From Monday to Friday, they functioned as a pair of childless socialites. Their parenting MO was one step on from the seen-and-not-heard ethos of the Victorians but it was a very, very tiny step – almost imperceptible to the naked eye. If we'd been middle class, we'd have been left alone in the back of a car with a bottle of Coke and the windows cracked open if the temperature passed 75. But we were rich, so we had Linda instead.

The modern belief that the world revolves around children would have been as revolutionary to my parents as the time Copernicus suggested we lived in a heliocentric universe. It took us nearly five hundred years to accept that theory – about half the time it would have taken my mum and dad to come to terms with the laws of modern parenting. There was a clearly defined line between where they were and weren't prepared to take their children and that line was drawn at any establishment with a children's menu.

My father travelled a huge amount on business – most often to the then uncharted waters of the Communist bloc. During the mid-60s, he was one of the first people to import and export goods from Russia. This was the height of the Cold War and his activities attracted the interest of both the Russian and the British intelligence services. His trips to Moscow were typically accompanied by a silent observer sitting somewhere behind a newspaper in the arrivals lounge at the airport. He was shadowed by the 'unintroduced' everywhere he went during his stay. As a precaution he'd always pack a spare bath plug to prevent the KGB from listening in to his conversations through the pipes in the bathroom. When it was the turn of his Russian trade partners to come to the UK, tensions were inevitably high and my father was adept at handling not just the trade end of his business but the paranoia that went with it.

One Thursday evening the Russian consul came for dinner at Pelham Place. I was duly presented before being whisked off by Linda for my bath, leaving my parents and their Commi friend to get on with dinner. Linda pretended not to mind when I squirted her with water from my empty Fairy Liquid

9

bottle. She was more annoyed when I extinguished the pilot light on the boiler above the bath with a far-reaching jet. For the next twenty minutes we were both slowly, silently, being poisoned by the leaking gas. Ever the professional, and sensitive to the delicate nature of the evening, Linda waited arguably too long before lifting my dead weight out of the bath to go downstairs for help. Appearing with an apparently lifeless child wrapped in a towel in the doorway of the dining room, Linda did nothing to calm British–Soviet relations. When she collapsed to the floor herself, things escalated quite quickly. My parents were less worried about Linda falling unconscious than convincing their guest we weren't in the midst of a political assassination attempt and the killer wasn't still at large in the house. It took my mother's well-honed hostessing skills and some very expensive dessert wine to convince him to stay for the remainder of the meal. I was sent to bed with some cough mixture and we all kept our fingers crossed Linda didn't die in the night.

Wherever my father went, my mother was by his side. He had a tag on the handle of his briefcase that said British Airways, First Class, because that was the one and only way he travelled. When we flew as a family, my sister and I sat in the back while our parents enjoyed a better life up front. If we were driving abroad, it was always my father at the wheel because my mother was too nervous to drive on the wrong side of the road. At home, it would be my mother or my father's chauffeur, Mrs Wilson, who drove. My dad was a brave man to opt for a Northern Irish driver in the 1980s, given the prevalence of car bombs, but Mrs Wilson was just that. At fourteen I assumed she was a fully paid-up member of the

IRA. This was largely because of her green uniform, which I interpreted as a covert signal to any passing sympathisers. Even if she *was* a political extremist, she was still a very careful driver and good company on a trip to the dentist. Every morning my mother would cook us all breakfast – bacon and tomatoes and a cup of tea with toast and marmalade – then Mrs Wilson would arrive at 9 a.m. to drive my father to work on Dover Street. Her wages weren't paid from my father's pocket, because that would be vulgar. A chauffeur provided by your firm was the only acceptable kind to have. Driving did not escape the unfathomable rules of snobbery, and cars that weren't German, cushions in the rear window, and hats worn by motorists were equally frowned upon.

In our house, returning with a present from your travels was an acceptable substitute for an absentee father. Dolls in national costume were a firm favourite and there was always a huge fanfare around the unveiling. My mother's performance as an advocate of this paternal policy was flawless: 'Look what Daddy's brought for you. Isn't he wonderful? He chose it specially.' The only thing I remember doing alone with my father was stargazing on our holidays in France. Before bedtime, we'd walk up the cobbled streets to the square at the highest point of the village and stare into the night. In my bare feet and nightdress, he taught me about Orion's belt and the handle on the saucepan. Even though I came to know the constellations as well as the lines on my middle-aged face, this ritual was something I never tired of. My father wasn't devoid of affection, but it was expressed on his terms. When it suited him. We knew he loved us but he only chose to show us when he had time.

This set-up didn't stem from my mother. My father's rules dictated their level of interaction with us. If she'd been married to someone else or in a different era she'd have been a very different wife and very different mother. She'd have been more available to indulge the love she had for us. As it was, my father had to be her first priority and we got in line behind him. I imagine the idea of her staying home with us would never have reached the discussion table and I think this must have broken her heart.

In the 1960s and '70s, the world of an 'important' man's home life wove seamlessly into his working one. If he didn't have the right house, silverware or wife, this could have a direct impact on his business reputation. Whilst commerce of the time was dominated by powerful men, their success or failure was often tied to the success or failure of their wives. If the soufflé didn't rise to the appropriate height, the contracts may not be signed either. The phrase 'a married woman' was key to my mother's generation and perfectly encapsulated her status as an owned object. Every morning at breakfast my father gave her a daily list of things to do. There were no questions asked. Their marriage centred around the needs and desires of my father and was defined by the social mores and customs of '60s Britain.

My mother was a corporate accessory, rolled out by my father on any important trip. In the same way that every upper-class businessman of note would own an Asprey briefcase or Smythson headed writing paper, he'd be all the more revered by foreign business associates for owning a really beautiful wife. My father knew this implicitly and never travelled without one. At that time, presentation of a wife was what passed for due diligence: validation you were the safe pair of hands you claimed to be. Single or, God forbid, gay, did not have the same ring as 'married with two children' in spite of the fact that many marriages would not have stood particularly close scrutiny. My parents' included.

Saying all this about my father makes him sound like a chauvinist monster. In fact, he was just a man living in the latter part of the twentieth century. Being a chauvinist was simply part of the job.

Their trips weren't just long weekends but often anything from two weeks to a month, and typically four or five times a year, so Linda's status as a 'just in case' was something of a euphemism. Had my sister and I been dogs, my father would have double-locked the front door and asked the neighbours to feed us once a day. As it was, he knew we'd scratch the furniture if left unattended for too long, so Linda was the equivalent of a professional dog-walker. Fortunately, I absolutely loved her.

At Pelham Place, my father, mother and older sister occupied the bedrooms on the third floor, while Linda and I slummed it below stairs in the servants' quarters. Having spent years juggling sleeping arrangements to accommodate anxious mothers in my own home, the fact I could not have been positioned any further from my own mother without actually sleeping outside does now strike me as darkly comic. Four floors down, entirely out of sight and earshot, seemed not to be an issue. From their perspective, they never left us alone; we never wanted for anything. We were always in the hands of someone loving and warm. It just wasn't them. In paying for others to love us, my parents successfully bought their own freedom. As a result, my nannies held the same position in my heart as my parents – a fact which never struck me as remarkable until now. Rather than finding this statement upsetting, I think my father would have seen it as confirmation that his plan had worked. Our emotional needs had been met. My mother was another matter: I know this arrangement was more a mark of the times than a proactive choice and I believe it was something that came back to haunt her in the years that followed.

When my parents were searching for domestic help, getting a reference wasn't a thing. Whether you were employing someone to take care of your children or your paperwork, the approach was the same. Word-of-mouth recommendations or inherited staff were the cornerstones of recruitment. I have no idea how Linda came to be our nanny, what she'd done before or where she came from. Like Mary Poppins she just arrived one day out of the blue. Prior to Linda, my downtime consisted of repeated examination of the latest issue of *Twinkle* and the occasional excursion to the corner shop for a quarter of pear drops. Linda's arrival opened up a side of things hitherto totally unexplored. It was as if the lights had been turned on when she entered my life.

Although I already had a big sister, by the time Linda turned up Annette had been shipped off to boarding school and I was living the life of an only child. From my perspective, Linda wasn't there to look after me, she was there to play with me, and my parents couldn't have picked anyone more exciting. I was besotted with her. My mother was glamorous but Linda was trendy and had a young person's energy which was electric to be around. She was as much an emblem of the modern world as my parents were of the past. My mother wore kick pleats and pearls and dressed for dinner, while Linda wore a crochet halterneck you could just about see her nipples through and ate her supper on her lap in front of the telly. I suppose I didn't recognise this for what it was at the time but, while my mother was beautiful, Linda was sexy and, even as a girl, this was totally intoxicating. I loved doing things with my parents in the countryside – it was a gentle, naive world and a place where I was younger than my years suggested. But in London, especially as I got older, Linda was the greatest ally a young girl could want.

On top of all that, she paid attention to me. She made me feel like I was the centre of her world. I never thought about the fact she was paid to do this, which tells you how good she was at her job. I bought into the whole magic show hook, line and sinker. I think Linda did love me but now realise that a live-in job, ten minutes' walk from the King's Road at the height of the swinging '60s was a pretty jammy coup for any twenty-two-year-old. Outings to the Natural History Museum dovetailed very neatly with a flying visit to Kensington Market. I felt like our days were designed around me, and Linda was able to incorporate a wide range of things on her bucket list. We both got something we wanted. Anyway, the alternative was three hours alone on an Etch A Sketch so there was never an argument from me. My school was fortuitously en route to Linda's personal Mecca and I sat patiently on a novelty toadstool in Biba's café while she tried out samples at the make-up counter. Linda and I were synchronicity personified and our relationship the very definition of symbiotic.

One of our favourite diversions was cappuccinos at Dino's

in South Kensington. In 1968 this was hands down the wildest, most exotic thing ever to have touched my lips. You'd be hard pressed now to find even the remotest of cafés without a babyccino on the menu, but at this point 'coffee' typically meant two spoons of Coffee-mate in a watery mug of Maxwell House. Filter coffee and an After Eight mint might be offered at a dinner party in middle-class circles, but it would be another fourteen years before the word 'barista' entered the lexicon. The only places to offer 'proper' coffee were foreign and sat within a three-mile radius of Soho. I liked to bastardise this rare commodity with a thick layer of white sugar poured ritualistically over the top of the froth before eating the drink with a long-handled teaspoon. A sort of poor man's crème brûlée. Thursday nights, however, were the highlight of our week, coinciding as they did with *Top of the Pops* on the black-and-white portable TV recently leased from Radio Rentals.

To my six-year-old eyes, Linda seemed to be well into her mid-forties, although by my calculations now she was closer to twenty-three. A redheaded replica of Dusty Springfield, her lashes were false, her lips frosted pink, her legs bare and her skirts never less than eighteen inches above the knee. She was the kind of girl whose going-out shoes came from Dolcis. Linda was never a hippy but gave a nod to the times in the decor of her bedroom. An Indian sarong hung over her bed like a canopy in a cheap brothel, a handknit blanket lay across a wicker chair, and a cast-off silk scarf of my mother's over the bedside lamp. The smell of joss sticks wafted gently into the small kitchenette of the basement corridor where she kept her Sugar Puffs and Snoopy mug.

Her hourglass figure was better suited to the pencil skirts

and tight-fitting mohair twinsets of the previous decade, when showing off shape without revealing skin drove trends in women's fashion. When Twiggy came along she threatened to fuck it all up for girls like Linda, but it didn't really matter. While fashion said flat chests looked better in a shift dress, men's taste in tits never changed. This was Linda's currency and she traded on it to the full extent. The Singer sewing machine in her bedroom ran up hotpants and A-line dresses to complement her PVC peaked cap and knee-high boots. Once she'd added a sheer mist of hairspray to the arrangement, you knew never to go near her with a naked flame.

All in all, Linda looked like a hooker and – as it transpired – she was.

Given that I was at school during the day and in the countryside every weekend, Linda had plenty of time to moonlight as a prostitute. She must have been wonderfully organised, because she managed to keep it under her hat until the day my parents returned unexpectedly from a business trip to find her and one of her regulars making good use of the drawing-room sofa. The first sign that something was amiss was an unfamiliar beige mac and highly polished shoes under the hall chair. A pair of horn-rimmed glasses sat with their arms neatly folded on the console table. There was no sign of a rush. This was clearly a visitor used to taking his time. Of course I was none the wiser but details of this (and other) arrangements trickled out over time. Howard, we learned, was a middle-management sort who worked at the Ilford branch of Bradford & Bingley, two levels up from a teller on the pay grade. He visited Linda on Mondays, Wednesdays and Fridays and came three times a week – provided stress didn't put him off his stroke. Although Howard was prone to sweating, he apparently brought his own towel and flannel. It was a well-rehearsed routine and an easily earned extra two pounds for Linda.

Despite her clandestine profession, my parents were extremely reluctant to let Linda go. She'd been happy to baby-sit at short notice and took minimal holiday so the final decision was a very close call. I think what pushed them over the edge was when I innocently mentioned I'd shared a bed with her and a 'boyfriend' one Saturday under the paisley eiderdown at her parents' house in Cheam. Whilst I don't remember much about that weekend, I did go on to develop a fairly extreme phobia of feathers, so it's anyone's guess what might have gone on. But that was the '60s for you.

Us & Them

Despite my attachment to her, when Linda left I was surprisingly buoyant. Children are very fickle and can switch emotional gears much more quickly than their adult counterparts. I suspect losing a cheap, flexible babysitter was more of an annoyance to my parents than me and Annette. After all, it was them, not me, who wanted to go to the theatre.

Linda had never come to the country with us. There was no need because my parents had employed someone else to look after me whenever we were there. Her name was Mrs A and she called me Susie-Anna. Her arrival would change the course of my life for ever.

It was 1966 and I was four years old when my parents

decided we weren't quite posh enough and, after much search-ing, my father rented a gentrified farmhouse called the Priory in Knipton, Lincolnshire, on the estate of Belvoir Castle – seat of the Duke and Duchess of Rutland. The word 'estate' is really meaningless unless you've lived in close quarters to one. The land belonging to the Rutlands was on a scale that's almost impossible to visualise: 16,000 acres of prime farmland – that's 11,000 football pitches – with a 356-room Gothic-revival fort-ress at its epicentre. Entire villages were owned by this family and countless homes. The Priory was just one.

Once again we regarded our house as 'modest'. It began life as a monastery on the edge of a castle park so this was clearly something of a misnomer. Nevertheless, given our proximity to the castle and the friendships I developed with the titled children within, I spent my entire time at the Priory feeling like the poor relation. With seven bedrooms, our house could not have been considered small, but theirs had over fifty, many named after the kings and queens who'd slept in them. When the Prince Regent came to stay in 1814, the Rutlands were obliged to gouge out part of the bath-room wall to allow his stomach to fit through the door. Sometimes I'd run my hand over the smooth dip or put my bottom into it if I visited the King's Room. The walls of the state bedrooms were adorned with handpainted wallpaper and their beds overhung with gilded coronets. Chinese silk framed their goosedown pillows like the curtains of a belle-époque theatre. Holbein's portrait of Henry VIII hung in the Picture Gallery, while the walls at our house were dotted with pastel landscapes painted by my father and a threadbare Dutch tapestry rug.

Rare pic of me and Teabag out of the saddle.

My best friend in the world was the daughter of the Duke and Duchess, Lady Theresa Manners. 'Teabag' or 'Teasy', as she was better known, would in all likelihood marry a title – just like in a fairytale. I knew I would marry, but with a Lady around, how could a mere Miss compete? Marriage for our class was a competitive sport. There was a clear brief and it wasn't about falling in love. Marriage was about acquisition, preferably of something handed down: a title, a seat, a business. And for that matter, the avoidance of anything damaging – madness, bankruptcy and scandal. Although like most young people I took it for granted I'd marry for love, equally I was never in a social situation where the boys were anything other than appropriate marriage material. The pool of young men I would choose from had been pre-selected and narrowed down. You'd never put an Aberdeen Angus with a Hereford cow and, just as with the farmyard, we were only ever put in the field with people of the same breed.

Theresa and I were best friends. If I wanted to watch a black-and-white matinée of Fred and Ginger, she was the person I chose to do it with. If I wanted to catch a ghost, she was the one who'd hold the torch. Theresa was always my first choice and we were inseparable. My parents were best friends with her parents and I believed we were all on a level. But outside, in the community at large, our family was *not* the same as theirs. Very much like *The Frost Report* Class sketch, there was a silent hierarchy in Knipton. As far as the tenants of Belvoir estate were concerned, the Rutlands were at the top. Everyone looked up to them. They were John Cleese with his Lock & Co. bowler and brolly. The Constantines were the Ronnie Barkers of the piece – standing in the middle, able to look both ways. While we might have been regarded as upper class elsewhere, in Knipton, where there was a duke and duchess to hand, we were very definitely considered middle class – a statement I still have to whisper in case my father hears from heaven. Mrs A was always one for talking about 'knowing your place', which, from the luxury of my own position, was something I thought of as absolute nonsense. I thought she could go anywhere with anyone. She was the best person I knew. No one would stop her, I reasoned. I failed to see that people like Mrs A were put in their place without anyone ever needing to say a word. No one had to talk about the pecking order for it to exist. Of everyone I knew, Mrs A was the person most likely to enforce it, even when that meant she would be the one to miss out. '*Och, no, I canna do that.*'

When I went to the castle to play with Theresa, Mrs A's daughter, Lorraine, never came with me. I could cross over into her side, but she didn't into mine. I know the Rutlands would not have thought anything of it had Lorraine come with me but Mrs A would never have allowed it. In her own words, she had her 'place' and so, by extension, did her daughter. The only time Mrs A went to the castle was as a paying visitor. Any time an invitation outside of her own environment was extended she would always refuse. It was the same with the Rutland family's nannies. They never came to our home once. They never came 'upstairs'. These were all people who stuck by the rules more than the people who employed them.

Inside the walls of the Priory, Mrs A was supplemented by our cleaner, Mrs Bemrose, who lived across the front field in a cottage. Collectively Mrs A, Mrs Bemrose and my mother were known as Mrs A, B and C. My mother loved them both, though I never saw them socialise together outside of the house. Theirs was a geo-specific friendship and their head-quarters was the Priory kitchen table. Although they didn't go to lunch or the hairdressers together, sitting with Mrs A, Mrs B and a cup of tea was actually where Mrs C was at her happiest.

'Our place' in the pecking order came up infrequently in our friendship with the Rutlands but I'm sure my father was keenly aware of it. Genuine toffs have no need to shout about their money or heritage, while those a few rungs down the ladder (i.e. my father) tend to be the bigger snobs. When my husband, Sten, and I rented a cottage on the Belvoir estate just after we were married, rather than help us install a much-needed central-heating system, my father insisted on paying for an extension to house the washing machine so it wouldn't have to be seen in the kitchen. We continued to freeze but were freed from any potential white-goods-related village gossip.

The mercantile class – of which my father was a part – was a meritocracy. He had worked hard for his position and was an exceptional businessman but spent his life worrying that he wasn't an aristocrat. He hung on tight to the fact that he came from old money and never tired of telling people that his family was in the Domesday Book – his ancestor was a manservant to William the Conqueror. The Constantins – without the *e* – were French commoners, but, in our world, longevity was key, so this didn't matter. He endlessly searched for links to the past among the roots of our family tree. He always said my mother was more royal than the Royals because she was a direct descendant of Charles II, though I think it's more likely to have been Nell Gwynn. He always wanted to be an aristocratic layabout but I think it was his middle-class roots that saved him from being an absolute arsehole. He never looked down on people but he frequently looked up and I feel sad he was never satisfied with his lot or appreciated himself for what he was: a talented artist with a brilliant mind, a loyal friend, funny and good-looking to boot. What a waste.

I had no real concept of the social order or that we sat very comfortably at the upper end of it. From my blinkered view, I was surrounded by lovely people who cooked, cleaned, washed and played with me. It never struck me as odd that I was the only person in the equation not paid to be there. I always assumed it was just 'us' and there *was* no 'them'.

Household staff were treated as prized possessions and it was considered hugely bad form to 'steal' someone from another family. This sense of ownership ran in both directions. Nannies in particular were fiercely protective of their families. For years I thought it a wonderfully happy coincidence that Lord and Lady John Manners' nanny – Nanny Manners – had the same name as the family she cared for. In later years I realised she'd obviously been asked to change her name to theirs for ease – a custom common among the upper classes. The best-case scenario is that this was to simplify life for the titled. The worst is that it was a practice with its roots in the slave trade.

Mrs A

As a four-year-old, all that really mattered to me was who fed me and who loved me and there were two types of people who provided this sort of thing: cooks and nannies. I was very proud to say we outdid the Rutlands on both fronts, and all the more so because we did it in the form of a single person, Mrs A. This unbreakable Glaswegian was our secret

Mrs A.

weapon – like something Q might have invented for Bond. The best of British design, she was reliable, dependable, as comfy as she was efficient, and came with a lifetime warranty. If anything, she outdid the brief.

She could cook, comfort and control both me and my parents better than anyone else, and when we were in the country, home life revolved around her. The first place visitors went was the kitchen. It didn't matter how old you were, she was like a healing crystal. You just had to be in her presence to feel better. She was the human equivalent of a tea cosy, which all combined to give the impression she was an elderly woman. In 1968 she was actually a thirty-six-year-old single mother.

She did little, however, to dispel this aged impression, spending most of her time in a flammable tabard and open-toed sandals to accommodate her bunions. She never wore make-up and made no attempt to hide her dry, scaly legs. She had a tidy haircut and her ablutions were limited to warm water and a flannel. I only saw her twice without her dentures and it aged her half a century. She was of the generation who had their teeth voluntarily removed, often as an eighteenth-birthday or wedding present.* That she could never eat chewy

---

* Historically, false teeth were made from animals, peasants poor enough to warrant selling their own, or taken from graves and dental collections. Often the quality was so poor these dentures had to be removed in order to eat. In 1815, 50,000 men died at the Battle of Waterloo, mostly young, healthy men whose teeth were in great nick. Their bodies were stripped of anything of value, including their teeth, which were shipped to the UK in barrels to make dentures and implants. The battle triggered a dramatic drop in the price of false teeth so that even the middle classes could afford them. 'Waterloo Teeth' was a Victorianism that meant the teeth from any dead person, whether they'd fought at Waterloo or not.

mints was her only verbalised regret. Like every other person in the same circumstances, she kept her 'teeth' in a glass by her bed to quietly fizz away overnight, submerged in their effervescent cleaning solution. Dentistry was expensive and painful and by going this all-out route, you circumvented the need for further, unforeseen pain and expense. What it must have been like having every one of your teeth pulled in a 1940's dentist chair does not bear thinking about. For me it's the stuff of nightmares. I was born with insufficient enamel on my teeth and yellow and grey patches caused by my mother having the antibiotic tetracycline during pregnancy. As a result I'm still constantly in and out of the dentist's and not a tooth is undrilled. I'm exactly the kind of person who'd love a set of dentures as a birthday present. I hope my husband is reading this as I approach sixty . . .

Altruistic in the extreme, Mrs A barely spent a penny on herself. Her only indulgence was that once a year she'd leave us to holiday in Skegness with Mrs B. After a time the donkeys that worked there began to winter with us at the Priory because Mrs A was so upset at the thought of their out-of-season lives. They were put in the front field but we never rode them because we knew they were resting. Our garden was separated from the field by an iron fence but this didn't stop them regularly barging through to eat the climbing roses that covered the front wall. Our uppity ponies, Dandy, Rolo and Smokey, hated these fleabitten interlopers and did their best to make them feel as unwelcome as possible. If the ponies were eating and the donkeys dared approach, all three would flatten their ears and bare their teeth as a brief warning sign before turning round to kick them. If you ever played

Buckaroo as a child, this is exactly what it was like. There was a hierarchy even in the field; it was the Class sketch all over again. I loved our ponies but have to admit they loathed Mrs A's poor old seaside friends. I doubt it would have made them feel any better to know they felt the same way about pigs.

Mrs A never ventured further than the boiler room, where she did the laundry, and the next-door stable yard to hang it on the line. I never bumped into her at the post office or saw her chatting to a friend in the village because whenever I was at the Priory, she was at home, waiting. It was as if she only existed *with* me and *for* me. She gave up a huge part of her own life for us. What she gained in return was being the first person anyone ever wanted to see or turn to when they most needed a friend. Every time I had a baby, she was the one person I wanted them to meet. But what she lost I'll never really know. There have been many peacocks in my life who've provided colour, flair and wonderful anecdotes, but it was Mrs A who gave me the backbone I needed to go out and experience these things and return home to the safety of someone consistently sane.

I know nothing about how she grew up, except that when she got pregnant with Lorraine, her husband left her and she somehow found her way to Belvoir. Mrs A had her own end of the house and would come into ours to work. Often that work meant comforting me or my sister. On paper she was our housekeeper but really my father paid her to be a substitute mother at a time in his life when he believed his wife was not up to the job.

My mother was a wonderful but very troubled woman. As time went on it would become clear she was a manic depressive. This was not diagnosed until many years later and so she managed her highs and lows as best she could with alcohol. Now we would say she was ill, but then she was just seen as a woman who couldn't cope and one that was slowly but surely falling apart. We all watched as it happened like a slow-motion car crash, paralysed and shocked on the sidelines. It was a long and winding process, and one that eventually killed her, but the woman she had been earlier in her life slipped away long before her death.

When my mother disappeared into her illness, Mrs A automatically stepped into her shoes. It was in her nature to nurture. And my father let her do it. That was in his. She cared for me and my sister unconditionally and this alleviated a huge amount of stress for my father. Never once did he consider, 'Now hang on, this is my wife and my daughters . . .' Someone else was handling it competently, which meant he didn't have to. He was excused. I know if my mother had been well, caring for us was not a role she would have let go easily, but sadly there is no other way to describe what happened and I'm sure this in turn fed her depression and drinking.

I spent more time in Mrs A's sitting room than I did in our own. For years I've described her as 'part of the family', but that is a trite, euphemistic label. What I really mean is, I loved her more than I did my own parents. I knew exactly how she felt about me, and what I saw in her I reflected back. I knew she loved me. I don't think it was contrived or forced, but objectively I see she wasn't part of our family. In another age, she'd have been considered our servant. She was a single mother who must have made huge sacrifices with her own child in order to fulfil her duties with us. What was Lorraine doing while Mrs A cleaned my cuts and dried my tears? I'm ashamed to think of it.

The Way to This Girl's Heart . . .

Food at Belvoir was notoriously filthy and mealtimes as an adult were a very stodgy affair. José, their diminutive Portuguese chef, was angry, and overworked doing very little. Cakes came courtesy of Mr Kipling, and lumpy mashed potato and watery Bisto gravy were thrown onto the plate and served up with attitude. On a bad day I've no doubt he was the kind of man to have spat in their food.

As children we fared rather better. High Tea was the evening meal the castle children shared alone at weekends and during holidays. Though unsophisticated, it was the gastronomic highlight of the day as far as I was concerned. For the upper classes, High Tea was somewhat different to Afternoon Tea. The latter had been invented at Belvoir in 1840 when the visiting Duchess of Bedford asked for a tray of tea, cakes, bread and butter to be brought to her bedroom as a bridge between meals. She enjoyed it so much she continued the habit on her return to London, often inviting friends to join her. Eventually the practice of pausing for tea in the afternoons migrated to the drawing room, where ladies would take it on their laps in low, comfortable chairs. Over the years, the tea party became a breeding ground for female independent thinking, and it all began at Belvoir.

High Tea, by contrast, was served at the table, in the first instance to the working classes who couldn't wait as late as eight for their dinner. On their return from a long day in the fields or factories they wanted something straight away. High Tea was the original working-class evening meal. The upper classes appropriated it for the days when the servants were off. Designed as something they could prepare and serve themselves without help, it took the best bits of Afternoon Tea and added fancy cold meats. So the High Tea we ate in the nursery was not only a conglomeration of both foods and customs, but also a mark of our lower-class status within the hierarchy of the castle walls.

Victorian in its formality, this meal was beautifully laid out on a linen cloth, stitched with apple blossom and the odd cotton-thread darn to mask its age. The food was a fusion of culinary clichés: crumpets and drop scones, baked beans on white bread, anchovy toast that repeated on you at will, Welsh rarebit and paper-thin cucumber sandwiches spread with a thick layer of salted butter that disintegrated on your tongue. There was no need for recipe books in the nursery nor, for that matter, an oven. Most things were rustled up in the toaster or under the grill, with the very occasional need for a hob. There were no hidden ingredients or exotic surprises. Tried and tested on generations of children who'd passed through these rooms before us, everything we were served was sure to please. This food was familiar, safe and comforting – a reflection of the spirit of the nursery itself. We drank from tiny bone-china teacups, so delicate as to be see-through, but there was no silver teapot at our table. Instead, the ever-present, brown earthenware pot stood amongst the finery – a stalwart friend with humble origins.

High Tea was held under a heaven-high ceiling, fenced by a simple cornice. The expensive carpet, threadbare in patches, bore the signs of hundreds of shoeless feet dancing, playing and learning. Chinese silks, swept aside by ormolu tie-backs, allowed the weakening 4 o'clock sun through huge sash windows into a room too big to heat effectively.

In the warren of cold corridors and thick stone walls, the nursery was like a warm womb. It was the only room that suggested the castle was a home and not a museum or piece of living history. Any family that's wealthy enough to have a nursery like this is one where children are destined for something bigger. To become 'someone'. But in the nursery, that had not yet come to pass. In the nursery, you were still no one, which is what made the relationships within its walls unique. It was the one room where staff didn't have to knock before they entered, which is exactly why it was so full of life.

Nanny Webb

Nanny Webb was as much a fixture of these rooms as the draughty windows but was too old to really take care of us properly. She'd been the Duke of Rutland's nanny when he was a child but was now more a souvenir of bygone times: a treasured ornament saved for best. Of middling height, her snow-white hair was kept in a perfect bun held in place with tortoiseshell combs and a fine-mesh hairnet. She dressed in only pastel blue or oatmeal, a box-pleat skirt, stockings and lace-up brogues. Wire-rimmed spectacles and a white apron finished off the picture. She was the cleanest thing I'd ever seen, like a polished, if not new, pin. Nothing was out of place. Everything was spotless, ironed and neat. I do

31

remember sleeping in her bedroom after she died and peeing in a Chinese vase. I dared not tip it out the window on account of the snow. In all probability it is still there now. Nanny Webb was a thoroughly loving presence in our lives but I can hardly remember a thing she did beyond sewing on name tapes. She was like a solid, reliable old tugboat, semi-retired and bobbing about at the edge of the harbour. Hardly anyone took her out any more but you got the feeling she'd be up to the task if the fancy boats ran into trouble and she were really needed.

Cherry

For our day-to-day looking after, Nanny Webb was propped up by Cherry, the novice nursery maid. If Nanny Webb was the tug, then Cherry was the speedboat. Though I know exactly what she did for us day to day, I'm struggling to recall what Cherry looked like. The only reason I remember her at all is because of her name. It was the name of a girl who'd walked straight out of an ice-cream parlour rather than one living in a small rural Lincolnshire hamlet in the mid-60s. It seemed so unlikely: like a ruby in the dust. I wanted to ask if she'd been named after a song but never dared. Whatever the reason, we couldn't have picked any-thing more perfect for a nanny. It was the sort of name we'd give our dolls.

Coffee & Walnut Cake

The castle held a special magic for anyone coming up to stay, but Mrs A's coffee and walnut cake meant we got our fair share of visitors too. Her every culinary adventure was a success and something about which I felt unashamedly smug. The Manners' children knew coming to the Priory meant being fed properly, which was a huge draw. There was a strict rota for her meals too so, if you were clever, you'd time your visit with your favourite supper. Monday nights were her signature barbecued spare ribs – done in the oven – a dish I think you'd unlikely be served elsewhere in 1968. Pork chops with a Parmesan crust and cider and cream sauce with mash potato was a particular winner, and her crème caramel was better than that of any Michelin-starred chef. Baked Alaska, brandy snaps, a tomato ring with prawns . . . I could go on. Everything she made was made from scratch without a single corner cut. Her signature pudding was a Clarnico Mint Cream crumbled on top of grapefruit segments; her signature starter, peeled and deseeded tomato, cucumber and melon balls in white wine vinaigrette. God knows how Mrs A got anything else done because she cooked us three meals a day. Her potato pancakes with bacon or herrings fried in oatmeal were recipes that I imagine came from the previous occupant of the Priory, 'Sir Arthur'. I never knew this man's surname because Mrs A simply called him 'Siratha' in her strong Glaswegian accent. She had looked after him before us, though I could hardly conceive there'd ever been a *before us* for Mrs A. She was such an integral part of my life that I'd show her off whenever possible. Right up until the time my dad died in 1997 and we stopped renting the Priory, anyone of any significance in my life was driven to Knipton for one of Mrs A's cakes.

When staff live in, a high level of trust grows between

them and their employer. For me and my family, the boundaries were very blurred. I spent my childhood thinking we were all on the same footing, but these people were not free to leave the kitchen table when they'd heard our sad stories a hundred times. If they had their own worries, these were unlikely to be discussed in the same way. They knew their own needs were secondary to the well-being of the family. Mrs A can have had little room for life beyond taking care of the Constantines. I hope we were a good family to work for, and I imagine there can have been few better options for a single mother in the '60s, but saying that only serves to highlight the choices she never had. She must have been a woman faced with some very difficult decisions, but selfishly, I am eternally grateful they resulted in bringing us together. I never felt alone with Mrs A. To have a single, constant person in your life like this is a huge privilege. Parents can be distracted with affairs, illness, work or divorce but this was never the case with Mrs A. She was always there, unencumbered. None of us could have known how deeply our family would need her when she originally took on the role of housekeeper. Every day I thank God he sent exactly the right woman for the job. Life would have been a very different proposition without her.

Fine & Dandy

The Priory was two miles from Belvoir itself, but all bar 200 yards of this was in the castle park, so I'd drive myself there through the grounds in an unlicensed, clapped-out, two-seater

Land Rover. Rust had devoured the floor so the tarmac was visible beneath my feet if I dared take my eyes off the road. I've no idea who owned it; it had always just been there for the taking. A Land Rover with a bench seat is a rigid, one-size-fits-all set-up. It was the Goldilocks of motor vehicles: you had to be just right to drive it. And so it was that leg length rather than the law dictated the age I began driving – which was thirteen. The prospect of getting arrested never entered my mind and, anyway, I never once saw a policeman in my whole time in Knipton. The arm of the law wasn't quite long enough to reach over the cattle grids onto the Belvoir estate so we enjoyed a freedom only afforded the children of farmers, dukes and gypsies.

Theresa and I had long been touring the vast grounds in her knackered, forest-green Triumph, but if she were indisposed and I needed to get somewhere without the aid of a car, there was always my faithful pony, Dandy.

Dandy, my first true love.

Dandy was the source of much happiness in my life, as well as the probable cause of my recurring pinworms. My mother had banned chewing gum for being common so I'd scrape it off the pavement instead. The playground just off Sydney Street in Chelsea, which I'd visit with Linda, was a particularly fruitful treasure trove, and I'm sure this couldn't have helped matters. Mrs A, however, was confident the worms came from the unwashed carrots I fed Dandy. It could equally have been from the apples he'd roll around in his mouth and plop back into my hands, dripping in saliva, for me to bite into more manageable pieces. I made no distinction between my dinner and his. I remember feeling reassured I must not be the only person with worms, given that you could buy family packs of Ovex at Boots.

Dandy was a rescue pony who used to pull an ice-cream cart in Derbyshire. Legend had it he'd been a pit pony before that. He was four years old when we bought him and was incredibly thin and fleabitten with patchy grey hair. He'd never been maltreated but he'd not been fed properly either. That changed with me. Any vegetables I didn't like I'd hide in my pants and sneak out to the stables. Leftover pudding would travel un-secreted in the same direction. Boxes of sugar lumps were doled out with gay abandon and, when I rode him to the post office, I'd get a quarter of lemon sherbets for me and humbugs for him. It only took a summer of this for him to become as lazy as a slug and fat as a walrus. Plagued by laminitis, he was told by the vet to go on a diet, which I ignored. How could I tell him I loved him if I couldn't give him his favourite treats? Eventually, his barrel tummy was so wide my legs stuck up and out like lolly sticks on a beach ball. The sustained tension created down below was what eventually caused my hymen to break in 1971. There was no ceremony. He and I looked like an illustration straight out of a Thelwell cartoon, but he was absolutely bomb-proof. With me on Dandy and Theresa on her pony, Crystal, we were the four amigos.

Our adventures on horseback were varied. At times it was your basic cowboys and Indians. At others, fleeing from the Nazis in the woods. We were united by our insatiable love of our steeds. They were warm-blooded toys with a beating heart and fulfilled a childish longing to love and be responsible for the needs of a living thing. Dandy's care gave me purpose and a sense of self-worth. He needed me. It was my job to look after him and I took great pride in carrying it out. In return he delivered bruises, sore bottoms, broken bones and hours of entertainment. To Theresa and me, there was nothing we couldn't ask of our ponies. Want to come swimming? (Rhetorical question.) No problem. Off came their saddles and our clothes and we'd swim clinging on to their manes as they horse-paddled into the lake, their muzzles wrinkling and blowing like walruses. We'd share our picnics with them, thrilled when they nuzzled into our laps in search of another ham sandwich or slice of pork pie. You weren't supposed to give ponies meat but they didn't know that and we didn't care. If we'd offered them a packet of raw sausages they'd have snaffled them up even though they hated pigs. Or perhaps *because* they hated pigs. Whenever we returned home from our adventures, Dandy and Crystal always gave a spirited little jump before bolting across the field into their paddock. However tired they were, this last leg of the journey was always greeted with a buck of joy. We later discovered there was a live electric current hidden underground being triggered by their metal shoes. Each time we crossed the threshold it was this rather than a longing for home that gave them that extra little burst of energy at the end of a long ride.

The reason I knew the countryside so well was because of these adventures. Sometimes I'd ride for hours at a time as far as ten miles from the Priory. I'd find my way through hedges and overgrown gateways, always using the castle as my North Star. Its position high on a hill with the Vale of Belvoir below meant I could never get truly lost.

Grooming was carried out with a wholly unnecessary level of excellence. Dandy would tip his head back and groan with pleasure as if having a couple's massage at a spa. Ponies that lived outdoors had healthy skin and hair and didn't need this kind of daily grooming. Boo sucks to that. We treated every ride like a special occasion, picking out and oiling their hooves, sponging their eyes, noses and bums with a damp cloth, brushing mud off their coats and towelling down sweat marks after an unexpected escape from an angry gamekeeper.

Dandy could read my mind. He knew when I was upset – which, at twelve, I frequently was. In fact I'd find any excuse to storm out in a huff so I could go and sleep in the stables with him. The biannual defrosting of the freezer was one of my most onerous tasks and always something I'd do my best to get out of. Harvesting the Brussels sprouts came a close second as it meant laboriously picking them off one by one rather than yanking the whole thing out of the ground and chucking it in a wheelbarrow. And anyway, who wanted sprouts? Dandy and I both hated them.

Though Dandy was a mongrel, I treated him like Shergar. If Dandy had been horsenapped and ransomed for £2 million, I'd have done my level best to pay it. He was kept in the field most of the time, but when he came into his stable I made sure his stay was a five-star experience. A bed is made for a thoroughbred by banking straw high up the sides of the stable walls to stop the horse hurting itself when it needs to get up. Like a Tonka toy, Dandy needed no such coddling but I did it anyway. The bed was as much for me as it was for him. I tried to get him to lie down with me but he never would. He insisted on sleeping standing up. I did try going to sleep on his back but this too was unsuccessful. I'd wake myself up every time I began to slide off like a satin eiderdown. I never lasted the night with Dandy and always ended up back in my own bed, but not for want of trying. I'd dampen his hay to get the dust off and stop him getting a cough, and painted his name on the stable, though I'd much rather have had a plaque. I nailed one of his old shoes to the door upright to keep the luck in. I didn't need a Barbie because I washed Dandy's hair and blow-dried it with my Morphy Richards dryer instead. If I could have put him in a dress I would have. I got very close at a gymkhana when he went as the King of Spades to my Alice in Wonderland in the fancy-dress class. I also put tinsel in his mane every Christmas Day and mistletoe above the stable entrance so we had an excuse to kiss. Presuming he'd know not to leave any little surprises indoors, I took him into the kitchen for some chocolate cake, which Mrs A vetoed immediately. I was very aggrieved: when Theresa had outgrown Crystal she took her new horse Henry into the kitchen at the stable yard all the time and no one said anything about that. This seemed like favouritism but I think it was just that the livery owner, Mick, had much lower standards of hygiene than Mrs A. Dandy and I chatted constantly but never about anything deep. I shielded him from the brutal truths of home so it was more day-to-day stuff. Primarily I wanted to know how he was. What did he like? What made him happy? People-pleasing started early with me and I loved the way it made me feel. This was a formula that worked perfectly with ponies. I've learned the hard way that people soon tire of being given everything on a plate, but not so Dandy. He lapped it up.

The fact was, if Theresa wasn't around, I had no better friend than Dandy. He was my world. He lived to be twenty-four and his carcass was eventually fed to the Belvoir hounds. I thought this meant he would hunt for ever. The perfect circle. In real life he'd been a dreadful plodder who refused to jump even the smallest obstacle. He could be his best self in heaven and avoid that dreaded diet. He'd had a lovely dot-age at home until the day he died, when he finally reached the

Dandy gets a wash and blow-dry.

point where he was full and refused to eat. We took this as a sign that life was no longer worth living and had him put down. I hope someone will do the same for me. Theresa on the other hand did not want Henry to meet the same fate and insisted he was given a full state funeral at the chapel. The castle chaplain read his last rites before he was entombed in the family mausoleum. I boycotted the event on moral grounds but I understand they left the service to the tune of 'Morning Has Broken'.

Dandy was just one in a long list of animals I've been best friends with over the course of my life. In a low, sad, dark or frightening moment, I've often found animals a greater source of solace than their human counterparts. I don't know what this says about my emotional maturity. I don't care. I knew the comfort I got from being with Dandy when my parents rowed; I knew how much better I felt when I got my rescue dog Archie during a break with Sten; I knew the hole I felt in my soul when Kimmy died, but the first adult to legitimise these feelings was Mick Toulson.

Mick

At eight miles away, Mick's yard was too far to chance in the illegal rust bucket, but the 50cc Yamaha moped I got when I turned sixteen was the perfect mode of transport. Before then I relied on my mother to drop me off. She never minded. Barkestone Farm was the go-to livery for serious riders wanting their horses stabled and looked after by the best horseman in the Midlands. Everyone wanted to be around Mick.

Mick treated me no better than a chimney sweep, which

suited me perfectly. There was no room for airs or graces. It didn't matter whether you were a duke or a dustman, suicidal or riddled with cancer, Mick Toulson approached everything and everyone with complete irreverence. He could turn a worst-case scenario into pure comedy even if you were the butt of the joke. This was remarkable given his own unique collection of problems. He was the textbook definition of dysfunctional. Barkestone Farm had it all – alcoholism, mania, closeted homosexuality and a bit of drunk-driving here and there. On paper he was a spectacular mix of all that was considered wrong in a human being, but somehow his charisma and sense of humour recalibrated these flaws.

The farm had been his home and livery business for fifteen years. Ever since he could remember, Mick had had a way with horses. As a boy, he escaped his father's belt buckle and took refuge at a local riding school. Cycling five miles on a dilapidated bike he'd nicked from outside the local grocery store, he would pedal furiously past his school and away from the bullies it taught. The riding school provided a safe haven, free from brutality, and a place where no one questioned his truancy. He was only fourteen when he ran away from his home in Yorkshire, paying his way south by giving blow-jobs to lorry drivers eager for company and a lighter load. Though his foul language was more suited to the deck of a cargo ship, his flare and fearlessness astride a horse – however wild or unbroken – meant he would not have been out of place jousting as a knight in the court of Henry VIII. The saddle was the only place Mick felt in control of life. He was drawn to the broken, and his ability to fix even the most damaged goods allowed him to overlook his own portfolio of problems. He always said horses and the people that cared for them were the only ones to be trusted.

I was not fleeing an abusive home, but Mick and I had much in common. I frequently looked to animals as a source of non-judgemental comfort at difficult, emotional times in my life and, at Barkestone Farm, I began to see I was not the only person to do this. Some grown-ups did it too.

My parents paid Mick to look after my horse and I, in turn, worked as his unpaid yardhand. It was a much better education than I was getting at school. Mick was the king of his own castle, and his word was final. While my formal schooling was teaching me to be passive, Mick was covertly instilling a work ethic almost without my knowing. I only wish I could have repaid him before he drank himself to death.

I worshipped Mick because of his skill as a horseman. I also trusted him implicitly. I repeatedly put my life in his hands, taking his advice over all others in matters related to riding. If you were going to pay for livery, you wanted to make sure your £80 a week was very well spent. With Mick, you knew your horse and your money were in good hands. You were much less likely to have an accident on a well-fed, well-exercised horse and that was exactly what you were getting with Mick. I have always been attracted to gifted people. Those I really admire are highly skilled in what they do; always the ones with something money can't buy. I think Mick may have been the blueprint for many of my greatest friendships.

When Mick landed at Belvoir he began living with Russell Tolladay, who farmed the land for the Rutlands. When Russell kicked the bucket, Mick inherited the tenancy for the

43

farmhouse and Russell was laid out in his coffin on what was now Mick's kitchen table. His teeth, nicotine-stained and stubby; his skin chalky white and cold when I leaned in to kiss his cheek. Mick had made no effort to tidy up for the occasion. Russell lay pristine in his suit surrounded by half-eaten cans of dog food, a greasy Aga, and dirty boots kicked off at the back door. It was always thus. Mick and Russell were not known for their domestic prowess in the kitchen. Upon entering the farmhouse, you'd climb over a variety of dogs and high-top boots dull with unbuffed polish, the smell of wet fur and drying leather filling all available space. The only room in the entire house that was kept clean was the sitting room, which resembled an old-fashioned parlour. The decor and its condition was in stark contrast to the debris-strewn surfaces of the rest of the house. It was a room straight off the set of a *Miss Marple*.

Mick and Mum could often be found sharing local gossip about Bambi Hornbuckle or the new milkman with a tumbler of whisky mac for their elevenses. His 'throne' was a high-backed upholstered chair, complete with white crocheted antimacassar draped over its back to protect the damask. Mick did not slick his hair purposely with oil but since it was thick with unwashed grease these doilies were needed nonetheless. From September to April the room glowed orange from the Victorian fireplace that passed as central heating. Tiny ornaments like the ones my mother put in my Christmas stocking covered every available surface: frogs conversed with owls, shire horses curled their necks around one another, miniature flowers and begging girls mingled with thatched cottages and grand ladies dressed in bustles. Clichéd tapestry scatter cushions cluttered the sofa where my mum liked to sit. 'Love me, love my dog.' It was a room based on his idea of what it meant to be welcoming.

Dukes, lords and princes stabled their horses with Mick and he was unfazed by them all because he knew he was a superior jockey, but, just like Mrs A, he would never have gone up to the castle socially. He never verbalised it but I think he had a sense that, outside of the stables, he would not have felt the man he was within their parameters. Off the back of his horse or out of his yard, his weaknesses were suddenly much more visible. Like buying a sombrero on holiday and getting it back to your bedroom: some things are best kept in their original environment.

Whatever devils lurked beneath the surface, there was definitely something about Mick. He was a bonafide equine heart-throb. He rode beautifully, was funny, good-looking and confident. His hands were huge, rough and dirty but his voice was as effeminate as any pantomime dame and he moved like a prima ballerina. For all these reasons I put him down as out-and-out gay, but I think he probably fucked anything available. His appeal, though, was about more than just good looks. He represented a certain kind of freedom for a certain kind of person. For those whose horses he stabled, it was respite from the pomp, ceremony and rigidity of their own lives. He had something money couldn't buy, which was precisely the reason people paid him. There were other stables to choose from but none like Mick's. He was as close as we got to a rock star. People wanted to be near him. My mother in particular.

Whenever I saw my mother with Mick she was unusually

happy and relaxed. I imagine this was at least in part because around Mick her drinking was not frowned upon. Far from it. As much as I loved Mick and he loved my mother, there's no doubt he used her and preyed on her vulnerabilities to normalise his own problems. Addicts need other addicts to legitimise their own habits, and in my mother Mick found not just a kindred spirit, but a willing and naive accomplice. They were co-dependent. Mick had an energy that drew people from all walks of life to him but, when the yard fell silent, he was nothing more than an alcoholic alone with his demons. I would come to know this sense of isolation extremely well myself.

It is impossible to get to the bottom of addiction. All the psychoanalysis in the world could only point me in the right direction of the root cause. Nothing can provide concrete, rock-solid answers. The best we can do is make an informed guess. I'm very open about my mother's illness, her alcoholism and, latterly, mine; I've talked about these things to the point they've become bullet points in my biography. Meaningless, almost. I feel like I had these things all sewn up – '*It's X; it's Y. I get it. I understand it. I've put it behind me.*' It's easy to intellectualise-away the effects of our emotional past. But just because we can explain or rationalise something does not mean we can undo the effect it had on us. I always thought of Mick as a fantastic character; the kind of guy who'd be great to write about in a book. I saw him drinking, and saw him drinking with my mother, and it was all OK. I saw him handling the horses; riding; running a business; dealing with customers, families, relationships. He did it all while he was drinking and he was still OK. When my mother joined him, and I saw her visibly relax in his company, I was relieved. I wanted her to be happy. My anxiety dissolved. Mick's yard was a safe place for me. Mick 'fixed' my mother. How he did it is another thing. As a child, when you see someone you respect do something wrong, it's nearly impossible to separate it out from the person you care about. Mick was my first glimpse of a real, live, functioning alcoholic. I can't tell you definitively if this had any bearing on what I grew up to consider as acceptable or normal. I can't *prove* anything, I'll never know. But I think now perhaps it did. It is certainly a tangled web to work through. In some respects none of this matters: where it came from is irrelevant. It can help you understand the problem, but won't solve it. It's what you do with this self-knowledge that counts.

The Knipton Set

I spent more time in my parents' orbit in the country than in London – at the dining table, in the car or on the sofa watching Dick Emery, Benny Hill or *Upstairs, Downstairs*. But socialising with the grown-ups was confined to the daytime over the weekend. This was when local friends came together for Sunday drinks or picnics in the woods. My parents were part of a self-styled group known as the Knipton Set. Comprised of five socially suitable couples, it was a deliberately exclusive club that accepted the occasional interloper by invitation only. Like an Agatha Christie novel, they were a predictable cast of fabulously posh caricatures. Stunning, blonde Lady Caroline Ogilvy was the bombshell, her husband

James the financial wizard. Lord and Lady John Manners, aka Johnny and Mary, the World War II hero and his fiercely clever and rather frightening South African wife. Etienne Maze was the son of Paul Maze, last of the post-impressionists, a talented painter in his own right and married to my godmother Margaret, a health guru decades before such a thing was all the rage. And then, of course, Theresa's parents, the Duke and Duchess of Rutland. Each one knew not to hold a knife like a pencil and the way to butter their toast was bite by bite. It was all in the breeding. We lived within a five-mile radius of one another so no one worried about how to get home on a snowy night or driving over the limit after three glasses too many – both fairly standard for a New Year's Eve in Knipton.

We rang in the new year with the same people, the same food, the same smoking jackets and frocks, drinks and party games, in the same houses every year. The Ogilvys' was the prettiest, but essentially the interiors of all the houses looked the same: faded chintz, Colefax and Fowler. Johnny was in charge of his famously lethal rum punch. Champagne was always Bollinger; white wine, Pouilly-Fuissé; and claret, Berry Brothers. Round trestle tables spilled into the hallway, and the scent of Rigaud candles filled the rooms. The starter was condensed consommé, Philadelphia topped with lump fish, served with Melba toast. Main course would be a pheasant casserole, and pudding crème brûlée followed by locally sourced Colston Bassett Stilton. The port was passed left by the men. The ladies drank glasses of Calvados or poire William before leaving their husbands to discuss something apparently more important without them.

In total we made up a party of thirty-two, the biggest

gathering I encountered as a child. Despite my chronic shyness, these nights were some of the happiest I can remember. I never felt closer to my parents. My mother and I would add the finishing touches to our evening dresses, and she would pick out a piece of her jewellery for me to wear. Not of an age to be able to buy my own clothes yet, I would put on a frock by Laura Ashley or a Victorian nightdress she'd found at her favourite antique linen shop in Grantham. The addition of her black Kenzo belt made me look less like I was going to bed for the night. In her floor-length Bellville Sassoon, I thought my mum looked like Vivien Leigh, but I was biased: that lady had reportedly put a copy of *Peter Rabbit* into my pram outside Pelham Place on a visit to our neighbour, so this added to the fairytale quality of the night. All the diamonds came out on New Year's Eve. Nothing too ostentatious, but all rose cut because this was the only way they could be cut in the eighteenth and early nineteenth centuries.

The Duchess.

This was the one night my mother's illness went into hibernation. Everyone would be drinking and she could enjoy herself without feeling watched. My father was free to let his still-thick hair down without worrying about how his wife might behave, because everyone behaved badly on New Year's Eve. Even he got sozzled, told jokes and danced like Gene Kelly, and I would polish off half-empty glasses of whatever I could find abandoned in the dining room. For one night only, the age barrier disintegrated. Adults crouched and children stretched to pass the orange from one chin to another and the room filled with screams as we became ever more competitive in games of charades. 'Auld Lang Syne' would be sung with gusto and uncensored patriotism. The Queen would be toasted and we began the process of moving through partners, hugging and kissing, in the moments after Big Ben struck twelve.

This was the Knipton Set at their most potent. A group who brought out the best in each other, bound by long-standing friendships and inherited privilege. Raucous. Entertaining. Beautiful. Glamorous and fun. All that is, I felt, except one: Frances, the Duchess of Rutland.

The Rules of the Game

Like Batman, I too had a nemesis. She was more twinset and pearls than capes and tights, but appeared to be fully committed to total world domination nonetheless. I felt it became clear she intended to destroy me and everything I represented when she was in her early forties and I was just about to start primary school. Her name was Frances Rutland but in my world she was known simply as The Duchess.

A hero's not a hero without a worthy adversary – it's a set-up as old as time: Holmes and Moriarty, Bugs Bunny and Elmer J. Fudd, me and Frances Rutland. I accepted mine with good grace. I had no choice; she was the mother of my best friend, Theresa, and her nursery was where I ate at least half my weekly meals.

When Frances Sweeny married the Duke of Rutland, 'The Duchess' was a title that came with the job. It didn't belong to her; she was its custodian and it was simply a role she played for a time, stepping into the costume of someone already well known in her social sphere: the aristocrat's wife. Like Christopher Nolan, she could modify the character but couldn't throw out the blueprint and start again from scratch.

Like all the greats, she met the super-villain criteria head on.

The Costume

The Duchess was considered one of the greatest beauties of her age and any photograph will show her 'costume' was that of the classic '50s starlet. She had her father's aquamarine eyes, which always seemed to be bloodshot by nightfall. Sitting for hours at a time in her corner by the fire, she'd tap out the beats of a lonely Morse code with the tips of her coral-pink nails. I can still smell her lipstick. Thick, triple-layered Yardley, both cigarette and wine glass permanently rose-rimmed as she alternated between the two. Her full lips were never still as she muttered to herself, pursing and releasing between silent words – *click, click, smack, smack* – as if blotting her lipstick in readiness for a rendezvous that would never materialise. Occasionally etiquette dictated a smile but it never appeared to reach her eyes.

From the neck down she was ordinary, but her face was beautiful, her hands small and delicate and her feet petite and elegant. Everything on show was inspection-ready. Camel cashmere, Hermès scarves and A-line tweed skirts to accommodate a valuable pair of childbearing hips. It was clear she slept on her back because her otherwise perfect hair, worn short, was pressed flat against the back of her head.

The Performance

The greatest super-villains must be played by actors who know how to steal a scene, and Frances did this effortlessly. Sadly, her energies were wasted on an audience who couldn't have cared less. I, on the other hand, had never seen a performance like it.

Frances was a woman who appeared to have everything and nothing. It seemed that all that had once made her desirable was now cast aside through no fault of her own. Otherwise unused and unnoticed, she made her presence felt by withdrawing, the weight of what she didn't say worse than anything she possibly could have. Her superpower was silence.

I countered with a Julie Andrews' level of joy. Relentlessly upbeat, I'd skip and sing tunelessly across the Aubusson rug as I passed her on my way to the breakfast table for egg and soldiers. I knew it would make her blood boil and that this was my best defence.

The Back Story

Evil without a past is nothing more than a maniacal, victorious laugh and the swish of a cloak, but with backstory we get nuance, balance and pathos. The moment we add a shred of sympathy to the mix we've introduced a sliver of hope that our villain may come good and this is what keeps us glued to the screen.

The child in me lives on in the coping mechanisms I developed to deal with The Duchess so it's impossible for me to review her character without bias. She wasn't ten feet tall on a silver screen. She was brushing past me without comment or acknowledgement. Objectively I believe the seed of this unhappiness must have been planted in her by someone else, but who and why?

In the rules of the game played by high society, Frances was a trump card: bright, good-looking and filthy rich. When the time was right, she was washed and brushed and sold at market to the highest bidder.

She became the second wife of Charles Rutland – a duke in need of an heir. Frances was young, nubile and in season. Intellectually, she could have given Alan Yentob a run for his money but her only real job was to produce an heir and then sit dutifully beside her husband on their letterhead. However powerful a titled man might appear, a wife is a crucial part of his equation: a duke is not really a duke without a duchess, a lord without his lady. If he cannot come up with a wife to give him a son, he's failed in the only job that matters – the continuation of his bloodline. A female counterpart with all the right working parts is the only answer for a progenitor.

The feelings of that lady are of little consequence to anyone at all.

Frances lived with the indignity of knowing that she was required but not really wanted.

Once she'd produced an heir she was added to all the other trophy heads that lined the panelled walls. You didn't have to be a duchess to find yourself in this situation; it had happened to my mother and, in all likelihood, the same could easily happen to me. We were all in training for the same thing: marriage. In our world, Frances did everything she should have done. She was well trained, acquiescent and she married the right man and gave him an heir. So what went wrong? I think the flaw in this plan is that it doesn't take feelings into consideration. It is my belief that Frances was unhappy and she seemed to project that unhappiness onto others.

But there may have been another reason too . . .

I don't know the truth of her marriage but from the outside it seemed as if she and Charles were just two interdependent people who happened to live under the same roof. I imagine the only time they found themselves alone together was at the top of the stairs after they'd dressed for dinner in their separate bedrooms in preparation for presentation to some or other audience. As they descended the stairs from bedroom to hall, they quietly became the Duke and Duchess of Rutland rather than two lonely people trapped inside convention.

Charles was as handsome as his wife. Oddly, separating his features made him quite ugly, but, when the pieces of the puzzle were reunited, he was a total dreamboat. Like most men of his generation, his thick hair was swept back from his face, seemingly held in place by natural oils and good old-fashioned values. He'd run his hand through it at intervals like a matinee idol, and when he entered a room, the temperature immediately rose a degree or two. This duke could charm the birds from the trees and it was truly dazzling to be the focus of his attention, but he appeared to treat his wife the same way she treated me: he barely seemed to acknowledge her presence.

I do know she wasn't the only woman in his life. Frances' mother, the Duchess of Argyll, had overlooked her husband's adultery and now it seemed Frances was doing the same. The duke's womanising certainly appeared to go unchallenged – at least from the outside. The tip she gave her daughter-in-law on the subject was a simple, 'That's just what dukes do,' which seems a fairly fatalistic way to suggest your son and his wife run their marriage.

Charles reputedly had a traditional method of honouring his infidelities and gave the same floral gemstone brooch to each of his mistresses. I suppose it was only a matter of time before one found its way into the jewellery box on my mother's dressing table. I was six years old but even I could see Charles adored her. She was the antithesis of his own wife, gentle, soft and vulnerable, the kind of woman men wanted to look after, and there was no way this fact could have gone unnoticed by Frances. I can well imagine that this was part of the reason for Frances' behaviour towards me. But I was not my mother's keeper. Nor, for that matter, her husband's.

In thirty years of living next door to Frances, I can count

on one hand the number of times she and I conversed directly and remember each with a shudder. As a child and even as a grown-up, she still had the ability to put the fear of God into me.

The Legacy

The reverberations of a really great villain are felt long after the lights go up. The world is forever changed by their actions, their legacy a fundamentally altered path for their adversary.

The silver lining to this tale is that I decided I'd rather be a first-class citizen in my own world than a third-class one in hers. I forged my own path even when it meant going against the social mores of the people I grew up with. I suppose I have Frances to thank for that.

Even as an adult, winning people over is my 'thing'. My party trick. To be liked, remembered or acknowledged is a secret challenge I set myself whenever meeting someone new. It's a horribly unattractive, self-centred strand of my personality that I believe started with Frances. It didn't matter what I did or didn't do, I could not win her over and it made me feel worthless. One of the greatest gifts she gave me was the resolve to never make another person feel the same way, least of all a child.

Frances was the product of the cumulative grievances of at least two previous generations. I imagine that, little by little, she absorbed heartbreak and loss until they became the root of her unhappiness. While I cannot forgive Frances, I've come some way to understanding her. The role she played was more important than the happiness and well-being of the person who played it. That's something I wouldn't wish on my worst enemy. Not even The Duchess.

St Mary's, Wantage

In light of what I'm about to tell you, you might find it strange that we made the decision to send our children to boarding school, but it was something we did with their blessing. When Esme felt homesick we gave her the option to come home but she wanted to sit it out. I was not given the same choice. Some people excel in these situations, but I was not one of them. For my children it was different. My son wanted to leave home and be independent as early as he possibly could. Esme followed him and then Cece followed her big sister.

In 1974, when I was twelve, I was reluctantly packed off to boarding school. Two hours and an eternity away from home.

Mumfie – a girl's best friend.

St Mary's, Wantage, was a school well known for accepting any old thicky so long as her parents spent weekends in the country and could afford the fees. I don't remember a single student going on to university unless they had detoured via a London crammer to sit their A levels. While it fell short on academia, it excelled in producing young ladies who were exceptional at taking orders. By the end we were lobotomised of all ability to think for ourselves. We were trained to live by instruction and learned to live without thought. The whole set-up meant no one could flourish as an individual – which was exactly the point. We were homogenised for the ease of others.

Boarding schools in the 1970s for boys supposedly offered a secure environment where students could focus entirely on academics, athletics and extracurricular activities, with the top prize a turn at being prime minister. The primary emphasis of a girls' boarding school was to prepare a young lady for a life of marital servitude.

Every second of every day was accounted for. Every task heralded by a bell or your name on a rota. Every waking moment was governed by rules. There was no time for high jinks or free-thinking. It was possible to glide through a term without having to remember to do a single thing for yourself. We actually had a child-labour volume of day-to-day chores and responsibilities, from tending the garden to managing our laundry, but these had to be done to the letter. Even our spare time was meticulously scheduled and controlled. I have not yet served at Her Majesty's Pleasure but there is no doubt in my mind that, should this situation arise, there would be no need to acclimatise after my four years at St Mary's.

We were all captive in a historic, listed building and there was no point in trying to escape. When inmates are processed in prison they are expected to hand over their possessions for the duration of their stay and things were much the same at St Mary's. Our home clothes and accoutrements would not be needed again until we were released back onto trains and into our cars for the holidays. Personal effects, together with loud talking, shouting, or any other unnecessary noises, were not permitted. We were entitled to a uniform, food, shelter and medical attention, but anything else was a weekend privilege. Unlike prison or borstal, we were told we were there because our parents loved us.

No One Size Fits All

Lack of privacy was the cornerstone of most domestic arrangements when I was a child. Teenagers needing their own space or dignity was not a concept that existed and at boarding school there was even less room to breathe.

We were washed and weighed regularly to make sure no one smelt or died, as either would reflect badly on the school. Baths were taken three times a week at the end of the school day after supper. A list was published with our allotted slot which we were to stick to rigidly. Our allocated tubs were separated by partition walls so there was at least a modicum of privacy. If you wanted hot water, however, it was essential you were on time so as not to be shunted to the back of the queue. To mark our places, a long row of Peter Jones towels snaked from the bathroom door, punctuated by floral sponge bags.

A side note on washbags: along with pyjamas and a teddy, these were the only things in our possession not controlled by the Kit List and, as such, an important tie to home. They were our way of saying 'Stuff you; I do have parents who love me and this was given to me by my mother, so there!' They were the only items over which we could exercise any free will. However, the dichotomy of wanting to be different and the rules of fitting in were very much in evidence in the world of sponge bags. Since all our mothers shopped in the same establishments, every single one came from either Nina Campbell or Peter Jones and still needed name-taping to avert a mix-up. Even their contents were a mirror-image of our mothers' vanity cases: Clinique's yellow moisturiser and pink or green eye-watering toner. A tube of Clearasil was the only item that united us with the teenage masses beyond our school walls. Our parents were all part of the same tribe and so, by extension, were their sons and daughters. Their style was our style and we were never, ever, bought anything that might suggest we were freestanding entities. The concept of being a teenager bypassed the upper classes entirely.

Even with our slots bagsied for our baths, the adrenalin to keep them would kick in over pudding. It's the same feeling you get when your plane has landed and you're waiting – hand on clasp – for the seat-belt signs to be switched off. No one wants to get stuck behind a plodding slow-coach and it was a race to scoff down our fruit cocktail as quickly as possible to avoid any such hazards. There was no running in the corridors though, so it was awkward speed-walking the minute you were free of the refectory. Once submerged it was an all-over wash with the soap-on-a-rope in the shape of a lemon that my mother always got me from Fortnum's, and a rinse down of the bath for the next girl on the list.

The only time we would shower was after swimming and this was a dreaded affair. Herded in and out of the tiled cubicle block, the code of practice was very similar to that of a 1930s asylum. There was always the chance a games mistress would appear, unannounced, to hover Nurse Ratched-style over proceedings. Typically, this was someone with just enough of a question mark over their sexuality to make you feel you wanted to keep your bra and pants on. Even without this element, being thirteen and undressed in company was enough to make you feel vulnerable.

The thing about being a teenage girl is, there's nothing uniform about it. In one year group some of us looked sixteen while others looked ten, and you had absolutely no control over it either way. Hairless and flat-chested until fourteen, I was one of the latter. If physical survival at boarding school centred around food, one's emotional well-being revolved around getting your boobs and the curse. Silently we divided ourselves into the haves and have-nots. 'Developing', like everything else at boarding school, was something you just had to wait your turn for. It was the cruellest of games because it wasn't something we could train or prepare for but everyone was forced to take part anyway.

Down There

How fast or slow you were going was both the most private and most talked-about topic of my adolescence. Girls discussed other girls and mothers warned other mothers. If you were staying somewhere for the weekend you'd be deposited with your overnight bag and an announcement about exactly where you were in your cycle – if you had one. Sanitary towels of the 1970s – or STs as they were commonly known – were notoriously huge so a telltale bag would accompany your every move. When I finally had a need for one, mine was fashioned from my mother's redundant Yves St Laurent handbag cover. My periods as a teenager were both erratic and heavy so I needed to be on high alert at all times. As a boarder I didn't have a satchel, so changing my STs meant a conspicuous trip back to the bathrooms in the dorm rather than a simple dash to the nearest loo. If you left it too long you ran the risk of standing up to reveal a blood-soaked chair and a Rorschach butterfly stain on your inner thighs. And that was if someone hadn't already got a whiff of it in passing. The whole thing was intense but still something we all longed for.

Like runners in a holding pen waiting to start a marathon, we jostled for position, unsure when the starting pistol would be fired. There was a tense energy about us and we remained in a state of readiness until it was our turn to begin the race. Only months before, I'd been happy making a home in a matchbox for a stag beetle I'd found in the garden but now all that childishness was forgotten. I was starting a new journey and all that mattered was the destination. The milestones on the way would be the same for every girl: boobs, pubes, period – but not necessarily in that order. Unaware we were being guided by our hormones, subconsciously we made bonds with other girls going at the same pace. Whether you were early or late starters was the tie that bound you. Instinctively we stayed in our lanes, driving at the speed we were most comfortable.

The Golden Ticket

For the lucky ones who developed early it was a golden ticket into the most exclusive of clubs. These girls were free to swan around complaining smugly about how much it hurt to be elbowed in the boob, while us bra-less late developers seethed quietly under our tunics. I eventually got so embarrassed waiting for this process to kick in I started using STs anyway and lied about it for a full year before the floodgates opened. I'd embellish the fib with little groans or a hand on my tummy now and again, just to make sure everyone knew the status quo. '*Oh God, I hope I don't leak*,' I'd whisper unnecessarily to a friend. My charade extended to the wad of tissue paper I'd wrap up and post into the bin marked 'Feminine Waste Only!' Though I'm sure this label never actually included an exclamation mark, I always felt it was more of an alarmist warning than pure signposting. The underlying suggestion was that what came out 'down there' could be lethal – like biohazardous fumes, medieval vapours or other witchcraft-related secretions.

A note on menstruation mythology: myths surrounding menstruation are quite fabulous if you're interested in going down a jaw-dropping wormhole.* Even now, Yellowstone

* Medieval Europeans believed menstrual blood could both cause and cure leprosy and that you could lessen the flow by putting the remains of a burnt toad next to your vagina. A wide variety of cultures believe that having sex with a menstruating woman can kill a man. The Mae Enga of Papua New Guinea are more specific. Contact with the menstruating woman will 'kill his blood so that it turns black, corrupt his vital juices so that his skin darkens and hangs in folds as his flesh wastes, permanently dull his wits, and eventually lead to a slow decline and death'. (*The Curse: A Cultural History of Menstruation*, Delaney, Lupton and Toff, 1988.) Oh dear.

Park has a page on its website dedicated to whether or not menstruating women might attract and/or be killed by a bear.* One of the chief historical proponents of the dangers of a menstruating woman was the Roman natural philosopher Pliny. In his *Naturalis Historia*,† Pliny gives a number of reasons to be wary of them. 'There is no limit,' he tells us, 'to the marvellous powers attributed to females.' A naked, menstruating woman could cause caterpillars and beetles to fall from the ears of corn simply by walking through a field – a sort of early insecticide. Hailstorms, whirlwinds and lightning 'will be scared away by a woman uncovering her body while her monthly courses are upon her'. Bees will apparently leave their hives, and a horse in foal could miscarry just by seeing a woman – even at a distance – who happened to be having her period. No wonder my friends and I called it the curse.

While this might now seem like hocus-pocus, as late as the 1970s its threads found their way into a debate on 'menotoxins' in the *Lancet*. In the 1920s, a paediatrician called Béla Schick was prompted to conduct a series of experiments after his maid supposedly killed a vase of roses by touching them while having her period. Intrigued, Schick tested this theory with other maids. They not only ruined cut flowers but

* In case you're planning on making a trip during your period, you should be fine with grizzlies and black bears, but a polar bear is more likely to kill you than your male companion. Yellowstone Park warns ladies not to create a Pavlovian Dog situation by burying used tampons. This, they say, would give bears the idea you're rewarding them for digging them up and encourage them to seek out other unsuspecting menstruators.
† Pliny the Elder, *The Natural History*, xxviii, 'Remedies Derived from Living Creatures', 23, 'Facts Connected with the Menstrual Discharge'.

bread-making too. Some sort of deadly effluvium, he concluded, was being excreted through the skin. When this theory was revisited in the *Lancet* in 1974 many correspondents reported similar, traditionally held beliefs from all over the world. It was not just bread these women must avoid; neither should they preserve meat, sow seeds or reap fruit. There was also no point in having a perm because the solution wouldn't take. Finally someone wrote in to point out that 'a 1924 photograph of a wilted daisy . . . and the unexplainable death of one Italian tree' were insufficient grounds on which to build a case against the modern menstruating woman. Cultural conditioning is a pretty powerful thing, even when it comes to something as supposedly no-nonsense as science.

I was always intrigued by the coquettish Victorian lady on the front of our sanitary disposal bags. Like a quaint Lladro figurine, complete with crinoline, hat and wicker basket, she holds up her skirts to show a flash of petticoat as if readying herself for a ladylike step over a puddle. Presumably she was chosen in an attempt to beautify something widely considered to be a bit yucky. If she sprung to life to remind me to dispose properly of my lethal waste I imagine it would be in the voice of Blanche DuBois.

Cherry Pips

Relatively speaking, we were all fairly late bloomers at my school and we justified our delay with the belief that common, greedy girls developed earlier than us posh ones. Preconceptions about class combined with a very patchy understanding of anthropology, and we convinced ourselves that too many cakes and a lack of exercise were behind their head start. In reality I imagine the sustained stress of being away from home arrested the development of many a boarding-school girl and that this had much more to do with our slow progress than Mr Kipling or the class system.

On July 23rd 1975 I finally felt a little cherry pip under my jumper where my ironing board of a chest used to be. Annoyingly, it was the summer holidays and I was in my bedroom at Cottesmore Gardens in London, where we moved in 1974, so there was no one I could properly tell. This was the most exciting thing to have happened to me in my career as a woman to date and the only person I could share it with was my out-of-school friend, Lucinda. She and I had been inseparable until I'd left for boarding school, at which point I barely saw her again. I loved Lucinda but with so much time apart, she wasn't sufficiently up to date with my pilgrimage to womanhood to be as excited as I needed her to be. Technology was non-existent, of course, so there'd be no Zooming the news to schoolfriends or Theresa. I could write them a letter or make a phone call but that wasn't visceral or timely enough. What I really needed was for someone to have 'a feel' to really get the measure of things. Back at school six weeks later and the sheen had worn off so I never really got my fifteen minutes of fame on this front after all.

By the time I got my period the hype was completely impossible to live up to. It was the anticipation I'd loved. The end point was a massive, slightly revolting anticlimax. An annoyance, even, and much less impressive than the brochure had led me to believe.

Use of the school bathroom typically included someone tutting outside the door, waiting their turn. The minute it was locked I began worrying someone was listening in, so doing a Number 2 was always a trauma. My strategy was to line the bowl with loo paper but the scratchy squares of Izal did little to muffle the plop. Izal was well known for being the least effective way to wipe your bottom – front or back. The glossy surface meant any liquid it touched ran straight off onto your hand and its lack of pliability made it useless at getting into the cracks. It was often likened to greaseproof paper but I think even that would have had better wicking properties. In terms of absorbency, you may as well have used tinfoil. All in all you'd struggle to find a product less fit for purpose than Izal toilet paper. The only time its resilience came in handy was when I used it to reach round the back, sheets in hand, and catch the poo before laying it quietly to rest in the pan. A complete lack of health or safety guidance in school meant it was perfectly acceptable to do this and go straight to tea, where I'd pass round pieces of toast without a twinge of conscience.

Unlike day girls, when lessons finished boarders didn't have the luxury of going home to shut ourselves in our bedrooms. 'Go to your room' was a very popular refrain at home and it was a punishment like no other. What it really meant was 'You are excluded,' but it also meant you could be alone. Your mind was free to explore things it otherwise may not have had the space to. Everything from award-winning novels to three-storey dens might be created during your exile. Often the row that had sent you there was forgotten by the time your sentence was complete and you'd bound down the stairs to show everyone the puppet theatre you'd made out of an old shoe box and some Juicy Fruit wrappers. At boarding school, there was no such relief. Even at the end of a long day you didn't get to go home. You went to your study, common room or dorm – none of which were what you'd call private.

If it were adults you were trying to avoid, the loos were one of two possible options. The other was the bike shed. This was where I attempted to carve out my own space with like-minded individuals. Whether you were into *Jackie*, *Smash Hits* or Silk Cut, you were bound to find your people in one place or the other. As adults this set-up is replicated in public houses and members' clubs but there was nothing quite like those original boltholes for a sense of belonging. The bike shed was where I went to smoke and drink Woodpecker cider by the litre – the floor strewn with white fag butts and the grass worn bare by an endless huddle of lacrosse boots.

The loos were where I went to cry.

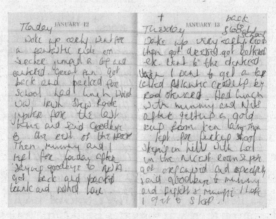

Teenage priorities – food, pets, Mrs A, Mum.

Crying in the loos was the lynchpin of my boarding-school life. Whether I wanted to be found and comforted or genuinely hide away, the loos were my sanctuary. The one thing you could rely on was that someone would come to look for you, regardless of intent. I tested this theory to the max by being homesick for the entire second term. Eventually people became immune to seeing my shoes under the cubicle door. I cried until there was literally nothing left and have honestly not cried properly since.

In life, the loos are where you have the highest chance of finding a woman in tears. The ladies' is its own microclimate; a place you may borrow, lean on or be leaned on. A place where it is fine to talk to strangers – expected, even. A huge amount of good-natured prying is done here too – 'Oh no, that's awful. Was it a stroke?' – but there's also a solidarity and unspoken code of conduct not found anywhere else in the world. You could meet the person who turns out to be on your interview panel and it wouldn't matter that you'd discussed her husband's vasectomy complications five minutes earlier, propped up by the cubicle wall. The loos are a safe space. A no-fly zone. I often wonder if the security we feel in them stems back to the fact it was here we first swapped secrets and easily transmittable viruses without judgement.

Pigeon Holes

While we were under constant scrutiny at school, we were also away from our loved ones. An hour after chapel each Sunday was set aside for letters home. My mother received an inordinate number of 'Love is . . .' themed notes from me in my time away, as we corresponded regularly. Often these were about hot-water bottles or whether we'd won the swimming relay, but homesickness was the overriding theme for me. My letters were split evenly between begging to be collected and, in the event that wasn't going to happen, asking for food to be sent instead. Food was one of the most closely guarded, highly valued items you could have – like razorblades and drugs in prison. So, in an effort to ameliorate my ongoing anxiety, my mother would send me regular supplies in brown-paper parcels. Each time one arrived I imagined myself a brave World War II fighter pilot forced to parachute into enemy territory when their plane was shot down. It was too dangerous for my regiment to rescue me but they could occasionally airdrop food to keep me going. Primula cheese-and-chives in a tube together with a packet of Tuc biscuits would have to tide me over until the next fly-by.

Virtually everything we did was motivated by the possible acquisition of food. At mid-morning break we'd descend on the refectory table laid with 'sticky willies' and pyramid cartons of milk. Within seconds the chequered cloth was stripped bare – like piranhas devouring a cow. We were constantly hungry. Part of the reason was because, with the exception of fish fingers, almost everything served at school came out of a tin. I think the cooks must have used the same menu planner as whoever was on catering for the Apollo missions. All vegetables were cooked for at least twice as long as necessary so it was very difficult to identify what was what from sight alone, and only marginally easier by taste. Colour-wise, food ranged between three or four Pantone shades, beginning with light green and ending with pale orange. Just like at Belvoir, the food at school was utter filth so you had to be incredibly resourceful if you intended to survive. Very little was eaten directly as delivered and most needed mixing with something else to make it palatable. Usually sugar or butter. Own-brand, bulk-bought cornflakes were crushed into a paste and mixed with Robinson's marmalade and Anchor butter and eaten with a spoon. Powdery Mellow Bird's was easily beaten into a froth with double the amount of sugar and passed off as a bargain-basement cappuccino. The only real reason to play netball was to get Match Tea after a game.

Using food as a source of comfort is something I've carried on with my own children. I am a feeder. As a child, food was used as a cure for every ill. It was the only thing that was consistent. It punctuated my day and distracted me from anything more emotionally amorphous. I think this is possibly the root of my ongoing fixation with food. One of the primary ways I express affection is through home cooking. From setting the table to chopping potatoes, I take huge pleasure in making a meal for my family. Even now I can't relax until I know what I'm making for dinner. It's central to my state of well-being. I can't even bring myself to get a takeaway because I feel like it's cheating. This isn't a judgement, it's about my own insecurities and how I see myself within my family. I've never had an eating disorder but food has played as central a role in my life as if I had. I feel sure this is in some way linked to being sent away to school and my mother's illness.

My mother knew very well how much I missed her but every time I tried to talk her into changing her mind she'd say, 'Don't be a silly goose. It will pass.' To an extent she was right. In time my begging letters got less frequent, but really I just resigned myself to my situation rather than embraced it. I found a way of suppressing my feelings, but every time I went home for the holidays, the return hung over my head like a sword swaying precariously in the wind. Night-times and mornings were the worst because this was when my mind was not occupied by day-to-day distractions. I was constantly anxious, sleep-deprived and on high alert. It was exhausting. The school day would divert me temporarily but when left alone with my thoughts, the same feelings descended on me again and again. I wrote to my mother that I 'woke up with a sweaty bottom', which would be laughable if it were not so innocently expressed, and the mother in me feels hugely protective over my younger self.

When my mother was ill I was her self-styled watcher. I policed her and all her moves and being away from her created huge stress for me. My children have had a security at home that I didn't. They knew their base was secure and wasn't going to go away, while I worried constantly about the stability of mine. I don't know why they felt differently than I had. Perhaps it was the fact they'd been given the option to stay home, or maybe they were fundamentally different people to me, but I honestly believe this security is partly what gave them the confidence to leave.

For me, the never-ending back and forth to school meant I had no choice but to toughen up. In one respect I'd say this taught me resilience, which has served me well. In another, all it did was suppress how I really felt about leaving the people I needed. Even as a grown woman I very rarely cry and am much more likely to paper over my true feelings. I imagine there is something in this tangle that informed my becoming an alcoholic. I don't know what my mum must have been thinking when I repeatedly raised my homesickness with her. People like us sent their children away to board no matter how unsuited they were, but, given her attachment to me, this must have been heart-wrenching. They say you are only as happy as your unhappiest child. Nevertheless, her well-intentioned, throw-away 'silly goose' eventually made me question the validity of my own feelings – something I've continued to do as an adult.

A Surprise Package

Food or otherwise, getting anything in the post at school was an event. We'd crowd around the message board each morning waiting to see if we'd been remembered. This may sound innocuous but it really wasn't given the feelings tied up in the whole process. Had you got a letter? Did you matter? You'd soon find out, and so would everyone else. A letter in handwriting that *wasn't* your parents' had the potential to be quite exciting. If it bore the postmark of Rugby, Windsor or Harrow that was enough to set us off like a brood of hysterical hens. If one of these letters was addressed to you, there was an unspoken agreement that the rest of the term could be devoted to planning your wedding.

In the whole time I was at St Mary's I never once got a letter from a boy, but in 1974 I did receive a dog in the post.

I realise this sounds like a terrible act of cruelty, but Kimmy was already dead when he arrived. It was kidney stones that saw him off. After much pestering and emotional blackmail, my mother finally agreed to send him to me for a 'proper burial'. If I wasn't going to organise that fantasy wedding, by God I'd do Kimmy proud with a funeral.

I have no idea how my mother managed to pull this off but I don't imagine she could have done such a thing without the support of a member of the Royal Mail. I should think her good relationship with Hilda, postmistress at the corner shop in Knipton, had something to do with her success. Hilda sat daily among the jars of sweets and A4 envelopes, peering out from behind her thick, clear-rimmed glasses and orange perm. She lived in the only modern cul-de-sac in the village and was always ready to do a favour in return for the gossip it might generate. Sending a dead dog in the post must have been a dream come true.

Taking the rules of animal decomposition into consideration, my mother must have moved quickly with her plan, the whole operation timed to the minute. There was no same-day service from Knipton so the best she could have hoped for was making the last post and paying extra for Special Delivery. (She did not go to this expense for my hamster Honey, who went straight in the deep-freeze and was forgotten by the time I returned home for the holidays.) Much like my pony Dandy, I considered Kimmy one of my closest friends and worthy of a well-attended service, so my mother knew Special Delivery was an unavoidable expense.

He was packed in a box like a contortionist from Cirque du Soleil. Although I'd known he was on his way, it was still a nice surprise when I unwrapped the tea towel at breakfast to reveal Kimmy's lovely little black-and-tan face. I honestly don't know whether my mother or father discussed this

Me, Nits, Kimmy, Teabag and Trinket with the Victorian cart I taught her to pull.

beforehand with the headmistress or if it was something we carried out under the cover of night with the co-operation of the groundsman, but I do know Kimmy was eventually buried under the mulberry tree next to the netball courts. I presume he is still there now.

Goodnight, Kimmy.

Hello, Dolly!

I met many grand ladies up at Belvoir Castle but the most glamorous was undeniably Theresa's granny, Margaret, Duchess of Argyll.

In fact she was probably the most glamorous woman I've *ever* met. Margaret had the looks of Ava Gardner, the balls of Bette Davis and the sex drive of Peter Stringfellow. As grannies go, she was quite a force to be reckoned with.

At fifteen she'd made the classic teenage error of getting knocked up. The perpetrator was gentleman heart-throb David Niven, though she is not mentioned in his autobiography. In a wonderful book, full of lascivious detail, the incident is conspicuous for its absence. After a secret termination designed to keep curtain-twitching to a minimum, she went on to become Debutante of the Year in 1930. Well done, Margaret. With four unsuitable engagements under her belt, she was eventually married off to Charles Sweeny at the age of twenty. The marriage was blighted by a series of traumatic events: a stillbirth, eight miscarriages and a near-death experience after she fell down a lift shaft. Margaret was reputedly never the same after. In 1947, the marriage ended in divorce.

Four years later, and she was back on the market. In 1951 she married drinker, gambler and fortune-hunter Ian Campbell, 11th Duke of Argyll. With his family seat in Scotland in chronic need of repair, the duke happily tapped into Margaret's family fortune to foot the bill. Twelve years later, with renovations complete and now suspecting Margaret of infidelity, the duke dragged her through the divorce courts in a case that was plastered all over the papers. In a bid to defame her, the duke employed a locksmith to break open her desk and rifle through her private belongings. Stolen diaries and Polaroids were used by his lawyers in the legal battle against her. Despite the fact that the duke had been unfaithful himself, it was Margaret's sexual liaisons that were the focus of the trial.

In the course of the hearing, the world learned that Margaret had supposedly slept with eighty-eight men in their twelve-year marriage and her old title was replaced with a new one. The Duchess of Argyll was now 'The Dirty Duchess' and there was one photograph in particular that caught the public's imagination. Among the Polaroids stolen by the duke was one of a naked woman kneeling at the feet of the man she was fellating. The photographer had been kind enough to crop the man's head from the picture and speculation about his identity ranged from Hollywood filmstar to Nazi bigwig. Margaret, on the other hand, was easily picked out by her trademark three strings of pearls. In 1963 the scandal became known as 'The Headless Man' in living rooms all over the world.

As a child I knew Margaret of Argyll well but wasn't up to speed with her sexual to-ings and fro-ings. She was my best friend's granny: high-society blow-jobbing didn't tend to come up much at teatime. Even so, when Granny pitched up, it was always an affair to remember.

My parents were away on another of their trips and I'd been seconded to the castle for a prolonged stay. Theresa had commandeered a safety pin from Nanny Webb's sewing box to prick our fingers and, after a rudimentary blood oath ceremony in the bathroom, I was initiated as a fourth sibling.

With formalities out of the way, we were off to the Nottingham Odeon for the Wednesday matinee of *Hello, Dolly!* with Granny. I'd only been to the pictures twice before. On the first occasion, under the supervision of the lovely Linda, I was thoroughly traumatised by Robert Helpmann's Child Catcher and on the second, with my mother, scarred for life by the withered legs of the Wicked Witch of the West. I approached the outing with some trepidation but was assured by Nanny Webb that Dolly was a 'lovely Jewish lady in a fancy hat' and to stop fretting. Nanny Webb was like a Battersea rescue dog: no one knew her provenance but she'd proved loyal and trustworthy in the past so I took her word for it. We were told to wash our hair, put on our party clothes and be ready for inspection at noon.

I had one dress whose style was replicated in incrementally bigger sizes each time I outgrew the last – a Liberty-print frock with puffed sleeves and a smocked front, worn with wool tights in navy or white whatever the outdoor temperature. We traipsed in one by one to spend a penny before flying down the stairs, three steps at a time, smack into a wall of Finnish mink pelts.

Granny's 'face' was painted on, ghost-white with kohl-rimmed eyes and claret lipstick that bled into the tissue-paper skin round her mouth in tiny rivulets. Solid black curls were held in place by fine netting embroidered with small velvet

'Granny' – the Duchess of Argyll.

polka dots. This was more for effect than necessity because, like every woman of her generation, her lacquered wash and set would stay obediently in place between weekly visits to the salon. Margaret did not wash her own hair. Pearl earrings the size of Maltesers framed her face and the notorious three strands – as ever – sat at her throat fastened with an enormous diamond clasp. There was a greedy extravagance about her that was a little overdone for an afternoon at the pictures.

This was the first time I'd worn gloves off the hunting field but Margaret was a stickler for both appearances and the avoidance of germs so we were instructed to keep them on come hell or high water. Cinemas were notoriously grubby places, especially if, like this one, they showed late-night pornos after the A and B reels had been safely packed away.

The smell of leather and satin-smooth ride of her Rolls-Royce meant that by the time we reached the Odeon I was ready to be sick. A tin of travel sweets was promptly produced from the glove compartment as a panacea.

Large, wonky letters announced *'Hello, Dolly!'* and her showtimes above the entrance. Outside the doors a line of flared jeans, platforms and leather jackets snaked towards the box office. Everyone looked just like Linda, with very little visible difference between the men and the women. I'd seen hippies before but never so close up. I may as well have landed on the moon. As the Rolls-Royce pulled up, a line of faces turned in unison to stare, open-mouthed, at the car and its occupants. I half-expected Margaret to give a regal wave. Instead she stood for what seemed like an eternity, cigarette held aloft, as she posed at the edge of the pavement as if waiting for a round of applause. This was a woman who'd been photographed and fawned over all her life, and allowing people time to properly admire her was something she did without a second thought or shred of inhibition. For someone used to inhabiting the shadows, this was beyond embarrassing for me. I was right in the middle of a 'them and us' situation and did not like the way it felt at all. For a start, 'them' looked far more exciting and interesting than anyone in our car and quite clearly none of them had been made to wear itchy tights or gloves.

Torch in hand, the usherette showed us to our seats in the middle of the stalls. Patrons already seated were obliged to accommodate our small, hoity-toity party as the duchess made no attempt to minimise the disruption or apologetically slide in sideways as is the custom. Instead she tutted loudly and repeatedly as she tried her best to avoid physical contact with the masses or a sticky drink on her crocodile shoes. She flipped down her upholstered banquette and flattened out a copy of *The Times* on its suspect seat pad before settling into place. No one talked above a hand-hidden whisper while looking in Margaret's direction. Even here, in this Nottingham picture-house, news had reached filmgoers of her most recent tabloid entry in which she fought off a band of thieves with a clothes iron.

The tittering hushed immediately the famous Pearl & Dean theme sprang to life – '*De da, de dah, de dah, de dah, de de dah*' – the onscreen titles outlined through the still-drawn curtains.

What followed was the most intense, exciting two and a half hours of my life.

Dolly was indeed a lovely Jewish lady, just as Nanny Webb had promised, whose gutsy spark set a little feminist fire in me. I resolved to spend less time masturbating and more time reading my copy of *Malory Towers*.

Private, Keep Out!

My greatest abiding memory of my time at St Mary's was the couple in the block of flats over the road who enjoyed having sex with the lights on and curtains open for the enjoyment of the boarders. We'd lift our nightdresses to egg them on. Whenever we saw the husband in the street, we'd take great pleasure in shouting '*Wanker!*' at him as loudly as possible since this was also something he liked to do at the window.

Before this time I had very little idea about sex itself but spent many hours lusting after Romanian tennis star Ilie Nastase. I was enough of a realist to know he was never going to be my boyfriend. He was twenty-seven and I was eleven. It would never have worked. I'd previously had a thing for Elvis but Nastase was more accessible in the summer months because, as the world's number 1, he was bound to be at Wimbledon. Nastase was a sexy, tanned trouble-maker as well as funny and flamboyant on court, a subliminal turn on – even if I didn't know what that meant at the time. He was an early example of something that gave me a funny feeling in my lower half, a sort of gateway drug to more blatant forms of titillation. He was in no way linked to the pornographic industry but from where I was standing, he did the same job. He was the perfect substitute for a dirty magazine.

The 1970s were the heyday of top-shelf pornography. Even as an eleven-year-old girl I knew not to look up when I got my copy of *Jackie* from the newsagent. Overall, people seemed fairly happy with its existence, just so long as it was out of reach for those five feet and under. Poor old Willie Carson.

Erotica

My dad kept his copy of *Playboy* unashamedly in the top drawer of his bedside table alongside his carton of duty-free Rothmans. I know this to be true because, from the age of twelve, I was leafing through one and smoking the other. I spent many hours happily occupied in this way. Until sex becomes hormonally relevant, pornography is met with the same exaggerated disgust reserved for Brussels sprouts. Either that or a forensic level of fascination. For Theresa and me, it was absolutely the latter.

Occasionally we'd find ourselves in possession of a nudie magazine, unearthed in a barn or under a horse blanket somewhere. Treasure in hand, we'd trek back to the castle nursery, where we'd create our own gallery, sticking the centrefolds to the bathroom windows with blobs of toothpaste. We'd grade and inspect the various pinups, giving marks for the biggest boobies or nicest hair. Even though they were 'in the nuddie', there was nothing rude about them from our point of view. Miss April, for example, was a two-time Playmate and, from memory, extremely wholesome. While I definitely had a crush on her, what I really wanted was for someone like her to be my nanny.

Once the relevant hormones kicked in, pictures were important but the addition of words was a much-sought-after bonus. Most straight men were happy with a picture of a naked lady, ideally with her legs open, but I'm inclined to think that, for women, getting turned on is a more cerebral activity.

In 1978 I left St Mary's and returned to London to sit my A levels. I became a day girl at Queen's Gate School for Girls, a bike ride from Cottesmore Gardens and near the Natural History Museum. In those days, Queen's Gate was the London equivalent of St Mary's – not your first choice if you were an academic but perfectly good enough if you were scraping through. I narrowly missed Trinny, who rocked up two years later having been at boarding school from the age of six.

The discovery of a cache of erotic literature hidden in the ceiling of the loos at Queen's Gate was testimony to a lady's need for cerebral stimulation to get turned on. I'm not sure which girl was the first to find it but it was well known that, by standing on the lavatory seat, you could stretch up to pop open the foamy white (possibly asbestos) ceiling tile and expose the void within. This only worked if you were tall for your age but, presuming you were, you had access to a whole stash of dirty books.

There was quite a range to choose from, but the one that really stood out was the *Story of O* – the tale of a woman 'taught to be constantly available for oral, vaginal, and anal intercourse'. Though I did my best to put the book to good use I found it too extreme and not erotic enough to really do the trick. There was not much debate about the true owner of this collection of erotica. We all agreed it must have belonged to the bewhiskered History of Art teacher, Miss Delalio. We had nothing to substantiate this other than the fact she wore a lot of corduroy and lived on-site, but even so, poor Miss Delalio never outlived the rumour.

Finding a stash of pornographic material was quite a community event. Unless we were going to *use* the magazines for something more private, it was the excitement of finding and discussing them that really united us. Even if we weren't old enough to be interested in the content, the clandestine nature of the whole escapade was tremendously bonding, and an Enid Blyton spirit of adventure accompanied their discovery.

'Hold on, everybody,' yelled Julian, 'there's a bag over here with some sort of dirty magazines inside.' The others rushed over as Timmy ran excitedly round Anne's legs, nearly tripping her up. There was a bit of jostling between Dick and George so Julian rather sensibly suggested they take it in turns.

For us, it was as much about camaraderie as it was ladies in the nude.

Most magazines had already had at least one careful owner – the identity of whom was unknown, but would nevertheless be hotly debated by every child in any village they were found. We had our suspicions about certain locals, though we based most of our predictions on gossip, folklore and Chinese whispers. My money was always on anyone who lived alone or had a beard, though I think this was largely down to the illustrations in *The Joy of Sex*.

Such was the secrecy around porn, an Ikea flat-pack

wardrobe would have been easier to smuggle in and out of the house than a copy of *Playboy*. I'm reliably informed that the best way to do it was in a standard-issue briefcase. A magazine could be ejected into any passing layby or ditch with a quick flick of a spring-loaded catch and no one would be any the wiser. Apparently, this was most commonly carried out on the way to work. If you wanted to rid yourself of a whole collection, though, that was another proposition altogether and one that required a great deal of forethought. Or a bonfire.

A bit of virginal Barbara Cartland was my touchstone for romance. I wanted to be the underdog heroine who ended up marrying the prince. For a girl who was (unwittingly) in training to be a society bride, it was the perfect reading material. Barbara taught me everything I thought I needed to know about relationships. Her leading men were wonderfully dashing and completely devoid of personality. Except for a change of name or title they were also identical in every book. I fell in love with them all. Harold Robbins was another favourite which I skim-read for the sexy parts, but I was also quite partial to Mr Rochester and Maxim de Winter. I fantasised about looking after Mr Rochester when he went blind and wanted to protect Maxim de Winter from Mrs Danvers after she burned his house down. Both men started out as gruff, broad-shouldered and seemingly impenetrable but were eventually won over by the lady's kindness and warm heart.

I now see this is exactly what happened with my husband. One of the greatest lessons I've learned is that Prince Charming is not a one-size-fits-all concept. Identifying exactly what it is you're looking for in a saviour is all part of the learning curve and largely dependent on what you yourself bring to the table. In my experience, that bit is harder to work out and it's taken me nearly thirty years of marriage to even think to ask the question.

I supplemented what these novels lacked in visual stimulation with the men's underwear section of Mrs A's catalogue, which she kept on her sewing table. Since most people didn't regard this as pornography, I was able to browse through it unmonitored in the comfort of her sitting room. I preferred the Y-fronts to the boxer shorts because the clear outline of their private parts made picking my favourite much easier.

At sixteen I found a copy of Anaïs Nin's *Delta of Venus* in my father's drawer. I read it cover to cover in one sitting on the floor of my parents' bathroom because this was the only room in the house with a lock. I had no idea how often he read it or how integral it was to his love life so didn't dare remove it from the immediate vicinity.

Outwardly, my father was a traditional, conservative man whose future had been predetermined by his family background. Had he been born at a different time to different parents, I think he may have allowed himself to be more bohemian – a sort of Henry Miller. Regrettably, he was pigeonholed by convention. It seems incredible to me that he had a copy of this book but perhaps I'm doing him a disservice. He was an extraordinarily creative man and I feel rather proud to think he owned something so progressive. I'd loved to have asked how it came into his possession. His owning it represents a side to him that I never had a chance to discover. In an interview with the *Lady* in 2017, I cited *Delta of Venus* as one of six books to have most influenced me, but sadly I don't think many women of my father's generation would have been given the opportunity to read it. My mother, I'm sure, cannot have known there was a copy in her husband's nightstand. Even as a very little girl I recall telling her about the 'funny feeling I get in my front bottom' as I fell asleep and how nice it felt. I don't remember her response but, as with every other awkward bedtime conversation, she no doubt put it down to eating too much cheese before bed.

Why Weren't More Women Codebreakers?*

Once I got into my stride, the list of reasons I'd masturbate was pretty exhaustive. It included, but was not limited to:

getting to sleep,
keeping warm,
nothing on the telly.

When I did do it, it was always covert and it seems I was not alone in this. Researching this chapter and hearing the 'secret' rituals developed by my allied fiddlers is one of the few times I've blushed in forty years. I've also not laughed so much since discovering Derek and Clive. The fact that women masturbate is not news – *Cosmo* and *Marie Claire* are filled with articles about 'The Need to Know Yourself' – but when I was a child, the topic was completely taboo. In the late '70s,

---

* While 75 per cent of people employed at Bletchley Park were women, only a handful worked as codebreakers. Many of the men felt this sort of intellectual activity would be beyond the ladies. However, Vera Atkins was a significant part of the team that broke the Enigma code, and Jane Fawcett decoded a message that led to the sinking of the *Bismarck*, so that told them.

Ann Summers muscled in on the Tupperware-party circuit and female desire was discussed with more freedom. These early childhood fumbles were something altogether different. Yes, most of us did it but, unless you'd grown up as part of the Bloomsbury Set, you were unlikely to be the first to admit it. The upshot was a wave of inventive, resourceful women adept at making do with whatever they could get their hands on to service themselves.

For boys there was more camaraderie. One friend told me their nightly routine at boarding school was to pass round a single copy of *Penthouse* after lights out so everyone could have a turn under a tented bedsheet. Another hid his father's edition of *Men Only* inside his own copy of Richard Scarry's *What Do People Do All Day?* Fed up waiting for its return, his father eventually marched into his son's bedroom, over to the bookcase, and retrieved his property. With an exasperated, 'Get your own bloody magazine,' he turned on his heel and left.

There were no such easy arrangements for the girls. If the boys operated in platoons, the girls faced the activity in isolation. Being a female masturbator required the skill and discretion of a spy – it was a lonely, solitary job with no one to turn to for advice. You knew instinctively that if you tried to contact base camp for help, you'd find the telephone lines dead and the headquarters deserted. You were on your own.

Learning how to make a success of it was like being locked in an escape room and told to get out using only things you found lying around the house. What I didn't realise was that all my friends had been given the same conundrum. Solving the puzzle required a lot of imagination, some knowledge of the laws of physics, and persistent trial and error. Why they

Watching the Calgary Stampede, British Columbia, c.1974.

Cookout at the OK Corral, Rocky Mountains, Canada, c.1972.

On board *Le Pistou*, St Tropez, c.1970.

Showing off my catch. It weighed nearly as much as me. Vancouver Island, c.1972.

Belvoir Castle.

Mum and Dad outside the Priory.
NB: high wire now in place to stop the
horses eating the hedges.

Dad's pastel of the Priory, which I now look at every time I have a bath.

The Knipton Set in the Spring Garden at Belvoir Castle.

Dad and 'The Duchess', Corsica.

Mum and the duke, Italy.

Mum.

A rare snap of me with Mum and Dad at my post-wedding cocktail do. The Orangery, Holland Park, 1995.

didn't have more female codebreakers at Bletchley Park is anyone's guess – we had all the necessary training.

Such is the embarrassment surrounding the topic, most women will take the secrets of their solutions to the grave. Even now, very few have been willing to come forward for the purposes of my limited research. I totally understand. I was only able to convey my own Enid Blyton-inspired method to my friend via text message provided she swore on her daughter's life to burn after reading. There are limits to what even I am happy to admit in print.

R&D

A friend of mine had a foolproof system incorporating the corner of her bedroom chest of drawers. The trick was to balance without slipping while maintaining enough pressure to close the deal. When the family moved house and left her beloved drawers behind she was devastated. 'It was my first real break up,' she told me. The doorframe was *my* first sexual partner. White-knuckled, I'd hang by my hands, breast-stroking furiously with my legs. A combination of tight jeans, friction and gravity meant I'd be done and dusted in thirty seconds. Another free-thinking friend relaxed with a roll-on cherry lip-gloss over episodes of John Thaw in *The Sweeney*, fantasising she was 'the brass who was his nark who he shagged occasionally'. More left of field was a girl we'll call 'Denise' who carefully selected the flattest, smoothest twigs to put down the front of her knickers. I wish I'd known about all this at the time because I'd have suggested she used a lolly stick instead. Had we only shared our ideas, we could have had so much more fun.

Sadly, guilt played a huge part in most amateur fumblings. One friend said her Catholicism meant she could only ever indulge with her Braun Epilady over the *top* of her trousers. The nun who taught her domestic science had no such qualms and spent most of the lesson rocking back and forth on the edge of the freestanding kitchen units with her skirts up. Navigating the waters between shame and desire is something many friends mentioned. One said the minute she got started she'd immediately imagine her grandfather hovering judgementally over her bed and be forced to stop. Drowning out the internal voices that tell you it's dirty, wicked or abnormal is an integral part of the process. I am convinced it's also part of the reason masturbation, like yoga, takes years to properly master.

If I could go back in time and give my younger self a piece of advice, it would be this: Go forth, study hard, work harder, get a good job and gain your independence so that one day, if you're lucky, you might end up with your own ensuite bathroom with its own lockable door. It may seem unlikely, but privacy is actually the answer to a surprising number of life's little problems.

The Shop Around the Corner

I doubt my parents ever once had a discussion about finances in the whole of their marriage. The only thing my mother knew about money was how to spend it, and even this only extended to the things she wanted rather than those she needed. It was my father's secretary who paid all the bills.

Aside from a few coins for the parking meter, my mother

never carried cash. There was no need. She had an account at Harrods and another at Peter Jones and a cheque book for everything else. Even in my twenties, when I entertained, I entertained at my parents' home (where I still lived) and put all the necessaries onto my mother's accounts. In order to do this I needed a permission slip from her, which she'd write on a piece of headed notepaper. I didn't enter a supermarket until I left home at twenty-three and realised that Harrods wasn't the cheapest place to buy cheese. The green-groceries and fish were purchased on Chelsea Green, and on special occasions she'd visit Pulbrook & Gould for flowers. Peonies and sweet peas were her favourites and, latterly, mine too. Everything else came from Harrods Food Hall and I knew my way around it like a seasoned chef. The prices were vastly inflated but, for my mother, it had the convenience of a supermarket combined with the personal touch of a corner

The cornucopia that was Harrods Food Hall.

91

shop. It also came with the advantage that everything she bought, she bought on tick.

If you've never been, the Food Hall is unlike anything you've ever seen. Were you to ask a set dresser at MGM to recreate a feast for the gods on Mount Olympus, Harrods Food Hall is what it would look like. Its imposing art deco, tile-clad hall covers at least an acre. Marble columns lift its high ceilings aloft like Atlas holding the skies on his shoulders. A vast, taxidermied blue marlin hung on the wall behind the lavish daily display of fresh fish. I always wondered whether he was trying to tell me something. And then there was the food itself. It's the only place I can think to describe using the word 'cornucopia' without it sounding like an exaggeration. Produce was imported from hotter climes, exotic and unseasonal, to the heart of Knightsbridge, strawberries in December, sprouts in June. Wicker baskets overflowed with bicoloured peaches and split pomegranates, disgorging their crimson seeds like a Caravaggio still life. Pears and apricots lay attached to their branches, and cucumbers and courgettes were proudly wonky and gnarled.

You'd expect Harrods to have prioritised perfection but actually the emphasis was on freshness. Customers knew it was the dowdiest or most imperfect that tasted the sweetest. And then there was the smell. Ray Charles would have pegged it as a greengrocer's the minute he crossed the threshold. You only needed to pick up a melon and smell it to know it was ripe. There was no plastic or packaging. Nothing was branded, except perhaps the smoked salmon. Harrods Food Hall was our version of an old-fashioned village shop. It's where Milly-Molly-Mandy would have got her shopping if she'd lived in Knightsbridge.

It was also the place that made my favourite birthday cake, an ice-cream one that came in a polystyrene box, packed in dry ice. I was warned repeatedly not to touch this, so I did and burned my fingers every year. Dry ice was a piece of scientific wizardry too mesmerising not to fiddle with. (The next time I saw it was at the St Mary's school dance. It curled around my feet as I stood pressed against the wall by a boy who, if I remember correctly, was called William and went to Radley. It was just as exciting then, though for very different reasons.) The Harrods orange and lemon sorbets served in their own skin were almost as exotic as the cake. In 1972 these were the height of culinary glamour, the kind of dessert you'd imagine Zsa Zsa Gabor might serve at a dinner party. They certainly weren't sold at the Co-op. Like so many other things, the only place I knew to get them was Harrods. The one time I doubted the department store's superior standing was on finding the Co-op sold Arctic Roll but Harrods didn't. I couldn't understand: Harrods could get anything! When Ronald Reagan telephoned their Pet Kingdom to buy an elephant the lady on the phone reportedly replied 'African or Indian, sir?' How on God's earth could they not sell Arctic Roll? When I questioned my mother about this inexplicable omission her response rocked me to the core: It wasn't that they *couldn't* get it, they just didn't want to. It was the first encounter I'd had with the class divide that actually mattered.

The last thirty years have not been kind to Harrods. A once awe-inspiring emporium, it has become a tourist attraction – a huge, expensive souvenir shop. But it wasn't always so.

To get to Harrods from my house I'd take the number 52 bus from Kensington to Knightsbridge. Pre health and safety,

London buses were doorless so you could hop on and off the back, swinging round the pole and narrowly missing the grumpy clippy with her ticket machine. A huddle would form at the open door of anyone not wanting to settle into a seat because they might be getting off soon. If you *were* getting off a moving bus you hit the ground running. A few steps were required to recalibrate your speed. If you didn't want to scatter your fellow pedestrians like skittles, you'd need to match their pace before reintegrating into the crowd. Getting on was much easier. As long as the vehicle had slowed to something approaching a halt, you could pick your way through the traffic and hop on. Bus stops were an irrelevance.

If I were taking the bus I'd do my best to wear jeans. The fibres of the carpet on the seats prickled through thin fabric so anything but denim was a no-no. A red cord that ran along the ceiling of both decks served as a signal to stop the bus with the ding-ding of a bell. As with the underside of most things in my youth, the bottoms of the seats were covered in chewing gum. An old lady, minus her dentures, might be sucking loudly on a bag of salt and vinegar crisps. Only the brave would broach the back seat with its snogging teens and YTS delinquents in their Burton suits. If you wanted to smoke you'd have to sit upstairs.

It's hard to describe the unique position Harrods held in the collective British conscience when I was growing up. The plain fact was there was a limit on what you could buy in 1979, but Baby Boomers didn't need Amazon Prime; they had Harrods. Its Latin motto – *Omnia Omnibus Ubique* – translates as 'All things for all people, everywhere'. Slight exaggeration – let's face it, it was no Woolworths – but if you couldn't afford to shop there regularly, it was the place you aspired to shop, somewhere you'd go as a treat, a destination. The 'all things' bit was absolutely true. Harrods was the place you could buy anything you wanted. That was its defining feature. However outlandish, exotic or hard to find, Harrods was the place to get it. It was the greatest concierge service in the world. It's difficult to imagine the novelty of this now. We live in an era where goods cross geographic and cultural borders with ease, where seasons and climate are no impediment to choice. The world was not always like this. If I wanted American breakfast cereal, the only way I'd get it was in the suitcase of a friend returning from their holidays. Other than feather-light airmail stationery, I got nothing in the post from abroad. Couriers were the preserve of millionaires and companies with time-zoned clocks in their foyers. There was no such thing as globalisation and without Harrods my world was correspondingly small.

Christmas Spirits

Christmas was always spent at the Priory. My dad would gather everyone round to decorate the tree and then refuse to let anyone touch it. For him, the tree was a work of art and he was meticulous about balance and symmetry. The lights had belonged to paternal grandparents, as had all the glass baubles. Every year they were packed away in tissue paper and kept safely in a cupboard in the guest bedroom. It was my job to go and get them down because the box was deemed light enough for me to carry (hopefully) without incident. I didn't need to be told how precious these were.

The tree always came from the Belvoir estate via the saw-mill. Ten foot tall, it was stood upright in a black rubber bucket of wet sand by Mr Taylor, our gardener.

Mr Taylor always wore a flat cap and tweed jacket and had whiskers that grew from his cheeks. He had one roll-up tucked behind his left ear and another, unlit, permanently between his lips. He didn't smoke. He hardly spoke either, probably because he'd *not* been given a set of dentures for his eighteenth birthday and was toothless. The roll-ups were a convenient prop. He looked exactly like Beatrix Potter's Mr McGregor. Every day he'd take elevenses with Mrs A in the kitchen. His son was the local butcher who made the best sausages I've ever tasted. Everyone on the estate was either friends with or related to everyone else. All our vegetables came from Mr Taylor's garden, caged in chicken wire. Every summer I'd pick the fruit there – raspberries, blackcurrants, redcurrants, gooseberries and strawberries, and the succulent white peaches in his greenhouse, which I'd eat straight from the branch. Every Christmas Eve, Mr Taylor would trudge through the house in his winter-muddied boots and put up the tree for us in the drawing room.

The first set of lights were put on top to bottom rather than side to side or wrapped around the tree, and always equidistant. My father had an eye for this. He considered coloured lights common so ours were all white. A second set was then put around the tree, not winding down but helter-skelter. It looked as if he'd mapped it out on graph paper ahead of time. You could have put a spirit level on any strand and the air bubble would have sat perfectly in the middle. I don't know what he did at the back of the tree to facilitate this but it always looked perfect from both sides. It was a true Christmas miracle. Then came the tinsel, which was all silver and put on to disguise the wires. When I was little I'd watch him doing all of this. It was part of the advent. Father Christmas would already have set off. Last but not least were the baubles, which is when we were finally allowed to participate. We would place them where the wires crossed and drape them outwards from there. Precision was key. We had six miniature crackers that had never been opened and these would be tucked carefully on branches. When I was small my dad would put me on his shoulders so I could place the fairy on the very top. I'd usually put it on wonky and he'd have to go over my work. I knew this was going to happen but it didn't matter, it was part of the ritual. Finally, we'd congregate to light the lights which was always met with an *Oooh* and an *Ahhh*.

Once I'd learned that Father Christmas wasn't real I discovered that the bell I'd heard as he flew past our house had been my sister all along. Mrs A would give me a homemade mince pie to put out for him, together with a tumbler of her cooking sherry. I'd write my Christmas list on a piece of paper which we'd set fire to before watching the smuts get sucked up the chimney. Our stockings were old shooting socks laid at the bottom of our beds. I was so convinced of his existence, I swore blind I'd seen the lights of his sleigh go through the sky. I also claimed I'd seen him coming into my bedroom with his sack. When I failed to give a more detailed account of this, I said it was because my eyes were so tightly shut. Everyone knew he didn't leave presents for children who were still awake when he came. These tales went unchallenged long after I'd stopped believing in him. There seemed no need to spoil the lie.

After Mrs A had prepared, served, cleared and tidied our Christmas lunch it was on to handing round the presents, during which she'd sit collecting torn-off wrapping paper for the bin bag. We'd give her our presents and she'd give us hers. All the while her own daughter was waiting in the next room for her mother to 'get home from work' so they could have their own Christmas Day once ours had finished. It never once occurred to me to wonder what Lorraine was doing while we were having our lunch. I took all this for granted – I thought it was just 'what Mrs A did'. Put another way, my parents never gave their housekeeper a Christmas Day off. Looking back, this does not seem quite so idyllic.

Finally we'd settle down to watch a catalogue of television shows that have not fared well with the passage of time.

That Christmas

Church with the Duke and Duchess of Rutland – aka the Manners family – was a cornerstone of Christmas Day. Getting the right seat was a critical part of the equation because it said something about who you were in the pecking order. The congregation was made up of people from all over the Belvoir estate so it wasn't just a church service, it was a celebration. It was Sunday Best and best behaviour for everyone. The Manners family sat in the front pew and it was a race to make sure you got a seat as close to them as possible. God forbid we should be late and end up at the back. In all other respects, the Mannerses were like family to us. The parents were as much friends as the children.

Theresa, Eddie (in his Eton togs), David (today's duke), the Duchess and the Duke of Rutland – aka the Manners family.

We went on holidays together, ate together and learned together. The only time we were not treated as family was on Christmas Day in Bottesford church. We didn't walk, drive or arrive there with them. They took their place at the front to signify they were the most important, revered people on the estate. The church belonged to them. The vicar was employed by them. They paid the wages of many of the congregation. They parked their car outside the Rectory while we parked ours in the street. This mattered to my father and his indignance was palpable throughout the morning as we drew closer and closer to leaving the house.

Over the years I've become a shameless, outspoken star-fucker but this was always done with humour. When I met Kate Bush at Elton and David's wedding, the first thing I did was call Trinny to show off. When I met Sam Fender at the Isle of Wight Festival, I made sure I got photographic evidence.

I've enjoyed every moment of this and had fun with it. I don't think my father did. His anxiety, I believe, came from a genuine need to fit in with the people he wanted to be around. He'd always been insecure about his lack of noble heritage. I never cared about any of that. I didn't care that my best friend was a lady or that she lived in a castle. It was meaningless to me. But not to my father. I wish he were alive now because, at the time, I didn't think to empathise or understand him. His stress over getting the day right just annoyed me.

We were usually on time and his anxieties unfounded but, one particular Christmas Day, we *were* late and he was furious. The paths were icy and the soles of my mother's new shoes were leather. By the time we reached the path to the church she was also drunk. When she slipped and fell and hit her head on a gravestone, it was a curt 'Pull yourself together, Mary-Rose,' rather than an affectionate 'Are you alright?' that fell easily from his lips.

Pull Yourself Together

I'd heard my father use that phrase on more than one occasion. 'Pull yourself together, Mary-Rose.' We all knew she was drunk but no one else was there to see it. No one else would even have known had he not said it. But he didn't comfort her or reach out to her. What he effectively told her was 'You've failed', and more specifically, 'You've failed *me*.' She was a disappointment and you could hear it in his voice. She was being scolded.

I know that when I think of my father, and my anxiety around being told off, what I really feared was disappointing him. Letting him down from some imagined level he'd set for himself and, by extension, us. I had my father on a pedestal so his approval mattered enormously. I was proud of him – for his intelligence, his artistic eye, his humour. He was a very entertaining man. I wanted to please him so he'd feel the same way about me. I did not want to be scolded. Though I can't remember him ever being particularly unhappy with me, I do remember him being unhappy with my mother. When this happened I absorbed his anger as if I were the cause. I couldn't shake the feeling his displeasure was my responsibility. I learned to be scared of my father via my mother. The way she showed her fear was by doing everything he told her to do and by lying about it when she hadn't. I did exactly the same. It is a pattern I am still trying to break.

The handle of my mother's hunting crop was antler horn with a monogrammed silver band. It was engraved with her family crest and had belonged to her mother before her. One day I took it and went into the woods. In my make-believe game, I was the huntsman and Piglet – my dog – my trusty foxhound. Somewhere on our travels, Piglet and I lost the crop. When my father found out, he was predictably enraged. It was a textbook 'Come into my study' moment. When I told him I hadn't touched it he believed me. The matter was dropped but not over. My guilt wouldn't allow me to let it go. I assumed he was hiding his anger and lived in fear of being punished anyway. I may just as well have told the truth. This was exactly the predicament my mother was so often in. It must have been exhausting. She lied constantly so he didn't trust her. I repeated her behaviour and assumed he didn't trust me either.

When my parents rowed it was always behind closed doors but we'd know perfectly well there was trouble. Mum would come out not in tears but just sort of empty – like she had disappeared somewhere. You could tell he was angry but there was no slamming of doors. He'd light a cigarette and read the newspaper, retreating into himself. They both did. Then I'd quietly retreat too. I'd go off with the dogs into the woods, or visit Dandy. The way I dealt with emotional confrontation was to remove myself from the situation and a silence would fall on the house. We all ignored it. That's how our family dealt with everything.

The way my dad responded to my mother's drinking was unsettling for us all. His withdrawal changed the atmosphere in our home. The cloud that hovered over us was palpable. The fact he didn't shout was irrelevant: his silence was just as audible. It was in my interest to hide her drinking. Covering it up was a form of self-preservation. Not upsetting the status quo was the driving force behind much of my behaviour and that's a hard habit to shake.

From the age of six I was to all intents and purposes raised as an only child. My sister had been sent to boarding school at twelve and effectively never came home. By the time she'd gone to finishing school, my mother was a changed woman but, in the natural order of things, Annette was ready to move on. Her approach was practical; she flew the nest, which I understood. She didn't feel like she could fix my mother but I was still naive enough to think I could. At six years older, Annette must have seen things through different eyes and known that there was nothing she could do to fix things even if she had stayed. She did exactly what young people are meant to do.

wake the children. Call 999. Fire and ambulance.' He picked up his wife, who lay limply in his arms. An empty bottle of sleeping pills fell from her hand and rolled under the bed.

I wish I could say this was the denouement of a cheap gothic novel. Sadly it's a sensational retelling of one of my mother's failed suicide attempts. Names and places changed for dramatic effect.

Two of my favourite novels – *Jane Eyre* and *Wuthering Heights* – have more than a touch of the gothic about them. Castles, or at the very least roomy mansions; a brooding man mooching about somewhere; ghosts, dreadful weather and women who've gone or go bonkers. I've never really thought until now about how closely my own life followed these literary conventions. Right down to the mad woman who sets light to her bed, it was all there; I just hadn't pieced the story together. I'd also never really considered why this genre paid so much attention to these themes or why it had such currency among female audiences. Was it that the gothic novel *happened* to reflect the repression of women or that it came about *in order* to illustrate these injustices? Women had had no voice to speak of, but the rise of literacy amongst those in the middle classes was beginning to give them one. They had been repressed and silenced for years – in marriage, education, politics and society as a whole. Were these stories a way of letting the world know how they were being perceived, labelled and treated?

It was the way my mother was treated. Had she lived fifty years earlier, she would have been a wife who was locked in an attic. For her, the themes of a gothic novel were not the stuff of fantasy; they were the world she grew up in. One that was completely ignorant and unsympathetic towards troubles in mental health. My grandparents *were* Victorians. Women who went 'mad' really were locked away without their consent. When Charlotte Brontë dedicated *Jane Eyre* to her hero William Thackeray, there was more than a ripple of embarrassment when she found out that, just as with Mr Rochester, Thackeray's own wife was secluded away after periods in the insane asylum.

A modern interpretation of my mother's behaviour would be that she was ill and, more than likely, treatable. Sadly, during her lifetime, her treatment wasn't so far off that of an inmate at Bedlam. A denial of her emotional needs, a reluctance to allow her to *express* them, electric shock treatments behind the closed doors of a sterile sanatorium. It was positively Victorian. She was Bertha Mason, Catherine Earnshaw, Jane Eyre and Mrs Danvers all rolled into one.

And, just as with my mother, it was the men in their lives who deemed these fictional women insane. Even if diagnosed by a doctor, that doctor would be a man. Women are quite used to seeing and coping with extreme emotion. It's not them who feel the need to shut it away in the attic. When faced with another woman's emotional outburst, women are unlikely to respond with, My God! We must call the doctor! As a child I was not able to apply reason to the situation. I took my cue from my father, who was both frightened and ill-equipped to deal with my mother. I now see her illness for what it was: she was a manic depressive who, mismanaged and unsupported, descended into alcoholism, mania, and finally dementia. It was a tale as old as time and one that had been told in many forms in the pages of my favourite novels.

Given my own experience, perhaps it was no coincidence I was drawn to these stories. There was definitely a comfort in knowing I was not alone.

Arrested Development

In many ways I was a capable and independent girl. I drove a car, rode a horse, swam in lakes, roamed the fields and came home after dark. I could have hit my head on a rock in the water and died and no one would have noticed till well into the evening. If I didn't turn up for Mrs A's dinner, that would be a red flag, but before that the alarm would not be raised. On another level, my mother point-blank refused to acknowledge I was growing up at all. I didn't wear a bra until I was old enough to go to the shops alone and buy one for myself because she never did. It wasn't that she refused, she just never discussed it and I certainly wasn't about to bring it up. Right up until she died, I would get tiny china ornaments in my Christmas stocking like the ones I'd loved as a little girl. This could easily be confused with nostalgia on my mother's part but not when you add the *Guinness Book of Records* and *Bunty* annual to the gift list – both of which she gave me well into my twenties. She was in charge of my stocking and this was filled with reminders of my young childhood. Long after I'd stopped looking after Dandy, there'd be brushes and tail bandages, a red and green velvet brow-band for his bridle from the local tack shop in Grantham. The Christmas I turned sixteen I opened a child's pair of pale pink ballet tights. I don't know what my reaction was. Not anger but weariness perhaps at the predictability of it.

My father was in charge of my main present. As a teenager this would typically be something practical or indulgent – a pretty pair of gold acorns from S. J. Phillips on Bond Street in London's West End where he got all my mum's jewellery. I remember sitting at her dressing table, taking out the pieces he'd bought from her jewellery box. An emerald and diamond clasp to put on a string of pearls, or an antique pair of drop earrings. The thing I wanted most looked like an Olympic gold medal on a watch chain. It was the size of a flat tangerine. For Christmas he'd always give my mother jewellery or art. A small pair of Ferneley oils – hunting scenes – or Old Master drawings. The one I really loved was of a woman on a chestnut mare riding side-saddle in her habit and top hat. When she was well my mother would have loved these things but, by the time she was ill, they were meaningless. They were really gifts my father wanted for himself.

There was a time when my parents were a properly functioning part of their social circle; entertaining and entertained. Back then, what the women wore was dictated by the men. If they were in smoking jackets or black tie, women would wear 'long'. If the men were in suits, it was cocktail. In London it might be a bouclé Chanel suit. For a dinner party in the country, a floor-length, wool-crepe Cacharel skirt, YSL shirt and Hermès belt. My mother was by far the best-dressed woman in their group. My father had plenty of money and she had wonderful taste, the perfect combination. Her favourite vintage shop was opposite Butler & Wilson on the Fulham Road, though I can't for the life of me remember the name of it.

I don't recall what Annette got in her stocking but I know it wasn't like mine. It wouldn't have been, because my mother didn't have the same relationship with my sister. Annette was already in her twenties and living in New York by the time my mother's illness was at its peak. I was still living at home. But it wasn't just this. Right from the time I was a little girl, my mother was fixated with me. She clung on to my childhood as if it were her own. My mother's illness seemed to have devoured the years between my being a child and an adult. At the age of forty-five, her clock had stopped and she never moved beyond the point it took hold. I wore a velvet head-band and she took to wearing them too. If she bought me a nightdress, she'd buy herself the same. On reflection I think she was trying to rewrite her history through me. It sounds a dreadfully unkind thing to say, but it was slightly unsettling. By the time I was a teenager she treated everything that was mine as if it was hers. It was almost as if she wanted to be me. On some level I think she felt she *was* me. It got to the point where I found it suffocating. I never discussed this with any-one, I just didn't want it to be happening. At the time it was an embarrassment. I covered my disgust with anger but the truth was I felt something between discomfort and fear.

It wasn't until I was sixteen or seventeen that I realised how ill she really was.

My mother had refused to get rid of many of my childhood clothes so they hung, unwanted and outgrown, in my ward-robe at the Priory like a shrine. I'd become accustomed to seeing them and justified their existence with the idea we were saving them for the day I had my own children. When I came into my bedroom to find my mother trying to get into one of my old party dresses, I knew we could never go back to pre-tending things were OK. It was the same Liberty-print frock

I'd worn to *Hello, Dolly!* Tiny mother-of-pearl buttons punctuated the back. It had hung on a child's padded hanger for the past ten years or so and now here was my mother trying desperately to get it on over her head, her own clothes making the task even more ludicrous. She was clearly in the middle of an episode. It was both pitiful and disturbing in equal measure.

Whatever I felt about seeing her in this state manifested as exasperation, which was a measure of how numbed I'd become to her behaviour. I wasn't unaffected; I'd just found a way to cover it up. She didn't react as if she'd been caught doing something wrong. The fact the incident passed without remark was a clear indication of how far things had deteriorated. It was a turning point in our already fragile relationship, the end of things for me. I didn't want her to be the child. That was supposed to be my job and I felt huge resentment that my mother had 'left'. From then on, there were bursts of normalcy, and every time they happened, I clung on to them in the hope she'd stay. I couldn't reject her completely, I loved her too much, but my feelings towards her were impossibly complicated.

The real education of my early years was learning how to cope without support. To get on with it. To harden myself to what I saw around me. I'd been alone in many ways since I'd left home for boarding school at twelve. I'd not been aware of my mother being ill before that time but looking at her behaviour from a distance, it must have started earlier than I realised. If nothing else, I see that sending me a dead animal in the post is not the action of a woman in her right mind.

My sister describes our mother as a persistent liar. Knowing Mum's past, I think it was rather that she created a parallel, fictional version of life to make the truth more palatable. I bought into this but my sister was too old to be able to ignore the truth. My mother had had both a troubled childhood and chronic post-natal depression, and, in the absence of anyone who really understood or was empathetic, her dark thoughts around these memories turned in on themselves. They created shadows around her that never left her side. They moved as she moved, stood between her and her relationships and living itself. No one came to her aid. When my father could not understand what she was going through, she withdrew further and further into this black hole. Whether through fear or a genuine lack of understanding, he didn't want to believe she had a drinking problem. Even when I came home one afternoon from school to find her passed out in bed, it took me calling the GP to take a blood test to prove to my father she'd had three-quarters of a bottle of vodka. 'I have to tell you, Joe, I believe your wife is losing her mind.' Still he refused to accept it.

My father hid the full extent of things. Friends knew she was unwell but it was an unspoken rule not to bring it up and to treat everything as if it were normal. The flip side of this meant there was no one for us to turn to. In any case, I never thought I needed to. It didn't seem justified. Even now I find it difficult to gauge when things are bad enough to ask for help. The feeling I don't deserve it is always lurking in the background. Do I really feel bad enough to call on another person? Asking for help is usually my last port of call when it should probably be the first. I'm sure I'm not alone in this.

When our son Joe was born I suffered from undiagnosed post-natal depression. My father had not long died and, while sorting through the furniture in his house, I had a severe panic attack. The doctor prescribed antidepressants for anxiety and for six weeks I took them without telling Sten. I was so ashamed of my weakness, I couldn't bring myself to discuss it with him. I was frightened I'd be labelled in the same way as my mother had been and the cycle would begin all over again. When he found the pills in my bag he was furious because I'd not trusted him enough to tell him why I had them. I was pre-empting how he'd feel based on how I thought my father felt about my mother. I'd seen first-hand what happened to women who fell apart. I didn't want anyone to tell me to 'Pull yourself together.' I didn't want to be told off. These patterns began in the years I sat in between my parents trying to decipher their unspoken emotional code.

In the past I always felt the need to be strong; always up, never down or depressed. Like my father, a lot of the time I've presented what I consider to be the perfect version of myself. Resilient, capable, without weakness. I'm known for being very empathetic, but if I saw a glimmer of neediness in someone, I'd panic at what might be under the surface. Like a form of PTSD, it brought back memories of my mother and I shut down. Over the course of my career I helped many people, but there was never any long-term requirement to be responsible for them. It was helping on my own terms. When my mother was ill I kept her at arm's length emotionally because the thought of the alternative was overwhelming – like I'd drown if the floodgates were allowed to open.

My mother's illness had swirled round my feet like water, the current threatening to pull me under for years, but as a family we collectively stood firm in the hope we'd survive.

With these psychotic episodes, any shadow of a maternal role model was conclusively swallowed up, and with them the last vestiges of my innocence. I could no longer pretend to rely on my parents for my security or strength. On a practical level I was grossly unprepared for adult life, but on an emotional one I'd seen and heard more than any girl of my age should.

Act Two

Ready for Absolutely Nothing

On June 3rd 1983, I became an on-paper adult and ticked all the boxes a trainee society wife should. With St Mary's and Queen's Gate behind me, my academic instruction was complete. I'd gone through the same token educational process as all the other daughters I knew. There'd been no anxious wait for exam results because we weren't expected to go to university; just to marry well within our tribe and produce an heir – ideally male. For some, including my sister, the final part of this charade was finishing school, which was where

I did it first.

you'd learn to lay a table and how to make a bed properly. My social class was in the business of manufacturing wives and these schools were where they went to have the finishing touches applied. Switzerland seemed an awfully long way to go and finishing school a very expensive method of learning how to make a bloody bed; Annette could have just asked Mrs A to show her. Then again, Mrs A couldn't have taught her how to get down a black run.

I'm not sure why it was never suggested I go to finishing school. Instead, I was given three possible options: a stint at Queen's Secretarial College on the Gloucester Road, Montessori teacher-training at Lancaster Gate, or Cordon Bleu classes in Paris. Though I later studied the Montessori Method, at this point I plumped for the one to do with food.

The Pot-au-Feu cookery school in the heart of Paris was a training ground for professional chefs. And me. It was the kind of place Raymond Blanc might have gone as an apprentice. I learned to make îles flottantes (a sort of meringue floating in rich custard), pâté de foie gras from fresh goose livers, and how to boil a lobster alive. As you can imagine, I use these skills constantly. If you weren't planning on running a Michelin-starred restaurant, you'd have to keep your fingers crossed you'd grow up to be the mistress of a chateau to have any hope of an ROI.

There were six of us and I was the only female. Everyone else wore chef's whites and I was lent a stripy apron to cover my jeans and t-shirt. Seemingly out of place, I actually felt very comfortable. It was Mick's stables again. These people had all come to work. To better themselves in their chosen field. There were no archaic hierarchies or pointless customs. It was an environment completely free from social pressures which allowed me to be the person I was below the surface. I was the shittest cook there, but a glimmer of the old work ethic found its way to the light again and I worked as hard as the best of them. I had purpose.

Even if I'd been top of my class, however, there was never any intention this might be something I'd do to make money, or as a career. In fact, there was never any thought of my having a career at all or even to make a living. It seems bonkers, but it wasn't something I'd ever thought about. It wasn't that I'd never contemplated work, but I didn't equate it with the need to support myself financially. Nothing I did was leading anywhere except marriage, which would, in theory, be the answer; the resolution to all life's questions. Any conversation about further education, therefore, was totally arbitrary because everyone knew whatever you did would be abandoned the minute you married. My mother had never worked and nor had her sisters. I was doing what had been expected of girls in my family for centuries. The world I lived in was so narrow and inward-looking I didn't realise I could be anything different. On 'graduating', I was essentially qualified to menu-plan a three-course dinner party and teach future children whether to use '*tu*' or '*vous*' when greeting a visiting French dignitary.

I could not have been called a debutante because post-war Britain had finally risen up against such blatant elitism and quashed the tradition of girls being presented at court like heifers at a county show. Had I been called on to go, however, I had the prerequisite Cornelia James gloves at the ready. My crowning glory was a full head of lowlights painstakingly maintained by Debrett's answer to Claire Rayner, Hugh Green on Ebury Street. His salon was a Chelsea institution, partly because of Hugh's Neil Diamond-esque vibe. All the ladies were in love with Hugh but he was too business-minded to ever once give it away. My exorbitant annual bill was bankrolled by my mother, who in turn was bankrolled by my father. Like many other women of the day, she'd been given her 'own' cheque book but this was financed and monitored by the man in her life. In the spirit of the age, she and I were encouraged to spend as much as possible on our appearance. International Women's Day was still some years off.

As a child I'd dragged behind my parents in whatever they did, like every other minor. In theory, when I hit my twenties, I'd begin the process of making my own decisions. Except there was no need. The people of my class were not looking to better themselves, or move up a notch. We were already there. There was no higher we could go. There was no desire to be anything other than what we already were, to rebel or strike out alone or propel ourselves forward. Yes, we wanted to move out of home, but not to do anything *different* than we'd be doing with our parents. Why on earth would we, when what was on offer was already the best you could get? Or so we were told . . . We were complacent, lacking the determination to break away and establish ourselves in our own right. It seems an incredible claim to make, but I had absolutely no opinions of my own.

In spite of everything we'd been given, we were a group of people virtually indistinguishable from one another. A production line of wives and brides. When the men came to pick, the aim was to look and sound as 'normal' as possible.

No one was looking for someone who might create trouble or throw the family line. The greatest value was placed on the woman who would give you an heir and not embarrass you by not knowing the salad from the fish fork. I wasn't a member of the aristocracy but my class mimicked their patterns.

As a gang we had a name, and that name was the Sloane Rangers, and we were divided into two equal parts – the Hoorays and the Nouveaus. What linked us was a private-school education and the sense of entitlement that came with it. I straddled both. Our uniform was described with words like 'effortless' and 'unambitious', which perfectly summed up a generation of young people with no need to provide for themselves. In the words of Scott Fitzgerald's Nick Carraway, we were 'careless people'.

At twenty-one, the degrading and demotivating truth was there was absolutely no expectation for me to amount to anything and I was on track to do exactly that.

I was just naive enough for life within the Royal enclosure. In my ankle-length, transparent skirt, Breton t-shirt and ballet pumps, I'd walked straight out of the pages of Ann Barr and Peter York's *The Sloane Ranger Handbook* and into the arms of earl-in-waiting David Linley – titled, supremely well-connected, and sixth in line to the British throne.

If I look at the traditional relationships I've had outside of my marriage, David Linley – Lord Snowdon – would be the most significant and, arguably, most tabloid-worthy. For most people, David was Princess Margaret's son and the Queen's nephew. For me, he was my first true love and ours was the partnership that defined my twenties.

And Then He Kissed Me

In May 1983, a month before my twenty-first birthday, I gave a dinner party at my parents' home in Cottesmore Gardens, Kensington. We'd moved from Pelham Place when I was fourteen but, even then, my bedroom was devoid of any indication it belonged to a teenager. For a start, it was never messy. Yes, we had Peggy to clear up after us, but equally I didn't *have* anything to make it a mess. Just my clothes and books – though most of those were at the Priory. I had nothing personal. No photographs. No toys. No stamp of individuality. Though the dormitory walls at St Mary's had been plastered with posters, I would never have dreamt – nor been allowed – to put them up in my bedroom at home. The wallpaper was far too expensive. My room may just as well have been a guest bedroom. There was nothing to suggest

David, not long before he kissed me.

who it belonged to. Ironically, whenever I travel now and stay somewhere for any length of time, one of my greatest pleasures is putting a personal stamp on my room. I love setting out my things. I also love personalising bedrooms for my own guests – flowers, a radio, a blanket or some magazines I know they'll like. Perhaps I'm making up for lost time. Cottesmore Gardens was very much my parents' house and my surroundings merely an extension of theirs.

I think perhaps I was always waiting to leave. I'd been at boarding school when the move was made and my mother's illness cast a shadow over the house unmodified by memories of happier times. Cottesmore Gardens was not a comforting place to be.

As always when I entertained at home, my parents made themselves scarce and sloped off to watch television in the study upstairs.

I want to pause a moment to reflect on this set-up. My parents subjugating themselves like this on my account was normal to me. At twenty-one I paid them no rent, contributed to no bills, and regularly asked them to absent themselves from their own home so I could entertain my friends. I had access to everything they owned and all the advantages that came with that. I was earning approximately £12,000 a year – nowhere near enough to finance the type of life I was living – and had choice and opportunity far beyond my own capabilities. On one level I had huge freedom, on another it was a subliminal, subconscious, entrenched form of control. Had my parents thrown me out on my ear and made me get a job at the local supermarket at eighteen, that would have been the end of the social life I knew. That would have been the end of the circles I moved in. That would have been the end of the path towards a suitable marriage. Left to my own devices, they would have had no control over my future. I don't believe this is something they did consciously or purposely, but I do see that while I had freedom, I had absolutely no independence, which made it very easy to keep me on my predetermined path to find a suitable husband.

On the day of my dinner party, my St Mary's friend Edwina Hicks called to ask if she could bring along her cousin David, because he wanted 'to meet new people'. Edwina was the daughter of David Hicks, the interior designer partly responsible for the graphic revolution in textiles in the 1960s. Amongst other things, his infamous brown and orange Hicks' Hexagon carpet is the defining feature of the hotel corridors in Stanley Kubrick's *The Shining*. Edwina was also the granddaughter of Lord Mountbatten so she had it covered from every side. Her cousin David was Princess

The Queen's nephew.

Margaret's son; nephew to the reigning monarch. Never one to be thrown by a last-minute guest, I laid an extra place to my left out of politeness and kept the place to my right free for the boy I was currently obsessed with. I knew who David Linley was – everyone did. I'd seen his photograph in the papers but it had made no discernible impression. Objectively he was handsome, though not jaw-droppingly so. He was short, not much taller than his mother, and had no reputation to speak of. There wasn't any obvious reason to get excited.

As with most memories, it's what I cooked that night which stands out: chicken liver pâté with Melba toast, and pesto butter-bean pasta with a crunchy Parmesan crust. While delicious, this menu didn't merit the grandeur of its surroundings. Like the rest of the house, the dining room at Cottesmore Gardens had been designed by John Fowler of Colefax and Fowler, with my dad as his able assistant. It was a homage to brown. Brown silk walls, brown deeply fringed velvet curtains and window-seat cushion, and a mushroom carpet that offset the gilded picture frames and ormolu candelabra. This sounds hideous but was a striking backdrop for candlelight and night-time entertaining.

I had learned from a young age how to lay a dining table. Cutlery placed in order of course from the outside in with a pudding spoon never above the placemat. Wine glasses on the right with the larger red-wine goblet taking precedence over its smaller white counterpart that sat closest to the table mat. Side plates on the left, twelve dishes of butter curls and six silver toast racks. So far, so predictable. But all this precocious preparation was completely lost on my public-school friends. Little did my parents realise, but half the people who came that evening would be using their downstairs cloakroom to mainline heroin. It seems so incongruous given its dirty reputation but, at the time, smack was the drug of choice among my contemporaries. By another name, heroin is just opium so perhaps it was the glamour attached to its literary heritage that drew them in. As if it would provide some higher form of freedom. Ultimately all it did was erode them like battery acid.

To my immature mind, heroin made these boys dangerous and desirable. I was totally seduced. Every night I'd ride my bike to the smack den on Hogarth Road in Earl's Court and sit around while the addicts smoked. It didn't matter whether you'd come from borstal or Eton, it ravaged you in the same way. I remember one boy being so smacked out he didn't notice when another poured the contents of an ashtray into his gaping mouth. The room was strewn with tinfoil from dragon-chasing and cheap takeaways. A basement flat filled with some of the brightest, most beautiful boys I knew, their pupils like black pin-pricks. It was horribly depraved but there was a morbid fascination that accompanied it too. When I asked one of them why he did it, he replied 'Life's such a disappointment.' I was the only one there not using and, given my addictive nature, I've often asked myself how I managed to avoid it. I think it was immaturity and that I was still living under my parents' roof. I was also scared. Drugs were something the big boys did while I looked on.

David was totally different. I didn't fancy him straight off but did my best to make him feel at ease, which was completely unnecessary. He was far and away the most competent, interesting person there and certainly didn't need babysitting. He was energetic; a thinker and, surprisingly given his family, someone who presented a world beyond the realms of my upbringing. Right from the off, it was clear he was going to forge his own path and had the ambition and passion to do so. There was never a question he'd toe the line; being a member of the royal family was not going to be enough for David. He had something to prove. He dressed differently too – cotton polo-neck and velvet jacket in contrast to the checks and tweed around him. That he hadn't gone to Eton or Harrow added to the glamour. Bedales was a school for creatives encouraged to think outside the box. The icing on the cake was his vintage Triumph Bonneville which, coincidentally, he bought second-hand from the village I now live in. The only thing better than riding pillion on that bike was driving through France and Italy in the pale blue Aston Martin DB5 bought by his father from Peter Sellers and then handed on to David. What I'm trying to say is, David was much cooler than you might think.

I'd had only one boyfriend before David – a holiday fling that had come to a halt the minute my train left Brussels six months beforehand. I had graduated from Queen's Gate in 1980 with a pitiful portfolio of formal qualifications and embarked on a gap year in Belgium to broaden my mind. It worked. I lost my virginity to a Belgian DJ who I'd never have met in a million years at Annabel's, let alone slept with. Philippe Jacobs wasn't the sort of DJ who'd play 'Mamma Mia' at a wedding. He was a post-punk conceptual artist in the business of light and sound. He choreographed laser shows for Jean-Michel Jarre and introduced me to the music of Yellow Magic Orchestra. When I met Eric Clapton years later at the Hard Rock Café I took great pleasure in telling him he'd ripped off their song 'Behind the Mask'. He was decent enough not to rub it in my face when he told me no, he was well aware who'd written it, and to look on the album cover for his acknowledgement. Evidently Philippe Jacobs was not the only person who had heard of Yellow Magic Orchestra. He was also nothing like anyone I'd ever met before and what he did was nothing like anything I'd ever seen. So the trip was a success. I had indeed broadened my mind, just not in the way my father might have hoped.

Philippe was the first boy I'd slept with but you couldn't really have called it a relationship. It was a hiatus; a sabbatical from real life. A chance for me to be someone completely different. It didn't really matter that we could barely understand a word the other said.

By the night of my dinner party I'd moved on. You may remember I'd saved the seat next to me for the boy I was obsessed with. Like me, he was a member of the Careless Class but had removed himself from reality a step further by becoming a heroin addict. Out of deference to his family, let's call him the Lotus Eater. He was a beautiful, talented Old Etonian with whom I was totally unable to converse. We both spoke English but he was so handsome I became tongue-tied in his presence. My obsession prevented me from ever relaxing in his company, which begs the question, why agree to stay at his parents' house for the weekend? I was both on edge and irrational for the entire forty-eight hours. On the first morning, as I tried to locate the cereal, he appeared, god-like, in the kitchen doorway, throwing me completely. In my befuddled state I accidentally poured myself a bowl of tiny dog biscuits rather than cornflakes. Even when I realised my mistake, and he'd pointed it out, I didn't want to look stupid, and ate them anyway. It was that sort of relationship. When it came to the poo I'd been holding in for the previous two days, things continued in much the same vein. I'm sure I don't need to explain why I wanted to make my 'deposit' before anyone else was up, and why I set my alarm accordingly. I also felt it necessary to do it 'off site'. So, at 5.30 a.m., I left the house armed with only adrenalin and four sheets of loo paper. Instinctively, I fell back on my countryside training: an animal in distress will always look for a sheltered, secluded place to die and I began my search. The back of a disused barn was the perfect spot. It was over in minutes and the relief intoxicating. Ever the good girl scout, I covered what I'd left with mud and tucked the used sheets tidily under a loose Cotswold stone. I was never too rushed to follow the countryside code.

The idea you might be able to communicate with a person you also fancied came as a total revelation. With David my shyness evaporated. There was none of the anxiety I'd experienced with Philippe or the Lotus Eater. David was worldly but, like me, hadn't been to university. He wasn't intimidating. He was witty and easy to talk to. With David, I could be myself and he seemed to like me for it. The evolution from friend to boyfriend, however, didn't happen overnight.

In the course of the next two months, the Lotus Eater receded into the shadows as David and I spent more and more time together. One hot Friday in June we set off on our first weekend away to the home of my friends, Vicky and Susie Bell. The Bell sisters were a fixture on the weekend Sloane circuit so I'd stayed with them and they with me many times in the past. Like all parents, Vicky and Susie's mum and dad did not approve of overt sex before marriage so David and I had separate rooms. This made the whole thing even more exciting and the entire weekend revolved around if, when and where we might finally have our first snog. At the top of a Ferris wheel overlooking a pig farm was not where I might have imagined this would take place but I wasn't going to argue. At least there was a degree of privacy thirty feet in the air. That we were wafted with the rich smell of pig manure every time we approached the bottom of the wheel just added to the bucolic tableau. The kiss, when it came, was good enough that we did another twenty or thirty revolutions on the wheel in order to keep at it.

We were both twenty-one but might as well have been two thirteen-year-olds who'd snuck off at the village fete to escape the prying eyes of their parents. We were children but would spend the next five years growing up together.

Like me, David was still living at home with his mother at Kensington Palace. There was never a question of David staying at Cottesmore Gardens as my parents were of the view that nice girls didn't sleep with their boyfriends. Princess Margaret was more open-minded and, so long as we were discreet, turned a blind eye to us sloping off to bed together at the end of the night. Quite often an evening with Princess Margaret meant dancing – invariably to her favourite song, Desmond Dekker's 'Israelites'. At the end of a dinner party we'd move to the drawing room, find a little space on the carpet, and dance like you might if you were alone in your kitchen with the morning radio. Princess Margaret would always be the DJ. With her chosen 7" in hand, she'd lift the plastic lid, blow the dust off the vinyl and pop it on the turntable. After the customary introductory crackle, she'd conduct us all with a wave of her hand before joining in from her position next to the record player. She loved to dance but was not the most energetic of groovers. She had rhythm but it was always slow and timely, even to the fastest pop song. She did have an amazing singing voice, however, which made up for anything she might have lacked in moves. The evenings would resonate with her throaty, chesty cackle. Some of my most treasured memories are evenings lost in my own world amongst the sofas and blue opaline lamps of her drawing room. The turquoise of her eyes was the mood-board for the entire room's interior decor.

You couldn't rock up and ring the doorbell at Kensington Palace but I got to know all the policemen who guarded it from their sentry box. They knew the number plate on my car and, as I turned off Kensington High Street and down the palace drive, the barrier would begin lifting in anticipation of my arrival. Staff and family could use the side entrance which went straight into the kitchen, and I did too. This is where you'd find Stan, who made the delicious mushroom omelettes we had daily for break-fast. After a time, I no longer needed to prove my identity at the palace. I could come and go as I pleased. We'd reached the point where David would have given me a spare key, except there were no keys at Kensington Palace. Like the whole of the royal family, it was never left unattended.

To the outside world Princess Margaret was often seen as the sad, lonely, barbed sister of our monarch. Some said she enjoyed humiliating people; that she used her royal status like a sabre to cut those she didn't trust or like. Certainly she didn't suffer fools. She had a sommelier's nose for sycophants and could reduce even the most powerful to a damp wreck. All this was a form of protection. Once she knew your motives weren't self-serving, there was no kinder, funnier, more loyal ally to be had.

The first meeting of a steady boyfriend's mother is always a loaded experience for a girl. The very fact it's happening is a sign things are getting serious and equally of how much rides on the outcome. There was a sliver more anxiety attached to

Princess Margaret and me at the opening of David's workshop near Guildford, *c.*1985.

this particular encounter. I met the enormity of the situation head-on with counterfeit nonchalance. She in turn brought a level of imperiousness I'd only previously seen in footage of the Coronation. I knew this was Judgement Day; I held my nerve as we circled one another, before her clipped 'Would you like a drink?' told me I could finally stand down. I had been accepted into the pack. We could so easily have been combatants but happily we became allies and I a foot soldier in her faithful army. From then on, I was always ready to take Princess Margaret's side in a fight and was very glad on one particular occasion to find she would do the same for me.

Every summer the princess would organise 'a trip'. Not to the theatre or ballet but somewhere other people had to queue to get in. Her private secretary would organise its closure for the day so she could go backstage and see the strings and pulleys that made these places run smoothly. From Snowdon's Aviary to the crypt of St Paul's, Princess Margaret had had a lifetime's access to some of Britain's greatest monuments and a hands-on education no amount of money could possibly buy.

The maroon Rolls and its careful driver, Mr Griffin, were given the day off. The outriders who'd usually follow like a convoy of army ants were swapped for a coach, some old bloke with a comb-over, and the joy of waiting at traffic lights on the Embankment like everyone else. We were off for a private tour of the Old Royal Naval College at Greenwich. This was a day to be normal. Of course, what was normal for Princess Margaret was still extremely formal by most people's standards. We still curtseyed on greeting and called her ma'am as her bodyguard hovered at a suitable distance, but this was as low-key as it got for Princess Margaret. She picked the place; she set the agenda; she was in control. Invariably she'd be just as knowledgeable as the archivist who'd been drafted in, with his white gloves and pen torch, from the vaults below stairs, and she loved it. It was a chance to spread her wings inside a cage that was a fraction of the size required to show her full plumage.

When you're invited to lunch as part of the royal party, teams of hard-working, passionate and excited people have slogged for days to prepare the meal that sits before you. Even a casual lunch at her home in Kensington Palace was never a bowl of soup and a roll at the kitchen table. It was always served in the dining room on a white damask tablecloth laid with bone-handled cutlery and crystal glasses. It might just be Coronation chicken and rice salad but it was delivered by a butler. Princess Margaret was happy to nibble a grated cheese and pickle sandwich on a tray table with the best of us, but that sandwich would still be prepared and served by staff.

I'm ashamed to say the details of Britain's naval history were lost on me and, as ever, it was the prospect of food that kept me going. Lunch was served in the mess, a big, airy room with a linoleum floor and trestle tables covered in white cloth. The basic cutlery and glasses were the hired sort but the napkins weren't paper and the wine was good because Princess Margaret had supplied her favourite Riesling. The gold banqueting chairs (also rented) had the standard red pads, and matching red and white carnations (Princess Margaret's least favourite flower) peppered the tables to add a splash of colour. The overall effect had the whiff of a Silver Jubilee street party or 1960s village hall wedding breakfast.

Three courses in and the combination of a lemon tart and Silk Cut chaser was just the ticket to get my bowels moving, and off I went in search of the nearest loo.

Ten minutes had passed with no sign of my return. When her Baked Alaska had come and gone and my Turkish Delight sat forlornly like a jilted lover in front of my empty chair, the princess began to suspect there might be something amiss and excused herself to investigate. It didn't take long for her to find me as I sat panicking in my cubicle, having produced something rather larger than the naval plumbing could accommodate. I didn't feel I could leave to get help lest someone discover the evidence in my absence. I breathed a sigh of relief as I heard the tell-tale clip-clop of a pair of sensible shoes. Of all the people I knew, Princess Margaret was one of the most pragmatic. Surely she'd know what to do. 'Ma'am,' I called tentatively, 'is that you?' I opened the cubicle door a crack, through which she immediately stuck her head. 'What on earth have you been doing?' she asked. 'Your coffee's going cold.' There was more than a hint of irritation in her voice – it was the height of rudeness to leave the table for so long – but the panic in my face quickly softened her up. 'What *is* the matter?' I looked to the loo by way of explanation. My predicament was immediately clear. True to form, she didn't even flinch. 'Susannah, go and get me a knife,' she said calmly. I didn't dare question her plan. I was just grateful someone who outranked me had come to take over.

Like every good foot soldier, I did as ordered and returned to the fray, scanning the trestle tables for unmonitored cutlery. Instinctively I knew this was a covert mission but even the slightest suggestion I was in need of help would be met with a swarm of attention. And then I spotted it, the steely blade of a cake slice glinting in the sun next to a quietly melting butter pat pressed into the shape of a naval frigate. I swooped in, expertly dropping my napkin over it, before seamlessly transferring it up my sleeve. I glanced over at our two empty chairs. There was only so long a princess could be missing before they sent out a search party and, given our location, it would be a full-scale military operation. I knew we didn't have much time before the alarm was raised. I moved across the cobblestones as fast as my court shoes would carry me, crossing the Greenwich Meridian Line triumphant in the knowledge I had done my duty. Phase one of the operation was complete.

Together, we stared into the lavatory pan in awe. 'I've flushed again but it still won't go down,' she said in the matter-of-fact tone of a country vet patiently awaiting the deflation of his bullock's persistent erection. 'Could we just leave it?' I enquired hopefully. Her answer was a resounding no. Etiquette prevented us from abandoning our post and blaming the fall-out on some unsuspecting civilian. There was nothing for it but to get this turd into manageable pieces and, like all great generals, she waded into battle herself and took up the fight head-on, attacking it with gusto. It was a tense ten minutes as I stood guard. As the last brown cube circled the pan she returned the utensil to her soldier, washed her perfectly manicured, delicate hands, checked her hair in the mirror and exited past the men's urinals with the composure of a serial killer who's just expertly disposed of a freshly mutilated corpse.

I looked at the weapon in my hand, now a little sullied, and contemplated what to do. It was a quite lovely-looking cake slice after all – the handle very possibly ivory and the blade most definitely silver. I couldn't possibly put it back. I wiped it with my napkin and returned it to my sleeve. I could always wash it properly when we got home.

What I learned that day was that Princess Margaret had the ability to rise above normal humiliations as if they simply didn't exist. Like a great silverback at London Zoo, she went about life in captivity oblivious to the endless train of gawping visitors with their noses pressed to the glass. She'd been conditioned to conduct herself as if no one was looking. Seeing her in action was the perfect illustration of the fact that, the higher up the social ladder you are, the less you worry about what people think.

Two Old Queens

I've always instinctively divided my adult friends into the 'children' and the 'grown-ups' based on whether they'd be the people I'd get into trouble with or the people I'd call when I got into trouble. Although Princess Margaret had a naughty streak, our difference in age meant she was very definitely a mother-figure in this scenario and it was through her that I came to meet the 'daddy'.

It was 1984, the summer I turned twenty-two, and I was spending one of many happy weekends with David and Princess Margaret at Royal Lodge, home to the Queen Mother. After a year moving in royal circles I wasn't fazed by much – I'd breakfasted more than once with the Queen of England. I'd found my stride.

The journey from David's house in Kensington to his

grandmother's in Windsor was short. The luggage was small and the music loud. A U2 cassette boomed from the newly fitted speakers in my black, soft-top Ford Escort. Her Majesty, having been tipped off by police at the gates, was waiting in the doorway, arms as wide as her imperfect smile. Her black and grey teeth were a monument to the lack of vanity of a woman who'd lived through both wars. Hers was a generation of women always beautifully turned out but never unnaturally polished. Women who simply rolled their sleeves up and got on with it. Her famous visit to the East End during the Blitz was really just the tip of the iceberg and so much more self-sacrifice sat below the waterline.

In all the years I knew her, I never once saw the Queen Mother in trousers. It was always a tweed skirt, cotton or cashmere twinset, pin-tuck curls and dependable shoes, navy or brown. I loved the tea-cosy warmth of HM. It was no secret she wasn't one of the great beauties of her age but she had the most surprising grace and poise. Unlikely as it seems, this lovely little pudding of a lady was actually poetry in motion. And the routine was ever the same: kiss, kiss, curtsey while the footman got our cases from the car. A cup of tea in the drawing room left just the right amount of time for the maid to unpack our bags, and then it was up to our usual rooms. Mine, of course, was not occupied by David. He had his own at the opposite end of the corridor. As usual, shared rooms were for married couples only. If you wanted to have sex at the Queen Mother's house, you'd have to run the gauntlet down a hallway of squeaky floorboards like everyone else and hope the dogs didn't bark – a rule I've extended to my own home.

Although Royal Lodge is huge, in the space of six years I only ever went into three rooms: the dining room, the drawing room and the guest bedroom I always slept in. It was a snapshot from a bygone era, pickled in the strokes of the hand-painted wallpaper, fringed and heavily lined curtains, and lighting so low it made it impossible to see yourself in the mirror after sundown. The double bed – its sheets with their hospital corners, its blankets with their satin trim – was protected from the moths by an embroidered voile cover and dusky pink silk eiderdown. A bed so made was subtle proof that this was a house with an army of staff to maintain it. A tin of ginger nuts and glass of water sat on the bedside table in case of any midnight cravings, along with an ashtray and book of matches for a pre-dinner smoke. Covers were turned down and nightdresses laid out while we enjoyed dinner, carefree, in the candlelit rooms below. Life at Royal Lodge was suspended in time.

This extended to the personal hygiene facilities. Showers weren't a 'thing' in the '80s and should anyway be reserved for public swimming baths. It was a quick dip in the tub or a stand-up flannel wash at the basin before dinner. If you wanted to wash your hair you'd have to take your chances with a pink rubber shower hose. This route had only two outcomes – ice cold or scalding hot. The fashion for carpeted bathrooms made the process even more hazardous as the hose had a habit of flying off the taps when the water reached peak flow. All in all, one was well advised not to arrive with dirty hair. The maid put out what little make-up I had on the dressing table next to a cut-glass bowl of talc complete with marabou dusting puff. The set-up was just like my grandmother's make-up station, except hers had the addition of two scent bottles, one filled with Jean Patou's Joy and the other with gin. Just like her daughter and granddaughter, my grandmother knew exactly how to hide her dark little secret . . .

Things rarely changed at Royal Lodge but this weekend was going to be different. Somebody I was more than a little bit in love with was coming to dinner. As with every Saturday night it was the custom to change for dinner. Black tie for the men and a frock for the ladies. I'd plumped for a black velvet cocktail dress trimmed in white satin and diamanté buttons. If the aim was to look like the middle-aged wife of a Home Counties bank manager – or my own mother – I pulled it off with aplomb.

It didn't matter what the Queen Mother wore, she somehow always managed to look the same. Sturdy and dependable, like a love-worn teddy bear with three-carat diamonds clipped to its ears. The shape of her dresses was repeated ad infinitum by Norman Hartnell in every conceivable fabric, pattern and colour. Nothing ever changed. This was the uniform of a woman who'd spent her life on display, and one she unthinkingly returned to. Tonight, dove-grey chiffon disguised her formidable bosom. Embroidered bugle beads turned this modest gown into evening wear, as did the sparkling paste buckle on her matching silk pumps. Her only make-up was a slash of badly applied coral lipstick.

To the layman we were done up to the nines, ready for the grandest of formal dinners. In fact an unspoken set of rules defined the limits of our regalia. Nothing flashy, nothing vulgar. Bare legs were for Eurotrash so it was 15-denier nude or black tights and no hems above the knee. Jewellery was heirloom only. The ladies among us were never without an evening clutch and ideally one embroidered by a long-dead and greatly revered member of the female line. Otherwise, something new and grudgingly bought from Peter Jones would have to do. For the men, nothing had changed since the 1940s; there was no way of expressing your individuality. (They didn't really need to.) No pre-tied bow ties or, heaven forbid, cummerbunds. Double cuffs with cufflinks and velvet slip-ons embroidered with your family crest were the only acceptable accessories. Waistcoats were the preserve of snooker and darts players, and after-shave that of the Gin and Jag set. No one wanted to smell like the type of man who played golf. A moustache was acceptable if you were in the military but a beard meant you were incredibly suspicious.

These unspoken rules were like secret recipes passed down through the generations. There was no possible way you could know the ingredients unless you were born into the 'right' family. Tonight not a single hair was out of place in our party and we reported for duty and drinks in the drawing room at 7.30 p.m.

The Queen Mother had her Dubonnet and gin – she'd wait till she was seated at dinner to move on to Crystal with ice – and Princess Margaret her Famous Grouse and Highland Spring. There was only one person missing. As a teenager my dormitory walls were plastered with this man's image on posters carefully pulled from the centre pages of *Look-in*. As I heard the telltale steps of the footman in the corridor I backed slowly towards the fireplace to let out a small, soundless, stress fart, knowing from experience it would be drawn up the flue. The door handle turned. I subtly edged past Lady Glenconner to get to the front and adopted a stance of casual indifference as we awaited his entrance.

French-blue ringmaster's tailcoat, matching balloon trousers, round bejewelled spectacles, and Gandhi cap accessorised with a sapphire brooch the size of a small baked potato; he matched Princess Margaret jewel for jewel. Clearly this man had not read the note about the dress code. It was 1984 but may just as well have been 1784. A rare talent had been requested at court to sing for his supper for the delight of the royal family and I had a front-row seat for the show.

The Queen Mother tugged down her décolletage as she prepared to be upstaged. Captain Fantastic had arrived.

His stage costumes were legendary – from baseball whites at Dodger Stadium to Donald Duck in Central Park; everywhere he went, he went in costume. Everything he did, he did in character and, as the years went on, it became ever larger and more extravagant. Elton John was the name he'd given his alter ego and tonight he was going to sing for his supper in front of another old queen.

Staggeringly, he'd managed to out-dress a room full of people who already looked like extras on the set of a costume drama. As I would come to find out, this was actually a relatively sober outfit for Elton. Not quite mufti but certainly one he considered conservative. This was a person for whom normal didn't exist. Every outing was a performance and tonight was no different. I imagine this was part of the reason he eventually fitted in so well with the Windsors: both

Drawing room at Royal Lodge, minus the grand piano.

been present throughout our earlier dinner was replaced with the confident look of a man about to step into his element.

No one spoke above a whisper. Powder compacts were quietly opened and closed and wine glasses put down on occasional tables with the utmost care. Princess Margaret expertly silenced the fire with a careful kick of her foot. The Queen Mother sat still in her high-backed, red silk chair awaiting the entertainment. Many people had passed through these rooms in her time, but even by firelight I could see the flush in her cheeks. The fact that he was queer and she a widowed octogenarian gave them both a free pass to flirt shamelessly without consequence. Though her ankles were crossed and hands appropriately folded in her lap, you could tell she'd rather have had her bosom pressed against the piano. If you could suspend your disbelief, this was her version of Michelle Pfeiffer in *The Fabulous Baker Boys*. I was of course suffused with such jealousy that, had it been anyone else, I'd have knocked her off her chair and pushed her face into the Aubusson rug. I held back; I knew she wouldn't be around for ever.

It's hard to convey the romance or magnitude of this moment. It was mind-blowing – like Elvis turning up at your house to borrow an egg or the resurrection of Jesus Christ in your living room. I wanted to stand up and scream, but at Royal Lodge the way to express your excitement was with a subdued but rhythmic tap of the foot. It was one of those occasions in life where, even in the moment, I wanted it to be over and done with so I could run home and tell someone what had happened to me.

Like a bottle of HP Sauce, the boy from Pinner who had sold more than 300 million records got the royal warrant that night. This, as they say, was the beginning of a beautiful friendship.

Fast Food

Going out with David meant handing my private life over to the press. I was public property and could do little to stop my face appearing in the papers. Ironically, only a few years' prior I'd spent months traipsing the streets attempting to sell myself to the highest bidder in a stint working as a model for Select. Embarrassingly, the only job I managed to land was the 'before' foot model for Dr Scholl corn pads and it soon became clear I was no Christie Brinkley. I didn't even find my way into Mrs A's catalogue – in spite of being on time for the

Me and Hugo Swire pretending to model for Burberry.

casting. I was pretty, but not pretty enough. A small fish in a big pond, I just couldn't swim fast enough to make it. I was also far, far too greedy. I'd intersperse my visits to the booker with a matinee at the next-door Odeon on Baker Street. I'd couple that with a family bucket that I'd plough through mechanically before the trailers came to an end. It was during one such episode I learned the lesson 'never eat without looking down' the hard way. By this point, I'd had so many tubs of fried food in the darkness I had a Helen Keller-like instinct about how a piece of their chicken felt in my fingertips. It was this training that made me pause on feeling an oddly shaped piece at the bottom of the carton. The alarm bells went off immediately. Long story short, I did *not* eat a battered mouse that afternoon but a less experienced scoffer may very well have done so.

'Being a model' is not something just any old pretty girl can do. The way you look is only half the battle. In the words of Jerry Maguire, it's an up-at-dawn, pride-swallowing siege. Being good at it means being flexible, incredibly hard-working and even thicker skinned. The end goal? I guess that's different for everyone, but certainly money, fame and the power to choose your jobs would be on most people's lists. Walking or sitting for the best designers and photographers is most definitely a factor too. Despite my failure as a model, the connections I made through David meant I ended up having my portrait taken by some of the world's most celebrated photographers, though the magnitude of this didn't register with me at the time. If my Irish grey, Clancy Friday, had been profiled in *Horse & Hound*, I'd have torn out the pages and Copydexed them into my scrapbook, but I don't own a single still from a single sitting or a dog-eared copy of any magazine in which my own portrait appeared. There is something peculiarly British about the inability to enjoy – or recognise – one's own accomplishments until the moment has so long passed you've effectively become a different person. Only then can you look back with admiration and not be accused of vanity or ego. It's fine for someone else to admire you but much more difficult to receive a compliment. Is there a dignified way to accept one? I feel sure someone in France would know the answer to this.

When David moved house years later and came across the box of prints his father, Lord Snowdon, had taken of me thirty years earlier, I rather stupidly told him to throw them all away. This wasn't false humility. Quite apart from anything else, they were two foot tall and the whole thing seemed absurdly self-indulgent – but had they been of anyone else I'd undoubtedly have kept them. It didn't matter who I was;

the fact they were taken by Snowdon meant they were a piece of social history.

What the photographers I sat for had in common was that they were all men and all at least twice my age. Where they differed has only become clear to me with the passage of time.

Hairspray

In 1960 Princess Margaret's great friend Colin Tennant gave her a piece of land on Mustique as a wedding present. When she and Lord Snowdon separated, Colin built her a house on it too. Les Jolies Eaux was the one home she owned herself and this was hugely significant. It was a place her friends could see her for who she really was and somewhere I spent many happy holidays with her and David.

Princess Margaret was one of Mustique's original residents – someone who'd been there from the very beginning when

Les Jolies Eaux, Mustique.

running water was a luxury and electricity not something you could rely on if you were thinking of making cheese soufflé. You took Mustique as you found it. Whoever you were, the drawbacks were the same.

One of its greatest unsolved mysteries was how her neighbour (and cousin), Patrick Lichfield, achieved his signature voluminous hairdo. Given the fact that no dryer could ever be coaxed beyond a cheap-hotel level of oomph while on the island, this must have been a constant source of anxiety. It looked like it took a leaf blower to create that kind of height so I'm not sure how he managed, to be honest. Oddly, his sister, Lady Elizabeth Anson, had chosen an almost identical style, which begs the question, who had it first? Whatever the answer, this synergy must have come in very handy if either were stuck without a can of Elnett at a party. Sadly, they're both dead now, so how they managed on Mustique is one of life's big questions that will remain forever unanswered.

Patrick Lichfield – just look at that volume.

at the 'casual' composition now, I don't imagine anything about it was accidental. In going barefoot, she couldn't have picked a more poignant symbol to sum up the peculiar state in which she found herself. Unused but not free; incarcerated by convention.

Chocolate-boxy and romantic, Patrick's portraits could have hung happily as a poster in any bedroom of any terraced house in Britain. In artistic circles he was considered safe – and not in a good way; a commercial snapper rather than a respected photographer. His aristocratic roots meant he lacked the fashionable working-class edge of his contemporaries. Much to his chagrin he was more Beaton than Bailey – but Princess Margaret was wholly at ease with her cousin. She was a famously volatile character and you could never be sure which side of her profile she was going to present on any given day, but with Patrick she was her best self and it shows. For all the criticism he faced, he took what in my mind is one of her most telling portraits.

But there was one last shot left in the reel and this one, worryingly, had my name on it.

That day I'd watched as Princess Margaret made the sitting for her portrait look effortless. The whole thing was over in less than an hour and when I see the photograph now, I love the fact that I was present for its creation. There's always more to the picture than what's framed in the viewfinder. Had you panned, you'd have found me sitting on the stone steps going down to the pool, puffing away on my Silk Cut and munching through a bag of crisps, waiting for my friend to be free for a swim. When she was finished and it was suggested Patrick take my photograph the next day I was flattered and terribly excited. My session, however, turned out to be rather less enjoyable. It was the moment I discovered I was much more at ease with the lens focused on someone else. I was far happier scurrying around in the background, fetching an out-of-reach Dunhill lighter or glass of Famous Grouse, than as the subject matter of the picture.

Patrick had wanted me on 'set' by 7 a.m., which meant missing Bessie's delicious bacon and eggs for breakfast. In response to his 'come as you are', I trekked over to his villa, shoeless, in my Pineapple Dance one-piece swimsuit. Things were famously 'open house' on Mustique so there was no one to greet me when I arrived, and I wandered through the house as the morning was being prepared. It wasn't long before Patrick appeared in his customary swimming shorts, Mother Superior-scale rosary, seahorse tattoo and fitted shirt, open to the waist.

Patrick had gained a reputation as a dandy – playboy, even – but for me there was something that didn't ring true. He could have been dressed from the contents of the costume cupboard at an am-dram production of *The Pirates of Penzance*. It was all a little contrived. There was never quite enough grubby sexuality to be convincing. He was a champagne Cockney, doing his best to infiltrate the closed ranks of the East End working classes with a well-researched uniform as his disguise. I think my take on him was probably influenced by Snowdon's slightly sneering view of his fellow snapper. Face to face he was a very sweet man, but I agreed with Tony; he definitely wasn't someone you'd jump into bed with.

And so here we were. Artist and model. I slipped into the

water, ready for what I thought would be an Esther Williams-style production. I swam back and forth from the middle to the edge of Patrick's pool approximately one million times in an effort to get the right shot. I think we were aiming for a sporty, essence-of-youth type energy but I was beginning to feel more like I was going for my bronze lifesaver's badge. There was none of the fun we'd had the day before at Princess Margaret's house.

She was still in bed. Even if she'd have been up in time to come with me, she would never have sat exposed that long in the sun. While her body was wonderfully bronzed, her face was fully made-up at all times. When I asked her why she bothered in such a private setting, she told me it was to protect her skin, which I have to say was exquisite. This was the era when slathering yourself in Johnson's Baby Oil and holding a tin turkey tray under your chin was the only way to sunbathe. No one knew, much less cared, about sun damage – except for Princess

Having just completed my bronze lifesaver's badge in Patrick's pool.

Margaret, who would repeatedly chastise me for not having any cream on my face. This was another golden nugget I added to the list of tips she gave me over the years. I still never submerge my décolletage in a hot bath based on her telling me this was how she kept hers so youthful. Thank you, ma'am.

At the time I only saw the Polaroids Lichfield took to gauge the light. What strikes me now looking at the finished portrait is how incredibly pure I look. How immature. It's hard for me to reconcile that the innocent girl in those pictures is the same person navigating such sophisticated social waters. I was being treated as an adult, an equal, but when I look at the photograph all I see is a child.

She Was Only a Grocer's Daughter

My mother had never been given the option to work and her lack of control over her own life was as much a comment on her class as her marriage. The separation of the sexes, as championed by the public-school system, meant two things. Boys were educated to lead and, with women stripped from the equation, were taught to do this without the need to listen to the female voice. From a young age, girls in my social circle were syphoned off and told to stand in a different queue. Apparently we weren't going to the same place as the boys: our end destination was completely different. My father proactively discouraged me from going to university. What was the point, he said? I'd be better off learning how to make a decent Beef Wellington. His words, not mine. Growing up, I didn't know a single adult woman I admired or respected for what she did. I didn't even know one that had a career. There was only one woman on my radar who was capable and independent and I wanted what she had: the courage to rise to the top.

In 1979, Margaret Thatcher became Britain's first female prime minister and I added her, along with my dog Archie and my pony Dandy, to the list of things I loved without judgement. If Archie ate my slippers or Dandy gave me worms (again) I forgave them. When Thatcher stole our milk, I didn't waver. She was my leader and I'd sworn allegiance at the altar. I worshipped her.

Even at the time she was a hugely divisive character but you didn't have to agree with her politics to acknowledge her strength. I was seventeen when she came to power and, up until this point, there'd been very few visible women with her determination and intellectual capacity. She was formidable. My daughters don't have to look far to find women they admire in the public eye but when I was a young woman, the

Margaret becoming Thatcher.

pickings were pretty slim. Anyone front and centre seemed to be either 'selling' sex or, if they weren't, came with a caveat of some kind that undermined their standing: Germaine Greer was clever but billed as off-puttingly militant and Joan Bakewell was the thinking man's crumpet. Why was a statement of her intellect framed by considerations of whether she would or wouldn't appeal to a man? Couldn't she just be clever in her own right?

In her youth, Thatcher had been quite pretty but, in preparation for her role as PM, she'd gone out of her way to purposely de-frill, raising her necklines and lowering the pitch of her voice. She was operating in a patriarchy and knew that to be taken seriously she had no choice but to man-up. Something as simple as the tone of her voice was an obstacle that must be erased. Thatcher made a profound impression on people but no one ever came away thinking 'I wish I could have jumped into bed with her.' She happily jettisoned anything that could have been considered feminine. Nothing was going to stand in the way of her path to power.

Thatcher was not afraid of being disliked and had the balls to say what she meant. As a child who suffered from crippling shyness, it was something I admired enormously.

The first British Parliament was formed in 1215 – all men of course. It took another 700-odd years for women to be given the vote – and even then, it wasn't all of them. A mere sixty years later, however, one of them became prime minister. What this tells me is that, even with a 700-year head start, the men got an awful lot less done than they should have. In 1918, 8.5 million female householders over thirty were enfranchised. To make sure the men didn't go off in a huff, the same

Act removed a number of other restrictions to ensure the male vote rose from 8 to 13 million. Thank goodness for that, otherwise we'd have had equality to contend with. If you can find me a better example of ego-stroking, I'd like to hear it.

Women had spent centuries confined to the outskirts of decision-making. While eighteenth-century men took their socio-political debates to the coffee house, women were barred and confined to their homes, stitching cushion covers. They didn't let that stop them. They simply invited their friends over for tea and no one thought to stop them. While the men were arguing about who was in charge, the women were quietly getting on with the task at hand and that task was securing the vote. Tea parties were the innocuous beginnings of the suffrage movement. You can get a surprising amount done over a cup of tea and a piece of cake. As I was about to find out.

I'll Be Mother

The first time I ever went to Scotland was in 1984. It was to be the full Highland experience – stalking, fishing, grouse-shooting and black-tie dinners each night. I'd been invited to two estates. One was Birkhall and the other Balmoral. The first belonged to the Queen Mother and the other the Queen. Birkhall had originally belonged to Victoria and Albert, and from the 1940s was shared for the summer between the Queen Mother and the Queen. George and the Queen Mum went for the first bit and Lilibet and Phil the Greek for the second. Just like a timeshare. Birkhall was a true home to the Queen Mother. Balmoral was the closest the Queen came to a holiday cottage, though it was nevertheless a fully staffed

It doesn't get much more Sloaney.

castle. However informal and relaxed it purported to be, there were unspoken rules to be followed. 'Casual' dress in royal circles still meant following protocol. I knew the drill. I was all over it.

I'm a Lincolnshire girl at heart; I didn't need to buy anything new. I could have packed that bag with nine minutes' notice. For a weekend in the country what matters is practicality. Anything green or brown in a fabric or weave that hides the dirt. If you can find something that dries quickly and wicks the moisture away from your skin, something that can keep you warm even when it's wet, you've hit the jackpot. This, my friends, is tweed, the Rolls-Royce of practicality. In the 1850s when Albert bought Balmoral Castle, he also designed his own tweed – and tartan, for that matter. The family were pretty uppity about who could wear it though. Everyone who lived and worked at the house and no one else. Other Highland estates jumped on the bandwagon and developed their own

she was genuinely not in control. While Dennis was actually very relaxed at Balmoral, Thatcher was awkward.

I didn't care. All I felt was her power, which was very hard to get past. As a fellow Grantham girl, I was on ready-made common ground to break the ice when our eyes met for the first time over the Dundee cake.

'How d'you do, Mrs Thatcher. I'm from Grantham too.'

'Oh, really.'

Tumbleweed rolled across the deserted floor. It was not the conversation-starter I'd hoped for and the whole thing fizzled out before it had even started. Perhaps I'd touched on something she'd rather not revisit. It didn't matter anyway. My pathetic attempt at camaraderie was soon to be blown out of the water by an unexpected stand-off. A power struggle so subtle it was only visible to the trained eye.

It was a beautiful Saturday afternoon. Anyone in our party not stalking or grouse-shooting was fishing on the River Dee. If you were inexperienced, or lazy, you'd have a ghillie – a guide who'd show you the best pools and which fly would most likely catch a salmon. The choice of bait varied depending on the light, weather conditions, speed and depth of water. These fish are notoriously hard to catch and wielding a 12-foot fly rod takes great skill and years of practice. Salmon-fishing isn't a sprint, it's a marathon. Once you're there, you're there for the day, moving slowly downriver, casting and recasting, waiting for your prey to take the bait. The riverside was dotted with tackle, waders and amply spaced anglers quietly biding their time. There was no conversation along the riverbank, but a bit like with cricket, the fly-fishers attracted spectators. Anyone who wanted to admire their work, enjoy the ebb and flow of the river, or mingle over a sandwich would come and go throughout the day.

The only sounds to be heard came from a little fishing hut set back from the water's edge. Around 4 p.m., tea would be laid on for anyone wanting to watch or take a break. It was a fairly basic offering. A few fold-away chairs outside if the weather was fine. A few more inside for anyone who might want to sit, though most stood, cup and saucer in hand, and chatted round the old log-burner. The hut was the size of a suburban front room but contained more than its fair share of clout. There can only have been six or seven of us inside that afternoon but one of them was the prime minister and another the Queen.

Tea and sandwiches had been brought from the castle. The anchovy-topped egg and cress were the ones I'd go for first, then the crustless cucumber. It was always self-service so I could scoff as much as I liked without judgement. Brown Betty stood proudly amidst the cakes and cups. Like the Queen herself, her teapot was unfrivolous, sturdy and practical. Fit for purpose. The Brown Betty was originally made from Stoke-on-Trent clay, which retained the heat, and developed its big round tummy to best extract flavour from the leaves. Bone-china cups that withstood the heat allowed the milk, as always, to be added last. All that remained was for someone to be mother. Dutifully, the Queen picked up the great brown pot to pour as I held out my cup to be filled. As if by magic, a redundant Thatcher appeared at her side like a spectre.

'Let me do that, Your Majesty.'

Without waiting for an answer, she put her hand under the teapot to take its weight, but her offer was met with unexpected resistance from the Queen. I lowered my cup a little. Maggie tightened her fingertips around the base and tried once again to take the pot from its owner, but no. She was not mistaken. There was definitely resistance. Evidently the Queen had no intention of relinquishing the fat, brown pot. A further, more determined, pull from Thatcher was met with an equally resolute hold from Her Majesty. We appeared to have reached a stalemate. I put my cup and saucer quietly back down on the table. If this were a film it would be the closing scene where two adversaries finally come face to face in a big old church or disused meat factory. You know one of them is going to lose. Possibly even die. I didn't imagine the Queen was actually going to *kill* Thatcher – it wasn't the court of Elizabeth I – but it was quite tense. I was desperate to get someone to watch with me but daren't move lest I scare them off. Then all of a sudden, without warning, the pot was free; released back to its rightful owner. Thatcher had thrown in the towel. Why?! Maybe because the Queen was on home ground? Or had she purposely let it slide; let her opponent win? I won't deny it; I was a little bit disappointed in my prime minister but secretly pleased she'd been out-mothered by the Queen. Order was restored. Clear brown liquid continued its journey from the Queen's pot to my cup as if nothing untoward had happened. In the calm after the storm I popped another couple of sandwiches on my plate.

The two most powerful women in the world had settled their score the way women had been doing since the eighteenth century – over tea and cake – and I could not *wait* to tell David.

Champagne Supersonic

On August 7th 1985 David and I were invited to join his grandmother on a private flight around the British coast on Concorde. According to the *Christian Science Monitor*, 'Queen Elizabeth, the Queen Mother, is marking her 85th birthday by breaking the sound barrier amid a whirl of activity typical of the busy life she leads.' Apparently 'she had always wanted to bust the sound barrier but was never able to find time to squeeze it in.' I took their word for it. She'd never mentioned it to me.

The royal cavalcade, complete with police outriders, pulled up on the tarmac and we stepped out of the Daimler one by

Everyone getting excited about their imminent trip to the Bay of Biscay.

one. The cabin crew and captain waited patiently to greet us as if this were the after-party at the *Royal Variety Performance*. My white linen dress was a sensible length and my Betty Jackson polka-dot jacket cut, unflatteringly, mid-thigh. My sleeves were slightly ruched and my shoes the kind you'd find advertised in the back of a Sunday supplement next to bed jackets and incontinence pants. The end result was somewhere between Victoria Wood and Sarah Ferguson. Despite our sixty-year age gap, I could have swapped outfits with the Queen Mother and you'd barely have noticed. My hair for the occasion was the ubiquitous half-up, half-down do, as was that of David's twenty-one-year-old sister, Sarah. Add a wicker basket and block of Oasis and we could have passed for two fifty-somethings about to give a talk on flower-arranging at the WI. To this day I'm bewildered by the efforts of a fashion movement that compelled a generation of young women to look thirty years older than they were.

On the basis that a return ticket from London to New York cost approximately £35,000 in today's money, Concorde's customer base effectively began with Elizabeth Taylor and ended with Gerald Ratner. Anyone outside this wealth bracket didn't have a hope in hell of ever seeing the interior of a Concorde cabin. Don't worry; I can tell you exactly what it looked like. Far from having the space to accommodate the demands of people absolutely rolling in it, it was like being inside a Havana cigar tube. Personally, I was a bit underwhelmed. It was the same way I would feel about the Pyramids on my honeymoon. On the basis of seat size alone, I'd question its reputation as aviation's greatest innovation. Having mounted the steps, the Queen Mother, her grandchildren and

I wedged ourselves in like sardines, buckled up and prepared for take-off. The stewardesses, I noted, all wore pencil skirts, no doubt to prevent them getting stuck as they slithered down the aisle with their tomato juice and hot towels.

All this aside, the trip was an official royal engagement and I was very touched to be invited. It was quite out of the ordinary for an unbetrothed love-interest to be included in such a high-profile outing. That did not stop me from being secretly disappointed we weren't going to New York. Instead, the flight plan for the birthday girl would be a lazy ramble around the British coastline with a brief burst of speed over the Bay of Biscay. Her celebratory itinerary also included a visit to the Sandringham cottages where she was scheduled to 'meet pensioners and spend a lengthy period chatting with them'. I made a mental note to mention I'd like something less like this from David when I hit eighty-five, in the event we were still together.

In spite of my blasé stance, the trip did provide two fantastic, lifelong memories. The first was like something from a David Attenborough Christmas Special. A typical 747 flies at 35,000 feet while Concorde reaches 60,000, and from this advanced height you are able to see the curvature of the Earth. This was one of the most awe-inspiring things I've ever seen and affected us all greatly. Everything was so clean and precise; the curve and the colours – oranges and pinks going into dark blue – like taking in all life from the beginning of time to the present day in one glance. It was extraordinary. It was at this point I reassessed my earlier judgement: Concorde's reputation was justifiably built on its technological excellence rather than its legroom or inflight entertainment.

The second was Concorde's famed supersonic surge. We were told by the pilot that flying the plane required extreme precision so that when it broke the sound barrier it caused 'nothing more than a ripple on a hundred glasses of champagne'. Imagine our surprise, then, to find that, after a loud thunderclap, we were thrown back into our seats as you might be on a fairground ride that leaves your tummy behind. Mrs A's dentures would surely have been sucked down the back of her throat had she been with us on the trip. Drinks and dry-roasted peanuts found their way into everyone's laps, which livened things up a bit. Bolts of white linen napkins appeared from nowhere. Stewardesses attempted to mop up Veuve Clicquot without any unnecessary touching of any royal privates. Apparently, this 'ripple' was as unexpected for the crew as it was for us. Since our jaunt was the equivalent of a ceremonial fly-by, the absence of luggage meant the plane was lighter than it would be on a commercial flight. Hence the miscalculation. Hence the dry-cleaning bill. Given my white dress, I was glad it wasn't red wine. Gladder still I was sitting next to the Queen Mother and not Joan Collins who, if the ads were anything to go by, would have been much less affable about it.

'We Were On a Break!'

After such a high-profile public engagement you'd be forgiven for thinking the deal was about to be sealed between David and me, but you'd be wrong. I was no closer to a proposal and heartily fucked off about it. We'd been together for two years and I wanted him to commit. Not necessarily get married, but to at least discuss the possibility. We'd had the 'Where is this going?' conversation and it hadn't come out the way I'd hoped. Like the heroine of a Barbara Cartland novel, I intended to change his mind by distancing myself long enough for him to realise I was irreplaceable. I decided on a large-scale gesture to make my feelings known, which I regretted as soon as I'd done it. We were splitting up and I was going to New York for three months. I said the words with no sense of conviction and cried for most of the flight while listening to Journey's *Faithfully* over and over on my trusty Walkman. Having made such a bold announcement, I had no choice but to go through with it. I was devastated.

I'd already lived in Brussels for a year and done a few months in Paris – all with family friends – but the concept of travelling anywhere without such a buffer was still unimaginable. While contemporaries had spread their wings in the Okavango Delta or as competent crew on round-the-world sailing trips, the furthest I'd got from Kensington was the basement smack den in Earl's Court. This was not only far less aggro than the average camp of a lost Amazonian tribe, but also a short bicycle ride home. It was no surprise that when I decided to up sticks and head 'indefinitely' to the Big Apple, it would be with the comfortable cushion of my sister already in place.

Nits, Jonathan and the Kaleidoscope

In the autumn of 1985, Annette – or 'Nits' as she was better known – was living uptown on 93rd and 1st on the borders of Harlem, a fairly bold choice of address in the mid-80s. New York was still a pretty lawless place, where a subway commute was something to be braved rather than relaxed into with the morning paper. In spite of the fact she was working at Christie's and her husband, Jonathan, for Lehman Brothers, their apartment was what I'd now describe as a hovel – if I was being generous. Roach Motel pest-traps were scattered in every corner of every room emblazoned with the reminder that, as a roach, you could check in anytime you liked, but you could never leave. Fortunately, Nits had inherited my father's impeccable taste and eye for antiques and filled their apartment with the rich pickings of New York's flea markets and skips. My bedroom was a linen cupboard in all but name and one I shared with a wealth of boxes that had no hope of ever being unpacked. My curtainless window ensured I was awakened daily at sunrise. Eventually I tacked up an American quilt over the light, only to find myself awake at the same time the very next morning. My anxiety, it transpired, was denser than any blanket and my body refused point-blank to move to New York time. Like me, it hankered after the green fields we'd left behind. I was lovesick and homesick and not even the mind-blowing two-hour laundry service was enough to convince me otherwise.*

I couldn't understand why my sister had settled for such tawdry living quarters. The first time I paid for my own drink in a bar, I realised very quickly what she'd long come to accept:

* America has always been ahead of us in terms of service, so I should not have been surprised by this. Even so, I never tired of getting my ironed knickers back boxed and wrapped in candy-striped paper. Even Mrs A didn't do that.

to live well in New York is a *very* expensive exercise. 'Out' is where New York happened. 'Out' is where home entertaining took place and 'Out' is where they spent all their money. My sister and brother-in-law were mixing with uptown Manhattanites and this meant the best and most fashionable of everything. When you went to dinner it was somewhere impossible to get a table, and when you went for drinks they were $12 each – $30 in today's money.

By the time I arrived in New York, Nits had already been living there for three years and was using the words 'elevator' and 'sidewalk' unironically. I worried England was losing her. In time she went on to get her Green Card, but even early on it was clear to me she had been brainwashed. Why else would she have made the sacrifices she had to move there? She could no longer get her sheets from Peter Jones, which was out-and-out heresy. The rules of naturalisation meant taking an oath of allegiance to your new home – accepting their ways, their customs, their passions – and Nits had clearly jumped into all this with both feet. The morning after my arrival I was forced to make an emergency call to her offices on Fifth Avenue.

'I can't find the kettle,' I said, with more alarm than was probably necessary.

'We don't have one,' she replied.

Panic rose in my voice as we to-ed and fro-ed about whether this could possibly be true.

'Can I go out and buy one?' I asked.

'Not an electric one,' she replied.

I pinched myself. This was turning into a waking nightmare. With no morning cup of tea, I was now fifteen minutes away from having a seizure.

What she suggested next was idiotic. Everyone knows that making a cup of tea with water boiled in a saucepan is blasphemy and the suggestion alone further proof she had crossed over to the other side. I won't relive the horrors of my cross-town efforts that morning. Suffice to say, in his heart I don't believe a true Englishman ever stops trying to find a proper cup of tea in New York, but there's only so many times you can be offered Lipton's with UHT creamer before your will is eventually broken. There are many differences between my sister and me but the one I have never reconciled myself to is the fact that she allowed this to happen. I felt like a little part of her had died.*

Nits and Jonathan were two of the least bohemian people I'd ever met and I don't think anyone could have really classed them as 'edgy', but with British heritage on their side, they moved in both unbelievably rarefied and creative circles. What my sister had going for her was that she genuinely didn't give a fuck. She was the *master* of zero fucks. Americans have a tendency to take themselves very seriously. Nits was the polar opposite and people gravitated towards her for this very reason. On top of that, she was a very bright, funny and entertaining English Rose, catnip to an American.

* The ritual of making tea for the English is something you mess with at your peril. As annoying as it is, even waiting for the kettle to boil has a kind of rhythm that's integral to our way of life. It's one of the first lessons in patience, and the electricity surge during the break in *Crossroads* was something that united us as a nation. While convenient, the invention of the boiling-water tap is fucking with the natural order of things and hence not something I'm prepared to allow in my home.

Her husband was the type of man you'd want leading you to your death, should you happen to find yourself bobbing in a boat on D-Day, and brought an element of aristocratic eccentricity to the table. He was steeped in the stuff. His cousin Peregrine Moncrieffe was both the first man to earn a million on Wall Street and the only person to commute to the office on roller skates in a kilt. At 6'1", Jonathan's mother, Lady Kilmarnock, was probably the tallest society hostess ever to grace the drawing rooms of Chelsea. With feet and hands the size of a docker's, she bought all her clothes from the Forgotten Woman on 66th and Lexington. Created by Nancye Radmin – 'Crazy Nancye' – the pioneer of plus-size fashion, this was a store that targeted New York's unfashionably large. A woman who herself had gone from a US size 8 to a post-pregnancy size 16, Nancye catered for women who, like her, found themselves unjustly pushed out of the upmarket, fashionable stores they'd previously frequented. Nancye took care of the full range of her customers' needs, with the inclusion of a Sugar Daddy bar where your credit-card-holding companion could wait while you spent. I should think this was also the perfect place to shop if you were on the lookout for a new husband. In the end Nancye successfully persuaded everyone from Oscar de la Renta and Bob Mackie to reproduce their gowns in plus sizes but, at up to $10,000 for a dress, this was a very niche market and somewhere you'd need to be both big and rich enough to shop. Later, when I worked in fashion, all the best catwalk models were six foot with huge feet and would often need their shoes specially made. Even now having big feet is something women tend to feel needlessly ashamed of. Nancye knew there were more women like this out there than New York would care to admit, and for this I salute her.

Classically posh but relatively poor, Lady Kilmarnock was part of the Jet Set and spent most of her fortune maintaining that lifestyle, so there was not much left for my brother-in-law after she died. The only thing she'd hung on to was the last privately owned home in London with a ballroom, although this sort of boast became largely redundant around about the same time Jane Austen passed away. Nevertheless, Jonathan was the Honourable Jonathan Boyd and so, on their marriage, my sister became the Honourable Mrs Jonathan Boyd and this was more than enough for even the most upmarket American appetite. As a result my sister's friendship group was peppered with a mix of the very wildest and very wealthiest – a group that straddled the buttoned-up, uptown Wasps and the grubby downtown drop-outs. Theirs was a social life that encompassed everything contemporary New York had to offer.

For me, the couple who best captured this rock 'n' royalty vibe was Cristina and Michael Zilkha. He was heir to the Mothercare throne and she one of Kid Creole's beloved Coconuts. She had her caché and he his and it mattered not a jot that they were two totally different currencies. Theirs was a kaleidoscopic union that personified the hedonistic tornado in which my sister found herself. Like all twisters, it passed through town, it didn't last for ever – it couldn't, it was too intense. Ultimately it was the tragedy of Aids that put a stop to this natural phenomenon – but my God, for a lot of people it was fantastic while it lasted.

Nits attracted a circle of friends who encapsulated the spirit of the '80s, but remained rock solid in her outlook. It didn't matter who or how famous, she was resolutely unfazed and nothing spoke of her nonchalance more than the time she was invited to the hen night of Madonna Ciccone on the eve of her marriage to Sean Penn. The only woman more recognisable than Madonna was the Princess of Wales, and even then I'd argue the former turned more heads than the latter when she walked into a room. Short of an invite to the wedding itself, a ticket to the hen-night was probably the hottest in town but the only reason my sister agreed to go was 'as a favour to my best friend'. This best friend was Nancy Huang, Madonna's hostess for the night in question. Nancy was the girlfriend of Funkmaster Generale, Nile Rodgers, who'd just put his heart, soul and reputation into the production of *Like a Virgin*. Nile was not only responsible for spreading funk throughout the English-speaking world, but reputedly the only person to successfully persuade my sister to thoroughly 'get down' whenever he picked up a bass.

Even when questioned now about Madonna, Nits has none of the salacious gossip one would hope to hear. The Madonna we see now has been polished and honed to within an inch of her life, but then she was still a misplaced rebel, out of her depth in most of the places she found herself. Plucked from the sticky dance floors of New York's underworld, she was dropped into an atmosphere more sophisticated than she was then able to navigate. Nits' abiding memory of Madonna was as the kind of person one 'saw' but never got to know. A woman who had no use for anyone who couldn't help her up the ladder, which seems to me a very sad but common comment on the price of stratospheric fame.

The Great Pretender

At thirty, Nits assessed risk based on its possible consequences. I was still making decisions based on whether or not I'd be likely to get caught, which should tell you a lot about how immature and ill-prepared I was for life in New York. My sister was someone I considered a proper grown-up and, for the next three months, I was going to pretend to be one too.

In theory I was fending for myself, but between my father's $25-a-week allowance and my iron bedstead in Nits' cupboard, my stay in New York was pretty cushy. When Nancy wangled me a job as a shopgirl on the second floor of Armani's flagship store on 69th and Madison, the chief difference between me and everyone else who worked there was that I had a safety net and they didn't. In three months I could count the things I sold on one hand (cashmere cardigan with collar) and no one seemed to mind in the slightest. I didn't even run this through the till because I never found out how to work it. I was not hired for my salesmanship but as window-dressing which, three decades ago, was a perfectly legitimate reason to employ someone. Half my working day was spent sitting on the table out the back of the shop, smoking a Merit and swinging my legs like Pippy Longstocking in the hayloft. Another 15 per cent of the day was absorbed by omelette and chips at the Gardenia – for which I was given lunch money by my employer. If someone very famous came in, I became conspicuously casual which made absolutely no difference to anyone involved. It was fair to say the Armani diffusion line was not going to collapse without me.

In the evenings I'd go out with Nits and her friends in my just-suggestive-enough see-through mini skirt, sequined Donna Karan body, and faithful Agnès B cropped box jacket. My uniform was a pre-prepared statement about who I considered myself to be. As I moved through New York's upper social strata, never knowing who I might meet amongst the crowds, it was the stamp of my tribe, an easy way of telling everyone a bit about who I was before I even opened my mouth. New York nightlife was very different to the safety of Annabel's and Tramp. I didn't know everyone I shared a taxi with and it was intimidating in a way I was not used to. Unlike in London I was anonymous and, as an inherently shy person, I hadn't factored in how stressful it would be to try and make new friends out of my comfort zone. The girl who came out of this experience was definitely not the same one that went in. The night the son of a Greek shipping magnate and a dreadful coke addict took me to dinner at Indochine in the Village was a very good example of an event that changed my outlook on life.

Andy

I couldn't really describe it as the night I 'met' Andy Warhol because although it was a dinner in his honour, I don't remember the exchange of a single word between us.

A moment in time exists in many forms and can be viewed from countless angles. Each person present will have their own story they tell their grandchildren. But whose names will stand the test of time and whose will be forgotten depends on who's telling the story. No memory remains the same for ever; it is jostled by other passing thoughts along its journey, like a little boat on the water, taken off by the current from time to time. What remains is not a record of the truth but a unique reimagining of a moment that once belonged to you. I don't imagine Andy went back to the Factory and told everyone he'd met a girl from Lincolnshire with no qualifications. Nevertheless, he is a tiny nugget of my history. The fact I wasn't on his radar is an equally interesting part of the picture.

I could have left the table that night without anyone perceiving the slightest shift in ambient temperature. I was a plus-one, another blonde in ballet pumps – and there were thousands of those on the streets that night who could have been called in to take my place. But for me the picture was a very different composition. Had I had the balls to take my Kodak Instamatic with me, the snapshot from where I

Andy, Basquiat, Jacqueline and Julian Schnabel with Kenny Scharf at the opening of Indochine, 1984.

sat would have incorporated not only Andy but Jean-Michel Basquiat and Julian Schnabel too. In 1985 there were very few places hipper than a green leather booth amongst the printed banana leaves of Indochine with Andy Warhol and his entourage. By that time he was more a barometer of style than style itself; Basquiat and Schnabel were already gaining on him. Two years later he was dead.

I wasn't surprised by his death. He was only fifty-six when I met him but he had the appearance and bearing of someone who'd been sickly as a child. There was a damaged, fragile air to him as if he wouldn't withstand close inspection or might turn to dust if you unpeeled his outer layers. Like a kind of Frankenstein's monster, perhaps needing the odd repair each evening after a day's work, a patch here, a stitch there. His skin had the look of a man rotting from the inside, as if he'd died years before and was recharged each night in his kooky private laboratory. Every morning his assistant would flip the switch and Andy would sit bolt upright, arms stiff and outstretched by his sides. Swinging his legs round awkwardly from the stretcher, dropping his feet to the floor with a light thud, he'd begin the day anew. He'd crafted a synthetic veneer for himself that he thought the public wanted – like an item packaged for sale. Just as with the Wizard of Oz, Andy, I suspect, was a small, lonely man behind a curtain doing his best to create an illusion of something bigger and better than the way he really saw himself.

The group he drew around him should have been formidable but somehow the evening was a sad one. There was something about Andy that both terrified and repulsed me in equal measure – as if you could catch a disease of the mind just by being near him, a self-destructive deviance you wouldn't be able to resist. Everyone there seemed to need an audience to be a version of themselves they were happy with, like a group of parasites feeding off one another even though their veins had long since run dry. I'd never gone out to a dinner where one of the guests being so gowched-out on heroin was not only acceptable but went unnoticed. It seemed it wasn't remarkable to anyone but me. I was doing my best to masquerade as an adult but the depravity of the evening frightened the life out of me. There was no warmth. No one you could turn to with an urgent, conspiratorial 'Have you got a tampon?' It wasn't my understanding of what friendship should be. We were more like participants in an art installation; holding still in our places until enough people had passed by and seen us. To make sure we existed. It was a very destabilising situation and one I would never put myself in again. I'd gone in hoping to be accepted by this enigmatic group but, seeing their grotesque, up-lit faces around the table, I felt grateful to be the girl at the back of the room – able to walk out and close the door behind me without anyone noticing I'd gone.

Many people would have given their eye-teeth for the experiences I had in New York, but for me it was a lesson in how to stiffen one's upper lip. My abiding memory of my time there was a homesickness I hadn't felt with the same intensity since boarding school. I lived on my nerves just as I had done at St Mary's. Manhattan was totally alien; a place where you couldn't see the horizon. I found the landscape both threatening and claustrophobic; the antithesis of what

I'd grown up with. It was a concrete jungle and I hated it. All I really wanted was for David to ask me to come home.

Christmas could not have come early enough for me and, when it finally rolled round, I could legitimately go home without shame or feeling I'd failed. I'd spent time away from England. I'd stuck to my guns. I had no intention of ever going back to New York.

The stress and relentless pining for my first big love while I was away took me from a UK-appropriate size 12 to a Manhattan-acceptable 8. On my return home ninety days later, I stepped onto the tarmac at Heathrow a thinner, if not happier, woman. My boss at Armani had become a great friend in my time there and, as was the custom of the day, wrote me a letter of recommendation to take back to London, where his colleague, Peder Bertelsen, was opening a franchise of the store. That January I traipsed down to Peder's offices in Smith Street, Chelsea, and handed him my letter. Mr Bertelsen, it later transpired, would end up being much more than just my boss.

The melodrama of our separation had gone some way to making David's heart grow fonder, though not enough for him to fork out for a ring. Realistically, if my plan to snare him had not worked by now it was probably never going to but we continued to play mummies and daddies for a while longer. For three months in New York I'd tried to look like a free spirit. It was a pitiful attempt that fooled no one but, in the process, I inadvertently picked up a few tips about the sort of person I thought I might like to be. I put them in my back pocket for later.

My mother had never worked a day in her life. I loved her but I didn't respect her and I think part of the reason was that she didn't have a job. Most of my friends' mothers didn't work either and I'd never really thought of myself as someone who wanted a career so I'm not sure where this disdain came from. Perhaps it was Thatcher.

The '80s 'greed is good' undercurrent must have had some impact on me though, because from around the age of sixteen I was perpetually coming up with money-making schemes. My ideas spanned everything from an early version of Uber to bringing ponies to London to give rides to Townies. I rarely thought through the logistics, and potential job satisfaction didn't come into it. My only goal was making money. In spite of this drive, by the time I returned from New York in December 1985, I was still woefully ill-equipped to put any of my schemes into action.

I'd never been in the red or searched for a job or a flatmate in *Loot*. I would come to identify an electricity meter but only because I'd so regularly neglect to pay my bills, the electricity board would insist I have one installed. I'd be one of very few quasi-aristocrats queuing at the post office to top up their key. When the wheels were stolen from my Ford Escort I didn't realise until I attempted to drive away. I'd accumulate so many parking tickets the bailiffs would eventually arrive on my doorstep. At first I'd pretend not to be in and ask my friend (and landlady) Lulu Blacker to answer the door – finally agreeing to give them a cheque only because the furniture they were threatening to take belonged to her and not me. I at least had a conscience about that.

The net result of my upbringing was that I entered my twenties with no regard for money or any idea how to live independently. The reason I didn't pay my bills was not because I couldn't but because I couldn't be bothered. I knew the consequences, as always, would be inconsequential. My father had taken very little interest in my future. I honestly don't know whether he was just relying on my getting married or that he just wasn't interested. Whatever the reason, there'd been no urgency around my finding a vocation. An education at St Mary's meant I was regarded as a dimwit and I slipped into a predictable range of courses for the under-qualified.

At twenty-one, I'd studied for a year at the Montessori Teachers' College next door to the Iranian Embassy in Lancaster Gate and got my first paid job at Hill House Nursery School on Flood Street. I abandoned this when Lulu offered me a job at the Montessori school she'd started on Dawes Road in Fulham because I knew it would be more fun with her. We'd been together at St Mary's but I don't remember anything about her from school because she was two years my senior. Quite justifiably, she remembers me as 'greedy and untidy', a reputation that clearly transcended year-group divisions. In spite of knowing this, on my return from New York she invited me to move into her new flat on Albert Bridge Road in Battersea.

When I'd left for the Big Apple I was still living at home. I had packed my bags from my childhood bedroom to embark on a rite of passage. When I returned with my tail between my legs, I was understandably reluctant to go back home to Mummy and Daddy. Lulu was the answer to my prayers.

Prior to my departure, David and I had been living like a pair of teenagers under our respective parents' roofs, still not ready to move in together. Lulu's spare bedroom was the ideal stepping stone. I was going it alone – though not quite. My brazen lack of accountability combined with her need to mother meant I moved from one cushy number to another. You could have detonated a bomb in my bedroom and it would've looked no different. Just like Mrs A, Lulu picked up pants and binned empty packets of Twiglets like the mother of a carefree teenage girl, which was what I still was at heart. We were both wild and unfettered, though Lulu did all the clearing up. But the relationship was much more than this. She stood by my side each time we returned home from a night out to find the answerphone lit up with chaotic, unhinged messages from my mum. Non-judgemental and as solid as a rock, Lulu knew instinctively when I needed someone to lean on.

I don't think anyone imagined I was going to go on to become Miss Jean Brody, and New York had proved a natural end to my career as a teacher. Nevertheless, I did still need to pay my rent and split the bills. With my letter of introduction from Armani safely in hand, off I went to meet a man called Peder Bertelsen.

The Backer

Peder Bertelsen is not a name the average man on the street would ever have heard. Even if you work in fashion it may

Classic Peder Bertelsen.

not be a name you know. He's not a designer or a model or a shopkeeper, but he did as much for the industry in this country as men like (that wanker) Philip Green or the lovely Paul Smith. Right up until the moment I met him, I had no idea who he was either or that he was to be the man who would launch my career.

Peder was an entrepreneur with his fingers in all sorts of pies – oil, property, basically anything legal that made money. In a different age, he'd have been described as a mogul. I have no idea how or why he went into fashion, but he was the first person to bring Italian designers to the UK and set them up in their own stores. Valentino, Dolce & Gabbana, Krizia, Alberta Ferretti, Ungaro and Armani. Up until then you could find these designers in department stores, but they have Peder to thank for their stand-alone shops. As a sideline, he also backed a number of smaller designers – but I'm getting ahead of myself.

All that was Peder on paper. Face to face he was larger

than life. A bon vivant. A maverick. A heavily accented Dane, he was charming, funny and exceptionally handsome, though not my type at all. One of the things that made him attractive was his spontaneity. Every year he would organise 'The Danish Lunch' – an event well known for schnapps and high jinks. At the end of one of these gatherings some years later, when I was too drunk to stand unaided, Peder held my hand as we crossed Knightsbridge, jumping from car bonnet to bonnet as we made our way to Valentino on Sloane Street. Once inside, I slumped into a puddle in the dressing room as he handed me items from the new collection to try on. We couldn't decide which ones we liked best so he bought the whole collection for me. The following day I received the instruction to 'Return all items' with the admission that the spree had been both alcohol-fuelled and ill-advised. Peder was the complete antithesis of my own father and everything I'd grown up with, and our meeting was the true beginning of my education.

Peder loved to shock. Not only was he handsome and charming but his accent introduced a lost-in-translation question mark to everything he said, allowing him to get away with things that might otherwise have earned him a slap round the face. He was a wonderfully naughty man. We were like two peas in a pod.

My boss at Armani had arranged for Peder and I to meet with a view to my working in the franchise he was about to open in Knightsbridge. In New York I'd got the job through Nancy, so there were no formalities. I turned up at 9 a.m. and started on the shop floor half an hour later. The meeting with Peder was the first proper grown-up thing I'd tackled.

In fact, it was the first interview I'd ever had and I was suitably nervous. Our meeting couldn't have lasted more than ten minutes and opened with the crushingly blunt 'There isn't a job for you at Armani.' Having explored no other avenues, this was a blow to me and I felt myself start to crumble. 'However,' he interjected before I had a chance to start begging, 'I've got a young designer who's just come from working with Karl Lagerfeld who's setting up on his own . . .'

That designer was Alistair Blair. I started working for him the next day.*

I had no CV, and was no great saleswoman. What I did have was a sterling pedigree and connections in all the right places, which was clearly why they agreed to hire me. Peder had an eye for young talent. In 1984, when his great friend Joan Bernstein (aka Mrs B of Brown's on South Molton Street) bought John Galliano's entire graduate collection, this was enough of an endorsement for him. Peder financed John as a start-up. Richard James, Patrick Cox, Katharine Hamnett – all these young designers were backed by Peder in their early careers. He had an eye like a hawk. The offices, pattern-cutters and secretaries for Alistair Blair were shared with Galliano and so, technically, was I. As it transpired I did much more for Alistair than I ever did for John. Though we became good friends, even I could see I was better matched to Alistair's brand. John wasn't

* 'In Peder's analysis of British designer fashion, he concluded that it fell into two categories – old and new money; old money was the Establishment, including the landowners; new money was in the City or in oil, and each identified with its own dress designers. Blair was categorised as Bertelsen's designer for the Establishment.' (Alistair Blair, Encyclopedia of Fashion: http://www.fashionencyclopedia.com/Ba-Bo/Blair-Alistair.html#ixzz79epSXM1d)

looking for his clothes to pop up in the Royal Enclosure but Alistair was and I was just the girl to make that happen. Even so, I would have loved to have done more for John.

Alistair was an auburn-headed Scotsman with a set of new teeth recently bonded to his old, unsightly ones. A soft-spoken, nervy, shy and handsome homosexual, at thirty he was only six years older than me but had already been Karl Lagerfeld's right-hand man in Paris's 7th arrondissement. Back in the UK, his studio was above a petrol station in Parson's Green. His niche was continental tailoring at ready-to-wear prices. If Boy George had introduced underground fashion to the masses, Alistair introduced them to off-the-shelf haute couture. He was beyond qualified to design his own label but what he needed to take things to the next level was money and publicity. He found one in Peder and the other in me. Prior to teaming up with Peder he'd been con-sidering an offer to work with Her Majesty's favourite, Norman Hartnell, but Peder wore him down. 'Before I knew where I was he was suggesting that he would back me and I was agreeing.'*

I always assumed I'd been employed as a dogsbody but recently learned from Alistair that Peder had sold me to him as a PR girl. Other than my connections and association with David, I was wholly unqualified to do this. But as Alistair said himself, 'She had little if not zero experience in PR but I had zero experience as a name designer.' We were in it together.

* Alistair Blair, Encyclopedia of Fashion.

Girl Friday

I worked for Alistair for four years, from his first month of business until almost the last. It was a crash course in turning talent into a commercial entity and doing it on the hoof. We were a very small team but the expectation was for us to perform on a level with the couture brands. His designs were not bespoke but the workmanship, quality of fabric and attention to detail meant they were the next best thing. His pleating was hand-folded and stitched, his sequins and bugle beads hand-sewn one by one. The skill that went into every garment matched that of any Parisian couturier. His clothes were not cheap but, if you knew what you were looking for, you'd understand why. They were made to last. During World War II, clothes rationing was based on how much labour and fabric went into a garment. A pair of stockings were only two coupons while a man's suit could be twenty-nine. Rations

'The Artist and His Muse' – Alistair and I trying to look edgy.

were calculated based on one change of outfit per annum and you knew the value of the item you were wearing. People got used to making and buying clothes that would stand the test of time. Alistair's were pieces you'd want to own for ever. Even so, while designers like Dior or Givenchy had a legacy that allowed the brand to sell itself, Alistair had to create a reputation overnight.

In the beginning, I was the closest thing he had to a royal warrant and I started wearing the collection out and about. My wardrobe and next season's samples were one and the same thing: I was essentially a sandwich board for the brand. My boyfriend was the Queen's nephew, which meant I was photographed everywhere I went and this gave Alistair a level of press coverage he could never have otherwise afforded. Lynne Franks was the biggest name in PR at the time but her fees were far too rich for Peder's blood. He knew that in hiring me not only would I *do* the PR, I *was* the PR, the 1980s version of an Influencer. The main difference was that I had the uber-paps of the day – Richard Young, Dave Benett and Alan Davidson – to take my picture rather than a selfie stick. I also had much less control over my image and absolutely no notion of my 'brand'.

Peder had taken an unqualified, directionless daddy's girl and turned her into a commodity. My job was to be charming and well connected. I'd held my own at enough high-society dinner parties to know this was something I could do with my eyes closed. Peder was the only person I'd met smart enough to recognise the value in this. To most people all racehorses look the same but it takes an expert to spot something special in an outsider. I thank God Peder had an eye for potential. The odds on my 'becoming' something were not great but he took a punt anyway and his faith in me gave me confidence. My upbringing had given me many things not afforded most people, but somehow girls like me were destined to be less than the sum of our parts. When you've been raised with no reason to try or make an effort, with nothing to strive for, where your opinion isn't important, valued or encouraged, it breeds a person destined to fade into the background.

Whatever Peder saw in me changed the course of my life in ways I could not possibly have predicted the day I walked into his office.

Alistair always joked I had a little black book that I kept in a safe, but my role liaising with the press was a wholly reactive one. Everyone came to us. This left plenty of time for other jobs and I quickly became Alistair's house model – not because of the way I looked but because I was the right size. In between seasons one of my primary jobs was to stand very still while he pinned toiles on me. I combined this with courier work in my shit-brown Ford Fiesta, delivering fabric to the beaders on Rathbone Place or collecting jewellery prototypes from Erickson Beamon on Ebury Street – it was non-stop. I never bothered with parking meters: I'd mount the pavement on a double-yellow and take my chances with the rest of the white vans. On my travels I had the privilege of getting to know some of London's greatest creative talents: Patrick Cox, Stephen Jones, Dinny Hall. The only area Alistair handled exclusively was fabric, all from Italy and every bolt chosen by him and him alone. Each sketch was pinned to the wall with its accompanying swatches – shirt, belt, skirt, shoes, buttons, zips and fastenings.

In 1988, when David Bailey was photographing British designers and their muses for a piece in what I think was *Vogue*, it was me Alistair chose to take with him for the shoot. McQueen would have Blow and Bob Mackie had Cher but Alistair didn't really have a muse. He was designing clothes for women like my mother so I was far too unsophisticated at twenty-four to be anything like his creative inspiration. I was a good clothes horse but I was more like a sidekick than his muse. However, I was also the best he had to offer.

For four years he and I were inseparable. I filled in his blanks and he mine. When Lady Diana came down to the studio, I was his safety blanket. His shyness was offset by my confidence around toffs, and this was exactly the sort of meeting where he felt he needed someone like me. He shouldn't have worried. I'd only met Diana once or twice before but she went out of her way to put everyone at ease. When I asked if she'd like a cup of tea, she offered to make it herself and one for me too. She was the kind of guest you'd find in the kitchen doing the washing-up or collecting torn-off wrapping paper in a bin bag after a game of pass-the-parcel at someone else's birthday party. Within minutes of her arrival you'd forgotten who she was. She was just a lovely young woman. She was also very clear about her own image. She must have read up on Alistair before she came because she was clearly very excited by who he was and what he could do. He was the new kid on the block and she wanted a piece of him. It was she who asked to see him, not a dresser or a stylist, and she was very decisive. She was about to go on tour and I thought she'd sweep up the whole collection, but in the end she only selected a few pieces. She knew exactly what she liked. Alistair and I were a team and this was a great example of our dynamic in action. There was nothing we couldn't do together.

Except perhaps this bloody photo shoot with David Bailey. I don't know what went on behind the scenes at all the other sessions, but the results suggest they found it much easier than we did.

Bailey was looking for a carefree vibe, but for two hours Alistair and I struggled to move much beyond wooden. Bailey was polite, though clearly unimpressed enough to feel we needed a prop, and some bright spark wheeled in a trampoline. These weren't the days when you could pop to Argos and pick one up for fifty quid, and it wasn't the type you'd find in a home gym. It was a full-size, community sports hall piece of equipment and must have taken some finding.

So here we were, Alistair grimacing through his newly minted teeth and me in my tartan box jacket. Both on the verge of a panic attack, we attempted to jump three foot in the air in unison while still trying to look like a couture designer and his muse. This is more difficult than it sounds if you're not an experienced gymnast. The main pitfalls were head-on collision or bouncing the other off into a by now very cross David Bailey.

Not every day was as eventful but, whatever it held, it always began with my bringing breakfast in the form of bacon sarnies and coffee in styrofoam cups. I'd done my Montessori teaching and had the Armani gig in New York, but neither had exposed me to anyone outside my social class. In this fledgling business, I was the classic Girl Friday, which meant interaction with a huge range of people – from craftsmen to receptionists, set-builders to hoteliers. The bottom line was I was mixing with people who worked for a living. I'd met plenty of skilled people growing up – everyone from the butcher in Bottesford to the blacksmith's apprentice. The difference now was that I was working too. These people were my peers. No one paid me any special attention and, just as at Mick's, I found it suited me very well. I loved working for a living and I liked being part of something bigger. Getting the business off the ground was a collective effort and I was proud to have some small part in it.

Ours was a close-knit team – the seamstress and pattern-cutters in the workshop, Alistair, me, Elaine and Limpet O'Conner in the office. Limpet oversaw everything from sales to buyers, Elaine was the office manager, Alistair was the talent, and I was everything else. Fellow Scot, Hugh, was Alistair's head pattern-cutter. An Alf Garnett lookalike with a less vigorous moustache, I remember thinking 'You're too old to be gay,' as if it might be something you grew out of. During a series of lengthy chats, I received an in-depth education on homosexuality as it existed in London at that time. No detail was too graphic. One day, on my return from getting the team milkshakes complete with straws, Hugh asked if he could keep my straw in addition to his own. The rationale behind his request still haunts me now. Apparently he needed one for each nostril because 'it's the only way I can breathe with my head up someone's arse'. I still don't know if that was true or if he was teasing me. I'm too scared to look it up. He also told me a third of those who frequented Earl's Court's celebrated leather bar, the Coleherne, were married men. Patrons wore

colour-coded handkerchiefs to indicate their sexual prefer-
ence. The positioning in a trouser back pocket gave further
information still. A handkerchief worn on the left meant you
were a 'top' – or active – lover. On the right meant you were
a 'bottom'. Black was S&M; dark blue, anal and light blue,
oral. Brown was scat; green, hustling or prostitution; grey,
bondage; red, fisting, and yellow, appropriately, water sports.
Trust men to formulate such a no-nonsense, cut-to-the-chase
path to fucking. No need to waste any time chatting before
you get down to it. In many respects, gay male sex is God's
greatest invention: given men's traditionally higher libidos
and complete lack of interest in small talk, putting two of
them together is frankly inspired.

Whatever went on in this establishment it was evidently
racy enough to necessitate its windows being blacked out.
The Coleherne closed for business in 2008 and reopened
later as a gastropub. What a sad end to such an illustrious
career.

The Shows

The expectation around Alistair's first catwalk show in 1986
was huge. Here was a designer bringing Paris to London and
the world's press descended on Olympia eager to witness
fashion history in the making. By the time I arrived on the
scene, we had three months left to prepare. The weeks leading up to the launch were a baptism of fire. We worked round
the clock. Alistair was the first person to bring international
catwalk models to the UK. The likes of Iman, Dalma, Marp-
essa and Linda Evangelista had never walked a London

catwalk before, but they came to support Alistair. His time at Lagerfeld had stood him in good stead.

At the time, a man named Kevin Arpino was the creative director at the mannequin designer Rootstein. Fashion isn't just about changes in the clothes but the body shapes that suit them. As beautiful as they were, you wouldn't put Marilyn Monroe in Mary Quant or Jean Shrimpton into Antony Price. And so, just as tastes in models changed, so did shapes in shop dummies. Rootstein produced two seasons of mannequins each year to coincide with designer collections and any trends in body shape that came with them. This was a first. Kevin knew and coordinated all Alistair's models. He too was at the start of his career when I met him but always came across as someone who'd been in the industry since the dawn of time. He lived and breathed it. He knew everyone. This came in very handy when deciding on what – or who – a shop dummy should look like in any given season.

Adel Rootstein had started her career in the late '50s making wigs and props in her flat in Earl's Court. She began creating handmade mannequins after realising the ones she saw all looked the same – a fact which did nothing for the clothes they were trying to sell. After employing a sculptor called John Taylor, they began producing mannequins based on real people. Adel booked models and John sculpted them from clay and these were then cast and mass-produced in foundries. When Adel booked Twiggy, that was the real game-changer. Rootstein became famous for their realistic creations and everyone from Joan Collins, Agyness Deyn, Joanna Lumley and Yasmin Le Bon sat for John Taylor. It was a great honour to be asked to model for a Rootstein mannequin. Naomi Campbell was only fifteen and had barely been discovered when she sat for John but sadly her dummy never found its way onto the shop floor. She did, however, make it into Alistair's show.

When her boob popped out of her top on his runway I thought she did very well to style it out given that – in spite of what you might read elsewhere – this was her first-ever cat-walk show. Arriving with her mum, Naomi was a shy, polite, nervous schoolgirl who had no idea who she was about to become. She was absolutely adorable and completely breath-taking to look at. As soon as she got onto the runway it was like watching a thoroughbred foal get up and walk. She knew what to do. It was second nature. Experience-wise the other girls were out of her league but, contrary to the supposed cat-fighting that goes on, were very protective over this new-comer. Naomi was the baby and they were the mothers. If they could have breastfed her they would.

Yasmin Le Bon and John Taylor in Rootstein's sculpting studio, London.

These girls might have *agreed* to do Alistair's show for love but they *walked* for money. A significant part of the reason they were classed as 'supermodels' was because they had control of their finances and knew the value of their brand. At the time this was totally lost on me. I assumed any old size 6 could be chucked down the runway and I would have done it for a fraction of the price. As Alistair was always telling me I had 'legs like a racehorse', I don't know why he didn't ask me. You've heard the soundbite about not getting out of bed for less than 10k a day. It was true. Thanks to these girls the cost of making the samples and producing the show jumped from approximately £50,000 to £250,000. Was it worth it? One hundred per cent.

The catwalk itself was covered in a slick plastic that gleamed like an ice rink. One of my jobs was to scour or tape the soles of every pair of heels to ensure their safe passage down the runway. The other was to pin handwritten numbers to each outfit. Every model had her own rack of fully accessorised ensembles, numbered in running order. In total there were about 120 looks ranging from daywear to cocktail to ballroom. The wedding gown was saved till last. The tradition to end a show with the bridal gown was one that now seems impossibly quaint. None of the menswear shows ended with a blushing groom. The 'bride' is usually a favourite model of the designer, and in this case it was Texan Dianne de Witt. The wedding dress never sold because customers always wanted something unique and most of them were already married anyway. There was also the question of superstition around wearing a wedding dress before your own big day and I secretly worried for Dianne. I needn't have bothered. She was married the following year while David persisted in not asking me for another two. Ironically it was Alistair who eventually made my own wedding dress in 1995, which I then promptly lost in a move.

By the time we reached the show I was pretty relaxed around catwalk models but was a bit taken aback to learn that no clothes were apparently required backstage. The models carried on blithely doing everything a person might do to get ready for work, but topless. Degas would have had a whale of a time if he'd turned up with his easel. These women were beautiful, languid creatures so it was actually quite a sight to behold. It was an odd kind of privilege to see them in their natural habitat, like being on safari and finding a herd of giraffes at a watering hole. They were a little like the royals in this respect, going about their jobs as if the world and his wife weren't looking on. They were consummate professionals and it fazed them not a jot. If the girls hadn't been so other-worldly, the pre-show set-up could have been a cosy pyjama party without the pyjamas. Everyone knew each other. There was no bitching, no competition, no nerves; just a gang of friends smoking, sipping champagne and having a laugh. Once again, I felt like I could have done it for much less.

The audience was rammed with global buyers and press, each seated in order of importance: *Vogue*, *Harper's* and other glossies front row, weekly press behind, and regional publications scattered in the gaps. Each thumbed through a press pack that I'd spent hours printing, photocopying, paper-clipping and assembling in the week before.

The models lined up as if casually queuing for the loo in a nightclub or breakfast buffet on a cruise while a visibly blanched Alistair made the final checks for his inaugural show. The lights went down but the adrenalin kept my heart in my mouth. The opening bars of ABC's 'The Look of Love' reverberated through the exhibition centre before Martin Fry's falsetto '*Ah, a-ha, ahhh!*' swept the first of our girls down the aisle. We were off. I thought I was going to be sick: it was more exciting than opening night at the Horse of the Year Show. Forgetting I had a job to do, I rushed impulsively round to the front to see the show from both sides. This was the moment I realised I could *not* in fact have done it better *or* for less. It was a masterclass in seduction. The models knew the important buyers and press and played to them depending on the proclivities of each. Every customer wants something different and they knew exactly what that was. It turned out these women weren't just models, they were businesswomen who understood the customer and just how to sell to them. They were worth their weight in gold.

It was my job to seat the press and the seating plans at these shows were a metaphor for the two parallel worlds that existed at that time in fashion. For John Galliano, someone like Caryn Franklin – fashion editor of *i-D* magazine – would be front row, but only warranted third from the back at Alistair's. His audience weren't interested in *i-D* magazine and *i-D*'s readers weren't interested in him. At this point she'd not yet been absorbed into the mainstream media with her role in *The Clothes Show*. I can remember being embarrassed by my background when I circulated with the likes of Caryn. I felt totally out of my league. I came from a world in which being a lady was still revered. Caryn came from a world in which creativity, individualism and rule-breaking were the cornerstones of success. She dressed for herself, not a man. At the time my tribe looked at that kind of behaviour as the preserve of tree-huggers. Left-wing, revolutionary, even. Alistair represented us, but, as incredibly talented as he was, in my heart I would really like to have been with Galliano. I had to live with the fact I wasn't really cool enough.

Another Shitty Day in Paradise

You might think being airdropped onto a tiny plot of land in the middle of the Caribbean would necessitate nothing but a sarong and a stack of paperbacks, but there was always *something* happening in Mustique. There was rarely time to kick back and lie on the beach with the latest Sidney Sheldon. Each day brought a new gathering and if there *were* a lull, we'd embark on one of Princess Margaret's favourite pastimes – snooping.

Mustique is renowned for its discretion. It doesn't matter who you are or how famous, it's somewhere you can enjoy unrivalled privacy. Unless, of course, Princess Margaret had the keys to your house and then she'd be up in your bedroom like a rocket. Yes, it was always open house on the island but I think most people assumed that was with the caveat you'd actually be home at the time. Princess Margaret's rank and longevity on the island gave her a kind of Mrs Danvers status – a regal caretaker with a big set of skeleton keys. She'd never bother going to the houses she loved – she could get an invite to those any day of the week. It was always those she wanted to inspect with no one looking over her shoulder that she snuck into, before returning home to quietly gloat over the juicy details. It was like an upmarket *Through the Keyhole* and the debriefings were one of my favourite parts of the day. Her harshest critique was reserved for Bowie's Bali-esque 'Mandalay' which, in his own words, was 'a whim personified . . . just the most delightful cliché'. That's not what she called it. Completely at odds with the distinctive sugared-almond villas that dominated and defined the island, Bowie's unorthodox house, Princess Margaret told me, 'would be lovely in suburban Tokyo'. Like it or loathe it, questioning Bowie's taste is just not something one does, which is no doubt why she had the good sense to do it behind his back.

After a brief visit in 1958, Colin Tennant had impetuously decided to buy the whole island. By 1986 it was technically no longer his but owned by a conglomerate he'd set up to finance

Bowie's house on Mustique – perfect . . . for suburban Tokyo.

its growth. Even so, Colin was still the big cheese as far as anyone on Mustique was concerned. Buying an island sounds much more glamorous than you might think. At the time his wife, Anne, lamented the complete lack of utilities – and indeed airport – but Colin had an eye for what it could be and devoted his life to making it happen. He was also known for being a bit spoiled and, in those early days, when he and Anne spent many years more or less alone together on the island, she had 'plenty of time to think of ways to murder him'.

The cornerstone of Mustique's success was arguably that Anne's best friend was Princess Margaret. Lady Anne (née Coke) had grown up at Holkham Hall in Norfolk, half an hour away from the Sandringham estate. Her father was equerry to King George VI, who stepped in after his brother Edward ran off with Mrs Simpson. King George's daughters – Princess Elizabeth and Princess Margaret – were

Anne and Colin Tennant on Mustique, maybe or maybe not in fancy dress – you never knew.

the perfect playmates for Anne. The families were sufficiently close that Anne was a maid of honour at Elizabeth's Coronation in 1953. When Anne married Colin Tennant in 1956, she hired a bloke called Tony Armstrong-Jones to take her wedding photos, which is how he bumped into her pal Princess Margaret. With her sister already taken, Princess Margaret was one of the most eligible women in the world but ended up marrying her friend's wedding photographer. This was typical of the Princess Margaret I knew.

The first time Princess Margaret saw Mustique was on a Caribbean cruise on the Royal Yacht *Britannia* with Tony directly after they were married, when Colin offered her some land as a wedding present. Eight years later she called to ask him whether the offer had been serious and, if so, would it include a house? How could he say no? Once he'd built the house, that was effectively the royal warrant on Mustique.

To live on the island in the early days you needed to be wealthy enough not only to buy the land but also to build a house. There simply were none. Or any real infrastructure. Colin was wealthy and well-connected, but not *that* wealthy, so his solution was to make Mustique a co-operative where homeowners were shareholders. Just like John Lewis. Luckily for Colin his friends included people like Mick Jagger and Bryan Adams and he approached them one by one with his idea. Each time someone bought in, a little bit more of Mustique became liveable. A little bit more road was built enabling the next buyer to get to their land. Mustique was a piecemeal effort. Colin employed Lord Snowdon's uncle, Oliver Messel, to plan the island and design its first homes. Messel had had a long career as an artist and theatrical set designer.

During the war his artistic skills were put to good use in his role as a camouflage officer – disguising pillboxes as haystacks or roadside cafés to hide them from the enemy. His architectural influence in the Caribbean can still be felt in his trademark 'Messel Green' on shutters and doors throughout the islands. In an odd twist of fate, Oliver's sister (and David's grandmother), Anne, grew up at Nymans estate in Sussex. In 2007, I bought the house next door.

Every February, David and I would fly out to stay with his mother. She loved to beachcomb for shells and would rub them with oil to make them shine. She had double-jointed fingers which allowed her to keep her fingertips bent back in the process, meaning she never disturbed her manicure. By 1986 I'd already been two or three times so was pretty relaxed at Les Jolies Eaux. Nevertheless, there are some things you only want to do in your own home and one of them is being ill.

I'll just say this now: sometimes I faint when I do a poo. Most of the time I'm at home and the worst that can happen is I knock myself out on the sink and lie there until Sten comes to brush his teeth. When it happened at the Peacock Ball on Mustique, not only was it the first time it had ever happened, but the fallout was significantly more high profile. I think it's fair to say that when you lose control of your bowels in front of someone, you ideally want to know them well enough to have got the pleasantries out the way. On this occasion luck was not on my side.

The Peacock Ball was held in honour of Colin's sixtieth birthday – the concluding knees-up to a week-long celebration. The theme was his beloved India, where he'd travelled in the lead-up to bring back saris, jewels and kurtas as costumes for his guests. He laid them all out in the *Wind Star* – the yacht he'd chartered for a seven-day cruise from St Lucia to Mustique – so guests could select their outfits for the evening ahead. The *Wind Star* was the largest sailing boat in the world and had been loaned to Colin in return for publicity. I remember being told it was the length of Beauchamp Place in London, which I can well believe. It had seventy-five state rooms and two on-board seamstresses in case of any ill-fitting emergencies.

Anyone without access to a home on the island stayed on the boat, apart from Raquel Welch, who'd borrowed her own boat from Maxim's in Paris – the *Maxim de Mer*. Princess Margaret nicknamed it the 'Mal de Mer' on account of the gaudy interiors, designed by Pierre Cardin. Raquel proved an unpopular guest that week. Mustique was an informal place but around royalty there was always a protocol to follow. This meant curtseys and ma'ams even if you were in your bathing suit. I don't know whether it was on purpose or not but Raquel succeeded in offending more than one person on more than one occasion. She'd invited Princess Margaret as guest of honour to a party on the 'Mal de Mer'. For one reason and another, stars were dropping off the guest list in quick succession, until even Raquel herself telegrammed Colin to say she would not be attending the party. It was an embarrassment for Colin, who felt a sense of responsibility for everything that happened during that week. Princess Margaret was pure class and would not have dreamt of letting Colin and Anne down and we went along to the party anyway. I livened up proceedings by lifting up my arms in my strapless dress every time she was engaged in conversation with another guest so my boobs popped out. She had a great sense of humour and I loved watching her trying to remain dignified with my nipples in her eye-line. 1–0 to the princess.

A treasure hunt was organised the next day by Colin's son Henry, which took us through the gardens of Bequia in search of clues. Beads hung from all the trees like Mardi Gras. I was so sure I was going to find the treasure and was furious when I was pipped to the post. I took solace by having a fag with Colin's eldest son, Charlie. Charlie was a hopeless heroin addict as well as acutely OCD. I'd often see him walking down the King's Road talking to himself as he avoided the cracks in the pavement. He was a sweet, sweet boy. I once saw the film *Nicholas and Alexandra* about the Romanovs and their haemophiliac son and remember thinking he was very like Charlie. You instinctively felt he was fragile; like he mustn't be bumped into or knocked lest he break or fall. Colin and Anne didn't embrace his addiction but they didn't ignore it either. It was just one of those things. They all got on with it. Charlie was one of the gang. The way other people treated him stemmed from the way his parents did. He looked truly terrible at the ball – pale, thin and gaunt, but beautiful at the same time. As we stood and had our smokes, he told me he couldn't roll his joint as he'd run out of Rizlas. I gave him the wrapper from my Tampax.

Colin was a flamboyant character but he was also very volatile. He didn't drink and I never saw him out of control due to substance abuse, but he found it difficult to manage his emotions. His mood could change on a sixpence and he was prone to explosions he couldn't control. Princess Margaret's contribution to festivities was a picnic party on Macaroni Beach.

The Incident

On the night of the ball, Anne, Princess Margaret and I dressed together in Anne's bedroom in the Great House. Their home was filled with treasures collected over a lifetime of travel but the jewel in the crown was their solid silver bed – unhallmarked, of course, hailing as it did from India. We all loitered in Anne's bedroom as we waited in vain for Raquel to turn up so that Princess Margaret could arrive last, as protocol dictated. Eventually we all trouped out after a clipped 'How rude' from PM. She certainly wasn't about to hold up the party.

Music came courtesy of the local steel band. Traditional Caribbean music occasionally strayed into something from the Stones. Staff fanned guests with peacock-feather fans and Basil, of the island's famed Basil's Bar, made rum punch. Prawns were served with fresh mango and guava. The rest of the food that night, however, was so spicy it was inedible and the resulting pain in my bowels so bad I thought I might throw up. On reflection, that would have been preferable. It was cramps rather than nausea that signalled the imminent arrival of an emergency. I knew I had to get to a bathroom post-haste if I didn't want to be an unannounced addition to the evening's entertainment. I battled my way through the revellers, throwing women and children out of the way. I cursed Colin for lining the walkway to his house with 200 metres of dusty, pale-pink carpet. I started chanting in my head, *Don't do it here; don't do it here.* The gods smiled on me, albeit briefly, and I made it to the cloakroom just in time, but this was where my luck ran out. The blood drained from me as I held the lavatory in my sights. The darkness rose from my feet to my head before my legs gave way beneath me.

I woke to the sounds of a statuesque blonde lady calling my name in a bold, Texan twang. Yes, it was Jerry Hall. How nice, I thought; she must have noticed I was unwell and come to find me.

When Mick had married Bianca in 1971 I remember being very put out. She was tanned and brunette and I was blonde. I was also about ten so the point was moot but I was cross nonetheless. I much preferred Jerry. She was beautiful, though not in the traditional sense. Her look brilliantly suited the excesses of the '70s and '80s, like everything had had one too many brushstrokes, but somehow it worked. The hair, the legs, the lips, the voice, even her sexy fluidity – it was all slightly OTT but perfectly suited to appear on camera. Alongside all this she was wonderfully down-to-earth, and

Me, Talita, Colin and Jerry in happier times before 'the incident'.

the only supermodel I've ever met to dye their hair with Sun-In. In private, she and Mick were quite homely. Mick was a big fan of dovecotes and she the epitome of a Southern, pumpkin-pie housewife. Though she's often defined by her men in the press, she was so much more in her own right.

I was less pleased to see Jerry when I realised that not only had I passed out but had clearly been emptying my bowels in the process. The floor was covered in poo, as was my pink sari, now bunched round my waist. I felt too ill to be embarrassed, though. It was the kind of moment I wished my mum would turn up with my teddy Gelatine and tuck me into bed. I have to say, Jerry was a pretty good alternative and threw herself into the revolting task at hand. While her friend Talita went off to fetch Princess Margaret, Jerry dowsed me down with a wet hand towel. She'd famously described herself as a 'maid in the living room, cook in the kitchen and whore in the bedroom'. I'm not sure about the rest of it but she certainly came good on the maid part as she tirelessly scrubbed away on what could have been a very nasty stain on Colin's floor. Jerry and Princess Margaret bundled me back to Les Jolies Eaux under the cover of night like a pair of hit-men disposing of a body. David, mercifully, was none the wiser thanks to the covert work of these two resourceful ladies.

Colin had pulled off something quite unique. The Peacock Ball had a charm that would be impossible to recreate now. Despite its decadence, it had a naivety too. A dressing-up party on an untouched desert island, complete with elephants, steel bands and treasure hunts through the trees. He was a difficult man but you had to hand it to him: he had a vision.

When I started going out with David in 1983 he asked his dad to take my picture. This wasn't any old father-in-law to-be, it was Lord Snowdon and, while this was an honour, in the event it was actually a rather sour experience. Princess Margaret was known as a divisive character – someone many considered spoiled and capricious – but I loved her unequivocally in spite of this. I did not, however, feel anything like the same affection for David's father. Like Princess Margaret, he was no doubt stifled by his position and I could forgive him his legitimate grievances. He was charismatic, handsome and talented enough to attract the attention of one of the most eligible women in the world, but his marriage simultaneously raised him up and tore him down professionally. His critics would accuse him of lacking the edge of his contemporaries, who used the relatively new freedoms of the time to make names for themselves at the cutting edge of popular culture. While Tony had to satisfy himself with a few audible gasps in aristocratic circles for showing the bare shoulders of the sister of a ruling monarch, his contemporaries were defining an era. The most powerful of his peers launched the careers of those they photographed. Twiggy, Shrimpton, Marie Helvin – we know their names because of the men who photographed them. They were the muses that inspired a generation of artists. By comparison, Snowdon's work was controlled; respectable compositions during the sexual revolution. And there was nothing more emasculating than that. The wife he chose and the world that came with her precluded him from artistic expression of the liberated man we now know him to be.

When Bailey was photographing *his* wife's high heel hooked erotically through the narrow gusset of her knickers, Snowdon was stuck straightening hems for formal royal portraits. There is a yawning chasm between the sort of photos Bailey et al were free to take and those considered acceptable for a senior member of the royal family to be producing. Had Tony ever seen a shoe tucked through a woman's knickers? He strikes me as the kind of person who might. Could he take a picture of it and sell it in a coffee-table book? Absolutely not. Creatively I imagine he must have felt very frustrated and trapped by his circumstances.

In my mid-twenties I was hardly in a position to comment on or appreciate his broader existential dilemmas but, fundamentally, I found him a thoroughly difficult man – sarcastic, condescending and a little cruel. When I correctly guessed the secret to his coin trick, he said 'Oh gosh, look how clever you are,' but stopped short of actually patting me on the head. If I met him now I'd describe him as hard to win over. But it was simpler than that: I was frightened of him and I think this says as much about me as it does David's father.

I don't feel at ease writing these negative words because I care greatly about David's feelings but Lady Glenconner has already testified to Snowdon's malevolence. Her revelations of his habit of leaving spiteful notes for his wife have already illustrated this side of his personality. 'You look like a Jewish manicurist and I hate you,' is not only spectacularly nasty but, equally, incredibly offensive to all concerned. Tony knew how to twist the knife and I felt it first-hand around him.

Even in the way he worked there was a strand of this malice. 'I'm not a great one for chatting people up,' he once said in an interview. 'I don't want people to feel at ease. You want a bit of edge. There are quite long, agonised silences. I love it. Something strange might happen. I mean, taking photographs is a very nasty thing to do. It's very cruel.' This may quite well be true but it's another thing to do it so knowingly and to so casually articulate your delight in the process.

On the day of the shoot, Mary Greenwell – then only twenty-five and at the beginning of her career – did my make-up and was instructed to add more and more layers as time wore on. 'One can legitimately accentuate certain things,' he once said, 'like a caricaturist,' and I now wonder what he must have thought of me. By the end of the session I remember feeling the only way he could bear to photograph me was if I were disguised as someone else. Was he caricaturing me as a kind of courtesan or marionette? I was so heavily made-up I could have left the shoot and gone straight to an audition for *Cats* without washing my face in between. I'd love to be able to look at these portraits now to see if my memories about the experience were justified. Stupidly, these are the prints I told David to put in the bin.

I'm not sure why he'd agreed to take my picture. He was not known for his generosity of spirit and I can't think he'd have done it for no reason. They weren't engagement photographs – I was alone in them – but I think they must have at least been a form of endorsement of our relationship. Of all the photos I'd had taken, these were the only private portraits I'd ever sat for.

*

David and I were still not engaged but things seemed to be moving forward nonetheless. It was time to meet the parents. Or at least one of them. Princess Margaret and Snowdon were divorced so Tony would not be included in the festivities. There was no way on God's earth my parents would have been forward enough to suggest such a get-together without the formality of an engagement, so it can only have come from Princess Margaret. Rather than one location, we settled on the idea of going to both homes in one night. Like a pub crawl. Princess Margaret was to come to Cottesmore Gardens for pre-dinner drinks and then we'd pile back to the palace for a bit of grub. This could have been Princess Margaret's attempt to make my parents feel important and at ease, but I think it more likely she just wanted the chance to nose round their house. It was no more than a ten-minute walk alongside London's glorious royal park but we drove in two cars instead.

Meeting the in-laws is stressful at the best of times but when one of them is Princess Margaret it adds an extra layer of pressure to the situation. My mother was on an almighty high that night and, though she was completely at home around the aristocracy, began an evening of compulsive curtseying the minute our guests arrived. It was difficult to maintain the flow of conversation given that my mum dropped halfway to the floor every time Princess Margaret so much as blinked. I think Mrs A would have been more composed had she been invited.

My dad went another way altogether. In an effort to prove we were as good as she was, he adopted a relaxed, Dave Allen manner. He didn't actually bring up our Domesday lineage or tell her that he thought the royals were a bunch of big-chinned Hanoverians, but if you knew him as well as I did, you knew it was implied in the way he sat languorously back in his chair. The only thing that prevented my father being a complete and utter arse that evening was the fear his inflamed haemorrhoids would leave a bloodstain on her sofa and it was this, rather than any deference, that kept him in check. The fact I'd behaved the same way myself on my first meeting with the princess was exactly what made me forgive him.

Thank God David and I didn't get married. I don't think my poor parents could have withstood the pressure.

Rangers vs Romantics

At the same time I was hanging around waiting to get married, another type of twenty-something was blazing a new trail. Plastered in blusher and draped in their makeshift, post-punk finery, these misfits were the New Romantics and they were out to change the world. We were two different species living in parallel time zones.

In London in the early 1980s, mainstream fashion manifested itself in very few forms. I could count the high-street brands on one hand – Miss Selfridge, French Connection, Kookai, Warehouse – so the clothes we wore came from a pretty small gene pool. For me, these were conveniently collected under one roof at Way In – Harrods' answer to young people. For more defiant sorts, there was Camden, Carnaby Street or Kensington Market. We were divided into easily identifiable gangs – recognisable by the clothes we wore and the

Clearly too full of myself to feel the need to wear trousers.

music we listened to. As far as I was concerned, you were one of two things: a Sloane Ranger or a New Romantic; anything else fell outside my peripheral vision. Dissect either group and you'd find the schools we went to, the streets we lived on and what our parents did for money. As a Sloane, the clothes I wore were bought and paid for by someone else. The clothes worn by the New Romantics were homemade, borrowed or saved for. We were two different tribes neatly representing Britain's social and economic divide. The Haves and Have-nots.

Both movements had their aspirations and their idols. The New Romantics wanted to marry Prince Charming while the Sloanes set their sights on the future king of England. One of us eventually bagged him, though it was not the fairytale ending we'd all discussed under the bed sheets by torchlight. Reputedly, Charles and Diana had only met thirteen times before they got engaged, which in my eyes made it an arranged marriage (but what other kind is there among the aristocracy?) rather than a Mills & Boon romance. I'm not surprised things went quickly south: surely the nursery at Windsor Castle is no one's idea of an appropriate setting to propose?

Even though it went against my background, I too was in love with Adam Ant. I couldn't help it. Not only was he exquisite, he was subversive. Different from the boys I knew. In homage to my love, I purloined my father's Coldstream Guards jacket, which was just long enough to cover my cheeks. Knickers and heels were the only accessories needed for a night out. It was the smallest seed of rebellion in an otherwise dutiful daughter. Had I told my parents I was seriously considering a union with a cross-dressing, working-class singer, they'd have thought it as preposterous as mating a chihuahua with a Rottweiler. One's course was so immovably plotted it would have been like driving down the motorway and suddenly deciding to swerve into the central reservation. Complete madness. I wish I'd known then that his mother was one of Norman Hartnell's embroiderers – that would have stumped them. My marriage to Adam Ant never did materialise, and two years later I'd rather predictably hooked up with my own 'prince'. The funny thing was, David Linley was far less Posh Boy than you might imagine. In fact his pedigree was quite diluted. His mother was more Hollywood than Balmoral, and his father a bedhopping bisexual. Just like Princess Margaret, David was a nonconformist. He was a rebel with the added benefit that my parents approved and Mrs A loved him even more than I did.

It was easy to track these tribes because each had their haunt of choice. For the New Romantics, it was a Tuesday night in the basement of a shitty Covent Garden nightclub, the Blitz. For me and my people, it was always Tramp or Annabel's.

Between twenty-two and twenty-seven I could always be found in one or the other. Though never on a Saturday. The weekend was a concept that mattered to us for different reasons than it did to the working classes. I was living with Lulu but we didn't use our Saturdays to do the weekly supermarket shop or run errands. We used it to return 'home' to the countryside, where there was nothing we need do but recover from burning the candle at both ends during the week. The only thing I had to get up for was breakfast cooked by someone else and laid up on the hotplate on the dining-room sideboard. By the time I hit twenty-five I'd seen 90 per cent of England's finest homes and fully expected to end up living in one. We were the Careless Class and the weekend was just an extension of an already carefree life.

To the uninitiated, it would be easy to lump Tramp and Annabel's together. To the initiated, the two could never be confused. Yes, they were both private members' clubs for the rich, the posh and the very famous, but the devil was in the detail. Trying to pick a favourite would be like re-enacting *Sophie's Choice*. I couldn't do it even now. However, what I will say is that, if I were going out in a gang, it was Annabel's. If I didn't want to bump into friends of my parents, it was Tramp every time.

Although I was going out with David for most of this period, he was typically holed-up at his carpentry workshop in Surrey during the week so I frequently flew solo. One of the things I admired most about him was his work ethic and skill as a craftsman. He was one of the few people I knew who actually deserved a weekend. My main accomplice was Lulu but I had a small pool of reliable alternatives should she be otherwise engaged. There was Dodi, of Dodi and Diana fame, someone I always felt was a little wounded, but very sweet; and Tim Jefferies, man about town and owner of Hamilton's photographic gallery in Mayfair. Tim was the man who introduced me to Edward Mapplethorpe, the lesser known but equally talented brother of Robert. We had a little fling. Years later he photographed my son Joe as a baby and the pictures now hang on my kitchen wall.

And then there was Ghislaine. Ghislaine Maxwell was the classic contradiction in terms: insecure and needy but over-powering and in your face. A girl with both an inferiority and a god complex. She was a bit like a Labrador; the more some-one kicked her the more she loved them. Ghislaine is the classic example of a person born with everything, given a huge leg up in life, but who sadly does nothing of value with it. Whatever these people became in time, during the mid-80s they were a group of bright young things who had the world at their feet. Some, like Julian Metcalfe of Pret a Manger or Matthew Freud of Freud Communications, clearly made better choices than others.

Tramp

Hidden inconspicuously behind dark-blue double doors on Jermyn Street, Tramp is an institution. This was an odd loca-tion for a nightclub given the rest of the street is wall-to-wall art galleries. Even in the '80s, most of St James' was double-yellows so Tramp wasn't a place with much passing trade. But it didn't need to be. Famed for its louche, rock 'n' royalty vibe, it was the favoured nightspot of Hollywood actors, A-list rock stars, and the sons and daughters of newly minted magnates. In short, Tramp was home to what my mother would have called 'The Fast Set'. In the 1950s, the club was known as the Society – somewhere the Queen Mother would supposedly go to celebrate a win on the horses. I'd love to think of her there with a Dubonnet and gin.

More than anything for me, Tramp was its host, Johnny Gold. The son of a bookmaker, Johnny was a savvy partner-in-crime to a man called Oscar Lerman. Even if you're unfamiliar with this name, you'll have heard of his wife – Jackie Collins. But, for the most part, Oscar stayed in the office and Johnny was the face of the club. Rough and rugged in both demeanour and appearance, he was

Golden-hearted Johnny Gold.

nevertheless a soft-centred sweetie. Like the safe-word in a sex game, I always felt he could be trusted. Despite the success of the club, there was nothing flashy or ostentatious about Johnny. If I didn't know, I'd have pegged him as a gangster or, at the very least, the kind of man who'd get you a good deal on a fur coat. Instinctively you knew he'd made it alone. He didn't hail from the crowd he attracted to his own establishment. He *became* a part of it but only *because* of it. Prior to all this he'd been employed by Oscar to run an earlier nighttime venture – Dolly's. Dolly's drew a fashionable crowd who faithfully followed Oscar and Johnny to Tramp. Their new club would be the backdrop to countless front-page stories.

When the remaining Beatles got together for the first time after John's death, it was at Tramp. When Michael Douglas and Danny DeVito arrived too late to find an empty table with Kathleen Turner, it was Johnny who got her a stall and made the two boys sit on the stairs. When Keith Moon was presented with a £14,000 bill after polishing off two dozen Pacific prawns, his somewhat understated response was 'They've gone up! I mean, I don't mind, but it's a bit much.' It transpired this was the sum of an annual bar bill he'd never been sober enough to settle at the end of an evening. Tramp's history under Johnny is overflowing with such joyful snippets. But, as much as Tramp was Johnny, Johnny was Tramp. He presided over every moment. Even after he sold the club in 1998 he continued to work on the door for another five years, greeting his friends each evening. In an environment where things could easily get out of hand, they never really did because no one wanted to displease him. We all liked him too much.

Top Table

The door policy excluded both riff-raff and paps but there was no question of a velvet rope downstairs at Tramp. The beau monde sat alongside hookers and hacks. But there was one seat everyone wanted and that was the one next to Johnny. Descend the stairs and turn to the right, and there you'd find him at the same table in the same seat night in, night out, till 4 a.m. It didn't matter whether you were Jack Nicholson or a nameless shopgirl, Johnny's table was reserved for the people he wanted to spend his evening with. Tramp was a meritoc-racy where the criteria for success was whether you had something interesting to bring to the conversation. If you were at his table, no two nights were the same. Absolutely anyone might rock up. For me this meant everyone from a bright orange George Hamilton to steaming hot chocolaté Errol Brown or Abergavenny's answer to Warren Beatty, Dai Llewellyn. In his own words, Johnny 'tried to treat the celebri-ties as ordinary people, and the ordinary people as celebrities', and this was something no amount of money could buy.

The Crowd

Tramp billed itself as a nightclub but it was more a dinner dance with a side order of Disco Inferno. In its heyday, the crowd was much more Jagger and Jerry but, in the nicest possible way, by the time I arrived it was a hair's breadth from seedy. No one minded, though. Escort girls propped up the bar, open for business. Moneyed old chancers after a bit of skirt dabbled in quid-pro-quo liaisons – a drink for a dance; a whole bottle if you sat on his knee. My girlfriends and I wangled cocktails out of men with deep pockets just by being twenty-two. We never felt used or vulnerable. If anything I felt guilty. There really is no fool like an old fool. Knowing I couldn't afford to get myself anywhere near as drunk as I intended, these gullible souls were the obvious solution. That we had no intention of following through on any of our implied promises was never an issue. It was a silent contract as old as time. The men enjoyed a turn on the dance floor and flaunting their readies and we benefited from their vanity. There was nothing edgy about it. Tramp was exactly like a large family wedding. You could drink and flirt, safe in the knowledge that someone's parents would inevitably be having coffee and an After Eight at their table on the other side of the room. I felt safe there. Years later, when I fell pregnant with my first child, Joe, he was 'Guido' in the womb in honour of Tramp's beloved maitre d' who'd kept a watchful eye over me all those years.

The Code

Unlike the buttoned-up dress code for Annabel's, Tramp was far more laid back. I was always a little suspicious about their claim that a man couldn't enter without a woman, given the number of free-roaming males on the make. Whatever the truth, a man certainly didn't need to wear a tie. At Annabel's, on the other hand, even the mighty Slash had to water down his Guns N' Roses persona with an Old Etonian tie borrowed for the evening we dined there together. He still managed to pull it off and brought a little bit of Angus Young to Mayfair. True to its broader ethos, Tramp was open to pretty much anything. As long as you were technically dressed, you'd probably get in.

Annabel's was another matter altogether. Today its dress code claims to be non-prescriptive but then reels off a list of explicit dos and don'ts. 'Gentlemen are required to wear a jacket at all times after 6 p.m., unless on the dancefloor!' – the exclamation mark making it no less pretentiously wanky.

Annabel's

If Tramp were a meritocracy, Annabel's personified the old-boy network. A closed shop, open only to those with the right surname. Had the Knipton Set moved their New Year's Eve party to town, Annabel's is what it would have looked and sounded like.

My subsection of the Sloanes was the Hoorays – old money and hand-me-down titles. The other was the Nouveaus; the young barons and stinking-rich offspring of Britain's captains of industry. A Hanson, a Maxwell or an Al-Fayed all sat happily in this category. I was one of a handful of people willing to straddle both sets. The Nouveaus were a bit more racy than the Hoorays so I'd go with them to Tramp. For the Hoorays, it was Annabel's.

During the day, Berkeley Square was full of nine-to-fivers coming and going from their offices behind the square's flat-fronted, Georgian facades. The days when anyone was wealthy enough to call these mansions home were long gone. Annabel's at number 44 was the next best thing. A flight of precarious ironwork stairs led to the entrance of what was once the basement of John Aspinall's famed gambling establishment, the Clermont. If you think you've heard the name

Loo & Soo escaping the paparazzi outside Annabel's.

before, it's because it was home to the Clermont Set, the group of aristos widely believed to have hidden the whereabouts of Lord Lucan after he vanished in the wake of the murder of his children's nanny, Sandra Rivett. Founded in 1962, the club's original members were an aristocratic *Who's Who*, and no one really knows whether they closed ranks to queer the investigation. Where the Scots have Nessie, Mayfair has Lucky Lucan – a mystery that will never be solved. Annabel's has since moved two doors down but for me its home was Aspinall's basement.

No matter how boring the dinner party or charity ball, there was always Annabel's to look forward to. It was the last stop of the night for the truly well-heeled. Consequently, I was usually pretty hammered by the time I got there. On a gradient calculator, the staircase to the basement felt like a 1:7. If you were as drunk as I was, it might as well have been an 80-degree bobsleigh run. Add to this a series of decorative holes in the treads, and the stairs were the perfect place to trap a stiletto and launch yourself face first to the bottom. The one time this *did* happen I'd had five screwdrivers and was luckily too pissed to go rigid, which softened my fall. I enjoyed the rest of my evening with the help of a medicinal brandy and the fact I couldn't feel my ballooning foot until I woke the next morning. The offending Charles Jourdan heels were put out to pasture in favour of a pair of Alberta Ferretti flats. I could now continue to drink like a sailor on leave with less chance of killing myself. Coming up the stairs was considerably easier, though often messier. If needs be, I could always do them on my hands and knees. I don't know why I never thought to go *down* them on my bottom. The night I staggered onto the pavement in my elbow-length, marabou-trimmed gloves and mini skirt was the only time I ever received a letter from my grandmother. 'I don't need to tell you what you looked like,' was her pointed response to the photograph that appeared of Lulu and me attempting to escape the press in the red tops the next day.

At the heart of Annabel's clientele were the usual lords and ladies, plus anyone whose education exceeded £10k a year and the whole of the Newmarket racing fraternity. Young officers of the Household Cavalry shacked up at Knightsbridge Barracks drank until daybreak before tacking-up for a canter round Rotten Row. The royals were never averse to a bit of Annabel's either. Princess Margaret was well-known for a knees-up, but the fact that Annabel's is the only nightclub ever to have been visited by her sister tells you everything you need to know about its cultural identity. When Fergie and Lady Di turned up at Andrew's stag-do dressed as policewomen, it gave everyone a glimpse into what they might have looked like as a pair of stripograms.

The Aesthetic

Like Tramp, Annabel's had one foot in the past. Named after owner Mark Birley's wife, Lady Annabel Vane-Tempest-Stewart, it was effectively an extension of their drawing room. Upmarket Laura Ashley interiors designed by Nina Campbell saw de Gournay wallpaper smothered in portraits of anonymous dogs and Derby winners. Every inch was packed with button-back banquets, velvet chairs, candlelit lamps and unnecessary fringing. Imagine the study of a sixty-year-old Old Etonian and you have it.

The lady's powder room was presided over by Mabel. In her uniform of pink and white stripes and crisp pinny, she was a ready ear for gossip and a shoulder for the tears of many a marital spat. Her domain was lit in a way that made even the most drunken, mascara-streaked cheeks look romantic. It was a reimagining of nanny's nursery for the tipsy elite. I knew that if I forgot my bag Mabel would happily put it in a taxi for me. She'd take delivery of the next day's papers at 1 a.m. and I'd go down the corridor for a chat and a debrief. She knew before me if I'd been in the tabloids with David. 'What a gorgeous frock,' she'd announce, as if I already knew my picture was in Dempster's society column. 'I don't know how you stay so slim.' I still can't decide if she was genuinely interested or just a well-placed, well-intentioned nosy neighbour, but the loos were a great place for an early morning round-up of the headlines nonetheless. If David and I were on a hiatus, I was just as likely to appear, except now the front

Love in the spotlight.

page would speculate on his new girlfriend and my level of heartbreak. For five years the press was relentless. What I thought about this differed with the circumstances. If I was chased by paparazzi on motorbikes because David and I had split up, it was horrible; if I was on my way to Valentino's launch party, I was prepared and it was fine. If I was being doorstepped, it was usually by paparazzi I didn't know and a violation that made me feel quite vulnerable. Whatever the circumstances, it was an intrusion I became very used to and I was on first-name terms with most of the photographers. I'd kiss them hello and they'd see me into a taxi if I was going home alone. They were decent people and there was a mutual respect between us, but it was an odd world to be living in nonetheless.

The dance floor at Annabel's was so tiny as to almost be an afterthought in the middle of the dining room. Uncoordinated 'Ras' whirled uncontrollably around the parquet floor shouting the words to 'Satisfaction' and 'Brown Sugar', and swaying to 'No Woman No Cry'. The older generation, noticeable for their fancy footwork and tendency to dance in couples, did their best to keep up. Robert Palmer's 'Addicted to Love' was as risqué as things got. The girls huddled into groups to mimic his leggy, wet-lipped backing band. The DJ never stooped as low as 'Tiger Feet', but equally knew which rudimentary beats would lure us up for a bop.

I danced every night at Annabel's but the music I really liked to listen to was being played for the New Romantics halfway across town at the Blitz.

The Blitz Kids

Around the same time I was nibbling my smoked almonds and hand-rolled cheese straws, a mile and a half up the road promotor Steve Strange and DJ Rusty Egan had lit a fuse to a new fire. The proletariat were about to set the world alight. For its loyal patrons, the Blitz was more than a club; it was a love affair. Its aesthetics were inspired by the flamboyance of Bowie and Bolan and the effete dandies of the late 1700s. Its door-policy of refusing entry to anyone not sufficiently bold or brazen bred a certain kind of creative competitiveness amongst clubbers. The make-up counters at Boots would not have met the needs of the Blitz Kids. I expect theatrical pancakes from Covent Garden's Screenface were more their bag. They weren't just dressing up, they were in disguise. While it was by no means uncommon to be outwardly gay at this point, it was still rare to be so overtly non-gendered. While men and women paraded their sexual question marks as androgyny, squat-dwellers hid their poverty under powdered wigs, beauty spots and Klaus Nomi lips. In my classically bland 'no make-up' make-up, the only time I attempted the Blitz I knew immediately I was out of my depth. I would never have had the courage to go out on a limb like this. I dressed to fit in, not stand out. Sophie Stapleton Cotton – my Queen's Gate schoolfriend – was the unlikeliest of girlfriends for Rusty Egan and surely the only reason they let me in. I did not return a second time. Unlike most of my friends, who considered the Blitz Kids ridiculous, I had huge admiration for their fearless individualism. It was a seminal moment in popular culture and one I was not a part of. I couldn't say I regretted this but they caught my eye. I was intrigued to know what was happening beyond the boundaries of my little life. Just like *Hello, Dolly!*, the New Romantics set a little fire inside me.

While other clubs expected customers to blend in, the Blitz expected theirs to stand out. Sitting between two art colleges, it was the perfect place for fashion students to experiment. Young designers like Judith Frankland showcased their collections inside its hallowed walls. While still a student, John Galliano used Tuesday nights as a substitute catwalk. 'All that experimental cutting led me to understand precisely how a jacket had been put together in the past; how to put it together correctly in the present and then, from that, I was led to dismantle it and reassemble it in a way that would point to the future.'* You could say the Blitz was what paved the way to a career at Dior. You only need look at his graduate show at

* Colin McDowell, *Galliano: Romantic, Realist and Revolutionary*, Rizzoli International, 1998.

St Martin's to see the cross-pollination between the club and his groundbreaking creations. The world of fashion owes a great deal to this Covent Garden dive.

But there was no place for the androgyny of the New Romantics among my tribe. Ours was a patriarchal society where the women lived through and for the men. We dressed like virgins because our goal was to find a husband. To have the best chance of attracting one, the aim was to be as boiled-chicken-and-mashed-potato as possible. Standing out or being different was just a way of cutting down on your odds of snaring one, and nobody wanted to do that. Someone like Galliano was looking to make his mark on the world; to lead and have others follow. We were waiting for the older generation to peg it so we could step into their shoes and repeat everything they'd already done. Looking back I suppose there was no need to distinguish ourselves from our parents when the end goal was to become them. At this point, I hadn't the faintest idea John Galliano existed but it wouldn't be too long before I did.

It wasn't until I started shoplifting in 1979 that I began to establish a style of my own. My career as a thief was short-lived – two years at most – but nevertheless intense. It wasn't done for kicks or out of desperation. Of all the people who didn't need to steal, I must have been close to top of the list. I had plenty of clothes, but they weren't the silver jeans or yellow dungarees I wanted from Fiorucci. There were at least two Fair Isle sweaters in my wardrobe already, but not like the Inca one Lady Diana had worn with Prince Charles at Balmoral and I now lusted after. Amassing enough pocket money to buy any of these would take far too long. The obvious answer was to steal them.

I had heard that the best way to forge someone's signature was to practise writing it upside down. Apparently this frees the mind to do it more fluidly so you're less likely to look guilty and be snagged at the till. My friend became really good at it and together we considered ourselves a pair of criminal masterminds. The world was our oyster. We developed a highly tuned, foolproof system. After a recce along Knightsbridge for the desired items, she'd return to purchase them with my cheque book. Five minutes later I'd telephone my bank from the phonebox on Knightsbridge Green: 'I need to report a theft.' By the time my cheque book was cancelled we were back in my bedroom deciding which of our stolen goods to wear while cruising the King's Road. We'd listen to the news on Capital Radio, terrified our names were going to be announced. Unbelievably, my parents never batted an eyelid about this sudden influx of new clothes, even though my only income at the time was their weekly allowance, paid into the same bank account I still have today. It also begs the question why the bank never wrote a letter home despite the frequency with which my cheque book was (supposedly) being stolen. Nevertheless, I think this is a good opportunity to apologise to both Benetton and Fiorucci for the hundreds of pounds' worth of goods I've removed from their shelves without asking. In the end it was the Queen who put an end to my career as a criminal. Shoplifting and the royal family are not really simpatico so, as David was phased in, thieving was sadly phased out.

When David and I rekindled our relationship on my return from New York, we both knew it had to keep moving or die. Though marriage was still not officially on the horizon, we went through the motions of moving forward. My parents had met his parents. His father had taken the closest thing I was going to get to engagement photos. But still he didn't propose. I continue to be very fond of David and look back on our relationship with great affection but there is no doubt I was not in control of our future. Eventually, at the end of 1988, it was finally over. Whatever we'd done had not been enough. The three years we had post our New York hiatus were great but, if he'd not proposed on my return, when would he? We'd both missed one another so much while I was away it was impossible to resist getting back together, despite the fact none of the issues we'd had had been resolved. It was easier to sweep them under the carpet and keep pretending everything would be all right.

Much of my relationship with David has already been played out in public, in the press and in whispers through the halls of England's great palaces and stately homes. When a member of the royal family courts a commoner there will always be gossip. There will always be opinions. As one such commoner, I learned to deal with this aspect of life pretty quickly. When the doors and newspapers were closed and the televisions off, David and I were just another boy and girl trying to navigate our own dynamic as the world waited expectantly for us to marry. It took having my own children to get a real perspective on how preposterous this notion really was. If my twenty-year-old daughter were to suggest spending the rest of her life with someone, inside I'd be screaming *Are you fucking joking?* I only need watch her trying to change her bedding to see just how unprepared for adult life a twenty-year-old really is.

David and I were playing mummies and daddies. The only difference was the doll's house we lived in was open to the public and you didn't need a ticket to get in. For up-to-the-minute news on our soap opera, you just had to buy a copy of the newspaper. Five years later, like the vast majority of romances between twenty-somethings, it ended.

Why it did is another matter. When asked that question now, I instinctively reply 'We were too young.' In reality, he'd simply never asked. In time, I was replaced by a new woman in David's life, which was an inevitability I accepted – life moves on. Letting go of his extended family and the world we'd inhabited was a more difficult adjustment than losing him alone. When things ended, so did a whole section of my life. We'd been inextricably interwoven but, without David, I became invisible to 90 per cent of the friends we'd made together. This had nothing to do with who David was, it was the by-product of the death of a long-term love affair. But an affair that seemed all-consuming at the time now seems naive and unsophisticated. It was a critical part of my journey but an L-plate relationship nonetheless. An introduction to love.

Ours had been a very public relationship and an even more public break-up. When I walked into David's wedding alone four years later it was one of the hardest things I'd ever done, but I wanted to stick two fingers up to everyone who thought I wouldn't be OK with it. I needed to give their marriage my seal of approval for my own dignity. It wasn't that I was still in love with David; quite the contrary. I'd already met the man I knew I was going to spend the rest of my life with. It was my age-old problem of needing to be liked and to be the one who got to make the decisions. It was an ego-driven exercise. No one else could have cared less about whether I was there or not.

From the vantage point of being close to sixty, I am relieved that I was accidentally extricated from a world in which I know I would have suffocated. I see my vulnerabilities as a younger woman and recognise my pat 'We were too young' as a form of self-preservation. It's only when you reach the point where a relationship genuinely no longer matters that you can look back at its disintegration and say 'He did not want me' and be at ease with that. When it ends, it's OK to mourn its loss and know that we will be weaker, less decisive, less confident and less in control for a time. If we can acknowledge this as a recognised stage of mourning, we can let the tide wash over us knowing we will still be standing when it retreats.

As life lessons go, this is one that can only truly be learned first-hand. I'd love to say I'll be able to pass this piece of wisdom on to my children, but if my own mother had tried to do the same it would have had no impact precisely because she was my mother. Had it come from David's mother, Princess Margaret, on the other hand, I may have been more inclined to listen.

As teenagers we begin the process of parting with

childhood. The eight or so years between snuggled bedtime stories and leaving home as a 'fully formed' adult take us from complete dependency on our parents to some level of self-reliance. When we hit our twenties, we're in that most potentially dangerous of times when we've cut ties with those who would protect us and launched ourselves into the real world with all the confidence of someone who has absolutely no idea what they're doing or of any of the possible consequences.

Relationships in our twenties are often made not just with our partner but with their families too. We attach ourselves to their parents as a replacement for the ones we've so rudely jettisoned in our teens. Having flown the nest, we immediately proceed to seek out another where we can rest our heads under a protective wing and sleep safely. For me, this was the home of David's mother.

Act Three

Ready for Anything?

So how was it I'd been so ready to settle down but failed to make it happen? The conditions were ideal but the seed just didn't take. As well as dealing with the personal loss associated with the break-up, it was like being sacked from my job. I'd been trained to within an inch of my life but couldn't close the deal. But why?

When David and I met he'd just finished his studies at John Makepeace's School for Craftsmen in Wood – later to become Parnham College – in Dorset. During our time together he set up a workshop and opened his first shop on the New King's Road. What was I doing all this time? Honestly, I have no fucking idea. He had a plan beyond getting married and I didn't. It's almost laughable now to think of it.

If you'd have met me in the summer of 1989 I doubt you'd have thought I was ready for marriage either, but I was certainly a different girl to the one who'd kept a space for David at her dinner party. For one thing I'd had my heart broken. And very publicly. When I met the photographer Terry O'Neill six months later, he caught this change on camera.

Unlike Patrick's portrait of a naive young girl, Terry taught me to 'look at the lens as if you want to fuck it,' which I found surprisingly easy. There is a case to be made for the

Terry O'Neill capturing the fact that 'I now belonged to someone else'.

notion that in order for a sitter to *look* like they might want to fuck someone, they have to believe the photographer wants to fuck them too. I had nothing of the sort with Patrick and quite a lot of it with Terry. A cursory glance over his work shows a plethora of people – men and women – who *all* look as if they'd either been to or would at least consider going to bed with him. Whether or not it was an act, it was definitely a part of what made him so great at his job. Lichfield played at being sexual, but Terry was the real deal.

It's a well-known cliché that many photographers go on to marry or bed their subjects and Terry O'Neill was no exception. His second wife was Faye Dunaway, who he'd first photographed in 1977 looking casually unimpressed over her post-Oscar breakfast by the pool at the Beverly Hills Hotel. That he was a diddy 5'5" did nothing to dampen his megawatt charisma and Cockney charm or diminish his ruggedly handsome face. A hobgoblin of irrepressible enthusiasm, he never

Alistair Blair, Terry O'Neill and David. Three of the nicest, shortest men I know.

had to rely on a 'look' to make himself more interesting. His voice alone was enough to elicit a bit of a downstairs surge. He was always watching, always observing, and had an inbuilt thermometer to gauge the mood and insecurities of his sitters. The old cliché of being able to make someone feel like the most important person in the room was something Terry could do with his eyes closed. As a photographer, he was the antithesis of Snowdon in every way.

You couldn't help but fall a little bit in love with Terry. It was as much his reputation as his manner. His confidence made him sexy. I was used to small boyfriends, having been out with David, but Terry – or El Tel – was a few inches too short even for me and this, luckily, put the stoppers on a full-blown affair. That and the twenty-two-year age gap. Not that I didn't fancy him – I did. Secretly, I'm pretty sure he felt the same way about me but this was a line we never crossed and thank goodness, otherwise I'm convinced we'd never have been such great friends. Even later in my career, I would always go out of my way to make the person behind the camera smile, and with Terry, there was nothing more rewarding than the sound of his gravelly laugh. The only note of self-consciousness I ever saw was in his attempts to conceal his teeth with his top lip as he cackled at my corny jokes and for that I loved him even more.

Beyond the fact his studio was somewhere off the north end of Ladbroke Grove, I cannot remember a single thing about the sitting you see in these photographs. What I do remember is Terry's warmth, humour and kindness, which was why we stayed friends for so long. It's a great sadness to me that he and I drifted apart after my marriage to Sten. The reality of life is that you leave people behind. Even so, I know that if it were possible for Terry to walk through my door today, it would be as if no time at all had passed.

Terry lived life to the full. He smoked voraciously, drank and worked with passion. That he died of prostate cancer was the most pedestrian thing he'd ever done. Terry, my love, you deserved a much more exotic ending. You were a person so full of life it seemed unimaginable you should die at all.

If we were to examine Terry's shot of me as you would a Renaissance painting, we're back to symbolism again and it's all there in these pictures. My face is cradled in my hands and the only accessory I'm wearing is a large Breitling men's watch. This belonged to a man who could not – or would not – acknowledge our relationship among his fellow countrymen and with whom I consequently had no hope of a future: Imran Khan. At £3,000, this watch was around the same price as the engagement ring I was never expecting to get. Choosing to wear it for my portrait was the best way to tell the world what I believed our relationship to be. Since the photos would appear in the pages of *Tatler*, it was also a very good way of letting David and all our mutual friends know I had most definitely moved on. I now belonged to someone else.

'When I Was a Rising Star'

The night I met Imran Khan we were standing in front of a bath filled with cash and carry wine in my bathroom at Albert Bridge Road. It was June 1989 and 'Loo and Soo' were having one of their Dos. This was perfect timing for me as I'd split up with David for the final time six months earlier and was on the rebound. Every year in June my landlady and best friend Lulu Blacker and I filled the bath with petrol-station ice and crammed 400 people into her two-bedroom flat for a knees-up. Loo & Soo's Dos began life as crisps, peanuts and boxed-wine affairs but ended up with enough clout to pull in the likes of James Hunt and good old Fergie – both A-listers at the time and not quite as funny as they sound now. The crisp and peanut bit didn't change. Our Dos remained as low-rent as ever, just with a better class of customer.

Space was at a premium on these evenings so there were no 'Out of Bounds' stickers on any of the doors. Though they could have spilled out onto the kitchen balcony, guests preferred to block the stairwell instead. A constant murmur of apology accompanied whatever music blasted from the stereo as they shuffled back and forth to let others through. This was a pre-digital era so the soundtrack came courtesy of the mix tapes we laboriously put together in the lead-up. Over the years the music barely changed because the mix tapes were limited to the CDs in our personal libraries – a revolving wheel of the Stones, the Monkees and the Everly Brothers was the staple backdrop every year. We never made an effort to become current.

Furniture was pushed to the sides and it was standing room only the night Elton arrived with Renate. Lulu felt about Elton the way I feel about food. She couldn't get enough of him, and her father, Bloggs, also there that night, knew this only too well. Bloggs was an eccentric with no filter. He was also very funny and willing to do anything to make Lulu laugh, even if that meant embarrassing her for the sake of the joke. Knowing how much Lulu wanted to impress Elton was too good an opportunity to miss. Elton and Renate were sitting on the edge of a single bed, which was masquerading as an extra sofa for the night. Elton had made the old faux pas of leaving the stickers on the bottoms of his new Versace loafers. Naughty old Bloggs spotted his error immediately and in a beat was down on his hands and knees, crawling across the floor. In his best effort to embarrass his daughter he picked conspicuously away at the offending price tag. 'Let's see how much you cost, Elton,' he said as Lulu contemplated the best way to pay her father back for his prank. With a glance to his feet, Elton eventually turned to Lulu and asked in the nicest possible way, 'Who on earth is that man?' 'I have absolutely no idea,' she replied, turning her back slightly on the offending gentleman kneeling on the rug. Lulu adored her father, but not as much as she wanted to impress Elton. Bloggs was an unpredictable creature and Elton was used to having people throw themselves at his feet so I might have known something like this would happen. With Bloggs safely back in his seat, it was time for more drinks and off I went to the bath on a booze run.

The Lion of Pakistan

A bottle of Chablis in each hand and another of tonic under my chin, I turned to find the bathroom doorway filled with the figure of a man I'd seen eyeing me earlier over the pretzels. He knew who I was – he'd come to my party – and I knew who he was. Everyone did. Lulu's father had told her about a handsome novice on the cricketing scene so, when she found herself sitting next to a rather attractive young cricketer one evening at a dinner party, she asked him, 'Are you the sexy cricketer everyone's talking about?' 'Yes,' he said, 'I am.' Imran knew he was exactly what it said on the tin.

For the party, he'd tagged along with our friend Jonathan Mermigan, who'd probably told him this would be a good pond to fish in. There was no need for introductions. This was Imran Khan – the Lion of Pakistan – and he was on the prowl.

He didn't have to go far. Without tooting my own horn, my bosoms were in magnificent condition in 1989 and Imran was a known boob-man. I was on rock-solid ground. There was

Imran Khan. Phwoar.

no faffing around; he jumped straight in. 'You have perfect breasts,' he said. I was absolutely thrilled. I was wearing a white wrap top and jeans, and he, his signature white shirt and stone-washed denim which, at the time, wasn't even a joke. I later went for lunch with him and Richard Branson only to find they were both identically – and as badly – dressed, which was a little off-putting. The Breitling watch with a green face and brown leather strap he wore was the one he would later give to me as a present and I would wear in my photo shoot with Terry. If there was one oddity I came to associate with Imran, it was the hole he'd cut in the big toe of his cricket spikes to relieve pressure when he was bowling. But, that night, he was wearing what I can only describe as hairdresser's shoes. None of these sartorial aberrations mattered. I got a loud and clear hello from below and was happy to proceed.

You didn't need to know this man was the captain of the Pakistani cricket team to sense that he was in charge. Whatever he wanted, you knew he'd get it. It was quite exciting – like one of my Barbara Cartland fantasies had leapt off the page. This is the sort of gender-stereotypical cliché I should be hiding from my daughters, but there we are. I can't rewrite the past. A handsome, charming man complimented my breasts and I was very pleased. No one called the police.

I had only two proper boyfriends before meeting my husband. In the summer of 1989 I was over one and about to meet the other. I was *over* David in the sense that I'd adjusted to our being apart, though 100 per cent not ready for him to be with anyone else. I was now in the unenviable/enviable position of having dated the Queen's nephew and an upgrade was going to be a very tall order. I'd gone about as high as I could go in the hierarchy of my world and didn't fancy my chances of finding anyone better amongst its ranks. The thing is, I was looking in all the wrong places. I'd forgotten that there is one type of person who tops a royal and that's a Casanova.

It's difficult to get the essence of a man like Imran down on paper. He's someone you need to experience first-hand to really appreciate. One of the most powerful things about him was that he didn't have a grain of insecurity. When a person regularly precedes what they say with the words 'When I was a rising star . . .' you know their self-esteem has never been in question. It doesn't matter what a person looks like, authentic confidence is one of the sexiest things in the world. When they look like Imran did, it's irresistible. Even his daily use of a hairdryer did nothing to undermine the appeal.

As far as I'm concerned, hands maketh the man and Imran's were sculptural, like Michelangelo's David. Always moving, exercising to keep supple, as if holding a ball ready to bowl. His mastery of the game was all part of the attraction. Imran was surrounded by gifted players but was truly a Rolls-Royce among an NCP full of Cortinas. If you know you're the best in the world at something . . . well, what does that feel like? What must that do for your self-esteem? Imagine what it looked like from the outside. Well, I didn't have to. Here he was standing in my bathroom.

For a year and a half, this was the only man I woke up to but it came at a price. I don't think I ever once felt completely secure in our relationship. If you went out with Imran, you read the writing on the wall before you entered the room. Knowing that the outcome of a liaison can only ever be heartbreak is an odd way to start something off but that is what I did.

In the end, it was me that drew a line under things. My heart had been broken by David and when I'd met Imran I was grateful that someone like him liked someone like me.

A break between matches on tour in Australia, 1989.

But as time went on, I knew I was moving into dangerous territory. I was falling in love and he wasn't. That didn't mean he didn't want to be with me or that we didn't have an amazing time together, but that's just not enough when what you really want is for someone to commit.

I Left My Heart in Pakistan

Funnily enough, I got over Imran pretty quickly. It was not the same thing I'd experienced with David. I would never have asked him to change. It was all part of who he was. I never expected to come out of our relationship with a ring on my finger. What he inadvertently gave me was something far more enduring and that was Pakistan – and I never got over her.

Imran was so incredibly passionate about his home that the first time I went it could easily have been a disappointment. But it was as wonderful and as rich as he'd made out. Just like Imran, his homeland was something you had to experience first-hand. It would take a lifetime to understand Pakistan – the politics, disparity in wealth and religion. It's a complicated country, layered like a silty plain with the gathering history of invaders, from the Aryans to the Mongols to the British. The city I came to know best was Lahore. It is the second largest in Pakistan, an ancient capital of the Punjab and home to around four million motorcycles with no chance in hell of meeting ULEZ emission standards. The streets were chaotic and lawless in the way you might imagine Victorian London to be. Anything from a bird to a lit cigarette butt could hit you in the face as you travelled the streets in your tuk-tuk. The sounds and smells were as thick as pea soup and the heat a constant source of oppression. It was so unlike anything I'd ever experienced, I've never been able to shake the impression it left on me. It was wonderful.

If Pakistan's cities were people, most would be easy to draw. Lahore is plump and relaxed, lying in his salwar kameez, stroking his beard over a feast of curried partridge. Islamabad cuts a more upright figure, holding court in an ornate drawing room, offering whisky and political gossip to his peers. Peshawar wears a pakol cap as he bustles among the stalls of an ancient bazaar. But Karachi is harder to draw. It has many faces: the booted businessman, rushing to his office; the poverty-stricken labourer who sends his wages back to his family in the Karakorum; the lithe young daughter of a dynasty, kicking off her sandals as she eats gaudy sweet treats.

When I think back to my travels through Pakistan, as much as I remember its beauty, its unique smells and its rich customs, what I remember most vividly is the cricket. For me, Pakistan is forever entangled with the game itself.

Cricket Whore

If you're not a cricket whore as I am, I feel I should probably give you a potted history of the rivalries that exist between India and Pakistan as a backdrop to my story.

Cricket had been established in British India under colonial rule. With the partition of the colony in 1947, Pakistan and India were created as two independent states. The cricketing teams of these two countries were now pitted against one another. Just as with a messy divorce, the family was broken up and made to fight on opposite sides. Political hostilities ran high and the cricket pitch was the only acceptable place these countries could do battle. On more than one occasion, actual war put a hold on matches between the two. In light of this intense rivalry, the two teams often played on neutral territory. During the 1989–90 cricket season, India played four Test matches and four one-day internationals against their rivals in Pakistan. If you're not into cricket, this doesn't sound particularly remarkable. If you do love the game, you'll know that it's a huge privilege to have seen this series in person. India and Pakistan have not played a Test match in Pakistan since 2008. Actually, no one has. There have only been fifteen Test series between India and Pakistan in total, so a ticket to an India vs Pakistan game is about as desirable as it gets when it comes to international cricket. When they played one another in the 2019 Cricket World Cup, 273 million people turned on their televisions to watch.

With my history lesson over, you can imagine how Lulu and I felt when we were invited to accompany the Pakistani team on tour. I'd grown up with a father who loved cricket and I'd spent summers watching school matches on the lawns at Eton, but it was Imran who really made me fall in love with the game.

Lulu was having a holiday fling with the world's fastest bowler – Wasim Akram – and I was the girlfriend of the team captain. We were the original Wags but, despite this, there were no spare seats for us on the flight from Lahore to Karachi. While the rest of the Pakistani cricket squad took their seats in the cabin, Lulu and I spent the trip in the cockpit. In a scene worthy of a *Carry On* film, we alternated throughout the journey between the captain and co-pilots' laps.* In a later shake down of Pakistan International Airlines, it emerged that a third of pilot licences were fake so it probably wasn't a real pilot whose lap we sat on anyway. No wonder he didn't seem to mind this breach of security.

When we reached Karachi I began to get the measure of Imran's standing in his country. Cricket is akin to a religion in Pakistan and, as the greatest player of all time, Imran their god. One fan appointed himself as Imran's bodyguard and slept throughout our stay on the floor outside the hotel bedroom door like an Alsatian, but with a revolver. He was so proud to be protecting his idol, Imran couldn't turn him away. There was nothing he wouldn't do for Imran and, by extension, me. At the match in Karachi, he lovingly plonked a chair for me right up against the boundary rope. Tensions were incredibly high and, as a woman, the edge of the pitch didn't seem like the ideal place to sit. After a round of polite 'thank you but no thank yous', I returned to join Lulu in the players' box instead.

I don't know what it felt like in the Colosseum waiting for the gladiators to come out and face the lions, but I'm guessing the feeling in the Karachi stadium was pretty close. You didn't have to have a boyfriend at the crease to feel the pressure. Ten-foot grilles separated the tourist fans from Pakistan's. The noise of banging drums, tin cans and bicycle

* This sort of lax approach to health and safety was probably why PIA are currently banned from many international airports, after it was discovered 'the airline was not capable of certifying and overseeing its operators and aircraft in accordance with applicable international standards.' (Pakistan International Airlines, Wikipedia: https://en.wikipedia.org/wiki/Pakistan_International_Airlines).

bells, whistles, jeering and cheering made it impossible to speak or be heard. The crowd were waiting for their heroes to emerge and answer their prayers. I'd been to Lords and I'd been to the Oval, which was all pretty sedate by comparison. In the UK, cricket is known for its teas, club ties and gentility. Watching India play Pakistan was how I imagined it might have been in the stadium for Millwall vs West Ham in 1976. Totally fucking lawless. I was glad to be safely tucked away in the players' box rather than out in the fray. I wasn't brave enough for that.

Earlier that year, Imran and I had trekked up through the Himalayas and across to the Karakoram mountains. Even in villages we passed where they'd not seen television or heard a radio, they knew this man. Children ran out into the streets to meet him. He was an icon; the Lion of Pakistan. Actually he preferred to think of himself as a tiger but you get the gist (hence the Krizia tiger jumper I bought him). We were in the furthest outpost of the North-West Frontier and he was mobbed. It was as if David Attenborough had just rocked up at the Natural History Museum.

In a country like Pakistan, food is the way you show your hospitality, share your culture and communicate. Imran was very greedy and hugely proud of his culinary heritage. He accepted everything offered with warmth and grace no matter how rancid or fatty. The people we met had nothing, but they shared what little they had without a second thought. Childishly, I spent a lot of time gagging behind my hand. Unable to stomach the inch of fat on everything put forward, I stuck to naan bread for the duration of the trip. By the time we reached our stopover that night on a mountainside above Fairy Meadows, I was ravenous and got out my secret stash of food. Ordinarily very calm, 15,000 feet above sea level is the only place I saw Imran truly enraged. With one tin of Heinz Baked Beans I managed to insult him, his people and his country in one fell swoop. It was like sitting down to break bread with St Peter and asking if he had any ketchup. It was back to the rancid meat from then on and I, predictably, came down with dysentery soon after.

When Imran was in his home country, in keeping with his faith, we adopted the segregation of the sexes and he and I didn't sleep in the same bed once. We didn't even share a tent when we were trekking. Back home in Knightsbridge, it was a different matter. He was like any other London playboy. His flat was decorated like Donald Trump's bedroom, complete with behind-the-bed, smoked-glass mirror. I don't know who it was that described it as 'A bedroom of great

'A bedroom of great expectations.'

expectations' but I salute them. There was a lot of leopard-skin upholstery together with a pair of handpainted tigers across the fitted wardrobe doors. A golden-silk-tented ceiling and pair of elephant tusks like bookends on the mantelpiece completed the ensemble. If Harrods ran a hotel, this is what a suite would look like. It had actually been decorated by a previous girlfriend and struck me as ego-massaging on her part rather than a directive from Imran. In Pakistan his home was simple and understated.

In London, Imran had his faith but he was only answerable to himself. In Pakistan, all that mattered was that we weren't married, and in public he was very respectful of his country's religious mores. He really was two people. His life was split between Lahore and London and I found the inbuilt, constant longing very hard to handle. There was no getting around it: Imran's first true love was his country and no woman was ever going to take her place, which is exactly why he went on to be prime minister.

Though I'd gone into the relationship with my eyes open, when I started falling in love I knew it was the right moment to get out, and left without warning.

Adelaide Oval, January 19th 1990, 4 p.m.

My timing could not have been worse. After the Indian tour of Pakistan, I'd flown home for Christmas with my family. It wasn't long before I was off again, this time to join Imran for their tour of Australia. It was my first time there and I loved it because it was the place I met my great friend Emma Gibbs. It was also where my otherwise rock-solid sexuality was briefly called into question. Tilda Swinton aside, I'm not someone who's ever leaned towards lesbianism. The Australian Tennis Open wasn't as exciting as the cricket but when I got back to the hotel and Martina Navratilova stepped into the lift with me, I went weak at the knees. Her gender was irrelevant; she was 100 per cent raw sex, one of the most magnetic people I'd ever been up close to. God knows what might have happened if the lift had broken down. Needless to say, when I told Imran about all this, he was absolutely delighted. Since Imran saved all his strength for the game, I had the memory of Martina to keep me going. I realise she might seem like an odd choice of sexual fantasy but you haven't been in a lift with her and I have.

By the time we reached Adelaide, we'd been touring for a month. Pakistan were staring at a massive defeat by Australia in the second innings. Imran's team were batting and when he came out to the crease, the score stood at 10 runs for 3 wickets. In other words it was a seemingly impossible mountain to climb. At a moment when I should have played the supportive girlfriend, I selfishly put my own needs first and booked a flight back to Melbourne to see Emma. This, of all moments, was the one I chose to leave Imran. I couldn't face saying goodbye in person. Annoyingly, I missed one of the most thrilling turnarounds in Test cricket. Imran thrived on pressure. It was the spark he needed to perform. I should have known he could change a game in a matter of minutes. While I flicked idly through my in-flight magazine, Imran racked up a personal best of 136 runs. His courage and commitment to the game, his team and his country was what made him the cricketer he was. Had I stayed, I would have witnessed cricketing history in the making, but I'd reached breaking point. I couldn't quash my insecurities any longer. Like a scene from a Danielle Steele mini-series, 'Gone to Melbourne. Speak soon' was the note I left on his pillow. For an added boost of melodrama, Simon & Garfunkel's 'I Am a Rock' hissed through my Walkman headphones as I closed the door behind me.

Though I was the one who walked out, it would be absurd to claim I left Imran. You couldn't dump a man like him. I left because I knew that, were the question posed, he wouldn't ask me to stay. In taking the initiative, I was paying lip-service to the idea that I had some control over our destiny. There are certain kinds of relationships that you know to be a part-nership. Where you're on an equal footing. Plans and decisions are discussed and made together. This wasn't one of them. Imran was always going to be the one to decide our fate so I took the most dignified way out I could think of.

Even now I think the concept of a no-strings relationship is an oxymoron. At twenty-seven I was completely ill-equipped to handle it. It was the sort of situation you needed to be a forty-five-year-old Parisian woman to deal with and I was far too unsophisticated to pull it off.

The upshot was I spent our entire relationship with my drawbridge half up and Imran knew it. 'You were always very closed,' he told me in his parting letter. I suppose I prob-ably was. Most people consider me to be a very open person but my openness is the buffer I use to protect my inner core. I'm very happy to talk more openly than most but it's a rare thing for me to truly bare my soul. Somewhere along the line I've erected a Chinese Wall between my conscious and subconscious self and even I'm not privy to the information on both sides. I'm not sure I'd learned much more than how to live through having my heart broken from my first relationship. The person I chose for my second was someone I knew would never fall in love with me, which I thought would protect me. I didn't bargain on falling in love with him. The lesson I took from this was that unless a person gives their whole self to you, it is impossible to give your whole self to them.

The Great Dane

I don't suppose you recall that stuffed blue marlin I mentioned in Harrods Food Hall? I didn't set much store by it myself at the time but it proved oddly prophetic and one of several threads that gradually pulled together over time and caught me in their net.

In 1993, an eight-year feud between shifty businessman Tiny Rowland and Mohamed Al-Fayed was brought to a close with the ceremonial installation of a 1,150lb mako shark from the ceiling of the Food Hall. The two men smiled on cue as the shark was hoisted up to the rafters in a PR stunt worthy of Edina Monsoon. The marlin I remember from my childhood had been joined by an even bigger fish.

Hooked off the coast of Mauritius, the shark would have broken the record for the largest ever line-caught mako but took so long to get weighed its mass dwindled in the hot weather. There are bigger sharks, but the mako is notoriously difficult to catch. This one had now found its way into the hands of Egyptian one-time cloth merchant Al-Fayed. He named it Tiny after the man he considered to be the biggest shark in the world, his old adversary and one-time friend, Tiny Rowland. Rowland had risen from Paddington station porter to loaded tycoon via a series of such allegedly dubious routes that Prince Charles famously refused to shake his hand, calling him 'the unacceptable face of capitalism'. In turn, it was an open secret in the City that Al-Fayed had shafted Rowland by refusing to give back the 30 per cent of Harrods shares Rowland had illegally parked with him while he was trying to buy the shop. Rowland couldn't admit he owned the shares because that would make it illegal for him to be buying more. Al-Fayed took advantage of this and blatantly pretended they belonged to him, knowing he couldn't be publicly challenged. I think many people would take issue over who was the bigger shark of the two, but Mohamed owned the fish, so he got to choose the name.

The man who caught the fish? Peder Bertelsen. Yes, that Peder. Unsurprisingly, Peder was a notorious and well-loved figure in Harrods Food Hall. Every Friday on his way home from work he would stop there for six oysters and a glass of crisp white wine at the caviar bar, and pick up a couple of Dover sole for his dinner. Peder was a keen fisherman and, with his friends Ric Wharton and Leo Kennedy, formed the self-titled Fishy Business. Ric had made a fortune by raising £50 million worth of gold bars from the shipwrecked HMS *Edinburgh*, while Leo was a rather louche photographer. As a team, they were the angling community's equivalent of the Brat Pack; a charismatic bunch who indulged their love of big-game fishing with annual trips anywhere from Guernsey to the Indian Ocean. Ric took the expedition out to catch Tiny, and Peder and Leo landed the fish. Leo then negotiated with Al-Fayed to pay to have Tiny shipped and mounted, which is how it came to hang from the Food Hall ceiling for the next four years. You can now find him living happily in the entrance hall to Deep Sea World in Scotland, just north of Edinburgh.

How do I know all this? In such detail? Well, a funny thing happened to me at a party.

Do you remember I told you about the night I was ghosted by Dolph Lundgren? How could you have forgotten? Not only had he ditched me but I spent quite a bit of time panicking I was dying of AIDS. Not because I suspected he had it but because that's how I felt about all sex in the '90s. I was as blindly ignorant as everyone else. The whole thing was a lesson on what sort of situations not to get yourself into.

The bottom line was, because of Beef Cake, I was now dateless for Alan Aldridge's party, but rescued last-minute by my friends Simon and Cosmo who agreed to come along. Alan was the father of our friend Saffron and a fantastic artist, much celebrated in the '70s having worked with everyone from The Who to The Beatles, as well as bringing Elton's Captain Fantastic to life on the cover of his eponymous album. Alan's style was Tamara de Lempicka meets *Crystal Tipps and Alistair*, and this evening we'd come for the launch of his fantasy novel, *The Gnole*.

I'd not long arrived when I noticed an arresting-looking man crossing the room. He was coming towards me. Though I was not in the mood for chit-chat, he was unbelievably good-looking so I decided to make an exception. It sounds like a dreadful cliché but it was love at first sight, for ever and ever amen. He was the most overwhelmingly attractive person I'd ever laid eyes on. In the years since I've thought many times about killing my husband, but I have never, ever stopped fancying him. However, I'm not sure I'd have felt as strongly had he not been wearing his Clark Kent glasses that night.

I was still at an age where I could get away with leggings and a body and was not looking half bad myself. My husband testified to this when he reminded me that I'd been 'Much slimmer then' and 'very petite at the time'. Despite this unpleasant truth, in the interests of impartiality I quizzed him further about his memories of our first meeting. His response was at least more flattering than Elton's, who replied with a simple 'Cannot remember. Sorry.'

It was a Thursday, and Sten was working in the City. He'd not wanted to go to the party but went as a favour to his friend Saffron. By 8.30 he'd put in his time and was ready to leave when he saw me on the other side of the room. *Oh yeah*, he thought, *that's interesting*. By his own admission he's not the type to act on impulse but thought he might just try his luck and go on a fishing trip. 'Do you want a beer?' he said. Of course I fucking didn't; what a stupid drink to offer a girl. I had one anyway. He was very dishy.

A north and a south magnet pulled through the debris to find each other. It was easy. We told each other anything and everything we could think of to stop the other leaving, falling over ourselves like two people who've just discovered they've been living on the same street for the last twenty years. Our friends left one by one as we rudely ignored them. I knew a Girl in Pearls was not going to cut the mustard in the world of

Sten Bertelsen. An even louder Phwoar.

investment banking. In fact I was more likely to be a joke and was determined he take me seriously. The thing I was most proud of was my burgeoning career with Alistair, so I made sure he knew how critical I was to the world of fashion.

'Oh, I know Alistair,' he said.

'Really,' I said, 'do you know Peder Bertelsen too?' – hoping to show off.

'Yes,' he said, 'quite well, actually. He's my dad.'

Cue the cartoon *Duh, duh, duhhh!!!* sound effect.

It wasn't until this moment I put two and two together. It was *not* just Morten Harket he reminded me of; I'd seen a flash of this man once before. Technically he'd been more of a boy at the time, still at university. He was nearly three years younger than me and dating another of his father's employees, Kate Chappell, who he'd come to see at our offices. In what now seems like a preposterously unlikely get-up, he was dressed in a purple suit and purple brothel-creepers and had fashioned his hair into a quiff – not quite Flock of Seagulls but easily on a par with Bananarama. This must have been one of the few times in his life he'd taken the concept of fashion and made an attempt to follow it. His father was on first-name terms with Armani and Valentino, but the night we met, Sten didn't know the difference between a dress and a skirt and described my eyeshadow as 'quite musky'. The only time I met a person with worse dress sense was some years later on *What Not to Wear* when Trinny and I made over Jeremy Clarkson.

There are very few surprises in an old, tired marriage, but the fact that Sten remembered more about our first meeting than me was one of them. And an oddly romantic one. The grand gestures and surges of energy can easily fade in a long-term relationship but when I heard my husband talk about the way he saw me that evening, I felt like a schoolgirl. I think I may even have blushed a little.

Unbeknown to me, Saffron called him at 8 a.m. the next morning at work to see whether he'd 'met anyone interesting at her party'. Let's face it, she'd never have got a job at MI5.

The First Date

Saffron had offered up Ringo Starr and Barbara Bach as add-ons to tempt Sten to come out with us again. I'm not sure if it was The Beatles or Bond that persuaded him but, given that neither of them turned up and he tried to kiss me anyway, I began to think I might be the real reason he came out that night. The kiss was an ill-timed lunge combined with a lizard-like flick of his tongue, for which I was completely unprepared. I also thought it was a tad forward and instinctively jumped back in my seat as if I'd been electrocuted. Instead of the romantic start this could have been, it was more like the efforts of a spotty teenager who'd been dared to French kiss a girl at the cinema. What an amateur. I'm surprised we recovered from this low.

Given the strength of our initial chemistry I decided to push through this blunder and called him the next day to invite him out. I set out to wow him with everything I had in my arsenal and thought backstage passes to see Lenny Kravitz at Wembley would be breathtaking enough for a first date. Whatever coolness I thought I may have garnered with this invite was cancelled in the taxi en route to the gig. Sten was excited because he'd 'always loved *Tiswas*'. It was then I realised he thought we were on our way to see Lenny Henry. That I needed to explain who Lenny Kravitz was detracted a little from the overall impression I'd hoped to make. Nevertheless, I still had one more trick up my sleeve which I'd saved for maximum impact. I held back the name of one of the friends we'd be going with so that when we arrived and the door was opened by Mick Jagger it would be funny to see the look on Sten's face. I was right; it was. However, surprise factor aside, Sten rolled easily with the punches. Dinner after the gig with Mick and Lenny at the Bombay Brasserie might as well have been a Sunday lunch with his in-laws; he was as cool as a cucumber. I decided I'd let him have another go at that kiss.

What I learned that night was that my future husband was not easily impressed. This was maddening to begin with but he's since proved a very reliable barometer. Someone whose judgement I can trust implicitly. There's nothing less productive than being patronised or patted on the head by someone because that's what they think you want to hear and, thank God, he's never been one to do that. As unpalatable as it has sometimes been, he's always told me the truth.

I'd been worried about how Sten would fit into my world but hadn't appreciated he might have the same reservations about me. In his job as an investment banker at Hill Samuel, I was not someone with whom he'd ideally want to be associated. Although the term 'It girl' had yet to be embedded in Britain's social conscience, it is the one that best describes how I was perceived at the time. I was a girl whose picture appeared regularly in the red tops, who turned up at all the right parties and who knew all the right people. While these 'qualities' might have appealed to some men, they did not appeal to a man like Sten. As an intellectual financier who'd never picked up a copy of *Tatler* or Dempster's Diary, our pairing was as unlikely as Lembit Opik and the Cheeky Girl. I was unaware of it at the time but Sten was embarrassed by my reputation. In the early days, when we went out 'together', I'd go alone and leave his name on the door so he could enter separately. I always assumed it was because he was working late but he's since confessed he wanted to keep me a secret from his colleagues. After about six months of this his boss, Sir Mark Wrightson, confronted Sten in his office: 'I didn't know you knew Susannah Constantine,' he said. Sten's initial, unspoken, response was a simple *Fuck*. This, he believed, was the end of his credibility in the workplace. But the worldly Wrightson was evidently much more broadminded than my husband. I have no idea how Wrightson knew about me but it was his seal of approval that eventually convinced Sten he wouldn't be tarnished by our association and he finally deigned to go public with his dolly-bird.

Three years later and he'd got over my reputation but had still, annoyingly, not proposed. It has to be said, I'd not had a great deal of success on that front. Even now, despite actually *being* married, no one has ever *asked* me. When it came to it, Sten responded to an ultimatum rather than a warm feeling inside.

The Proposal

I'd had my fill of hanging around waiting to be asked with David. I wasn't going to make the same mistake with Sten. There were multiple obstacles in my path, the largest being that it was obvious he didn't want to get married. He was still enjoying the idea of being a free man and, at the same time, not wholly detached from his mother's umbilical cord. He didn't really need a wife; he had his mum, Prue, and she did all his washing. I wouldn't want to leave her either but that wasn't the point. For someone who'd been in training for marriage since birth, at thirty-two I was knocking on a bit, so I told him: Unless he was coming round with a ring, he needn't come at all. Then followed what I considered to be a very long game of chicken. For three months I did my best to seem interesting. I did what I always do when I'm trying to get a man to marry me; I flew to America.

Only one seat left for Lulu – the captain's lap. On board PIA with the cricket team. Lahore to Carachi, 1989.

Boat trip on the Indus Delta, Carachi, with the Lion of Pakistan, c.1989.

Me, El Tel and his snaps.

Lulu and I on our way to a fundraiser for Imran's cancer hospital in Lahore. In the days before I knew about cultural appropriation.

Sten in Vietnam during the war wearing his obligatory dog tag, c.1969.

Wired for sound. An eighteen-year-old Sten, Greece, 1982.

Richard James, Elton and Sten doing their best to guess my charade. Elton and David's villa in Nice.

Classic Herb Ritts composition. Eric Buterbaugh, Calvin Klein underpant model Mark Findlay and me. Round the pool at Herb's ranch, Santa Fe, 1994.

Final fitting with Monica and Grace Tan at her studio in Kensington, 1995.

April 22nd 1995, Bottesford Church, Lincolnshire.

Promo for Sten and BJ Cunningham's Death Cigarettes, c.1993.

Jason – aka Jake Shears – and the woman that stalked him for three years.

In a sweaty club on the Gloucester Road with my original gay husband, David Furnish – a man whose friendship warrants an entire book. In the end there was simply too much to say so I said next to nothing. I love you C**t.

With David's plus-one at their house in Windsor.

Sten and I at Le Club 55 in Ramatuelle on holiday with David and Elton.

Easy like a Sunday morning.

Country girl, thrill seeker, swimmer, mother, housewife, writer, eater and dreamer. My many states of happiness.

First stop on the itinerary was the home of Herb Ritts in Santa Fe.

My old friend and celebrity florist, Eric Buterbaugh, was part of the Hollywood gay mafia so we travelled in style to Herb's mountain hideaway at 155 Ridge Road as guests on his private jet – a first for me. It was more cramped than Concorde but much more glamorous. For someone in need of a boost, this was the perfect holiday. As the sole woman and one of only two heterosexuals on the trip I was passed around like a Barbie doll. It was heaven. In addition to Eric, my room-mates were Herb's then-boyfriend Chris Cartozza, songwriter Bruce Roberts, photographer Michael Smith, and the comically beautiful Mark Findlay. You may not know Mark's name but you're bound to have seen pictures of him in his pants because Herb took loads of them. Mark was my straight compadre and it was pretty obvious he fancied me but nothing happened. Though his body was magnificent, like something from the *Iliad*, he had a peculiarly tiny head. Not as small as mine but almost; and he was 6'3". This wasn't the primary reason I didn't go to bed with him. The real explanation was that I'd only gone to America to get Sten to marry me. Even a Calvin Klein underwear model wasn't enough to distract me.

While I wouldn't consider myself to be uptight sexually, I'm equally not someone other women would find a threat. But I do love to flirt and it was on this holiday that I discovered the answer to guilt-free titillation is gay male friends. I was fancied and cooed over by a group of people that posed no threat to my status as a woman in love. I could indulge my vanity without upsetting my plan to get married.

I returned home from my holidays with an ego the size of a large birthday balloon.

The 'perfect' break is different for everyone depending on what they need at the time. For me, this was a massive dose of self-confidence so, when Herb took my picture and told me I 'had a better body than Cindy Crawford' I considered the trip a resounding success. Five stars.

You couldn't really call the photos Herb took of me 'portraits' because he used a disposable Fuji camera. While I pretended to be cool about it, you don't go to the house of a man like Herb Ritts and not secretly hope he'll ask to take your picture. I spent quite a bit of time draping myself languidly in chairs and looking wistfully out the window as I drank my coffee in the hopes I might prove irresistible. True to form I have none of the evidence to back this up but I was finally rewarded with an impromptu photo shoot and Herb's big compliment. I don't imagine I was his most inspiring muse but I can still technically say I've sat for Herb Ritts. If memory serves, Eric and I got the snaps processed at a drugstore on Melrose when we returned to LA. I doubt anyone behind the counter realised they were processing the work of the man I still consider to be the world's greatest photographer. The fact he took my picture on a disposable camera was the perfect metaphor for a friendship that would never be developed. Herb was way out of my league.

My escape to California was exactly the tactic I'd used when I'd broken up with David; I'd gone away in the hope Sten would see how much he needed me and fling himself at my feet. This time, it worked. Unlike with David, Sten and I had mutual friends I trusted, so I knew exactly what he was doing in the hiatus. To precis the situation, he went a bit bonkers and I was thrilled. Though he denies it now, I knew from our friends he was a delightful mess and, for the first time, I felt like I was in control of a relationship. I knew in my heart of hearts he'd come back and, moreover, it was right that he should. We were a fit. I was pushing him but for what I considered to be the right reasons. Over the years the power has shifted back and forth between us but this was one moment I felt I was in charge of our future and I needed to play bad cop.

I'm not sure Sten realised what was going on behind the scenes but it did the trick. After weeks of struggling to resist he eventually gave up and made the pilgrimage to Hatton Garden to look for a ring. Operating on the basis that a man should buy a ring three times his monthly salary, the one he wanted was three times his budget, which he duly told the dapper jeweller Tony Hirsh. Sten did his best to sweet-talk Tony into a deal but it wasn't until he said the magic words 'Peder Bertelsen' that Tony folded and gave him a hefty discount. Though Sten didn't know it at the time, Tony was the Bertelsen family jeweller and Peder a generous and treasured customer. Of all the jewellers in all the towns in all the world, Sten walked into Tony's. The moral of the story was that, as with so many things in life, Peder Bertelsen was the answer. I do still wonder whether the size of the discount was the real reason Sten decided to go through with the proposal. There was no sale-or-return at Tony's.

Even so it still took a large, fortified Sunday lunch to give Sten the oomph to do it and he finally arrived at my door with the discounted ring in his pocket after three hours in the pub. No answer. *Thank God*, he thought, *a reprieve*. But this, he knew, was merely a stay of execution. At some point he'd have to face the music. On arriving back at his flat he decided to get it over and done with and telephoned in case I'd been in bed. I was. When my flatmate handed over the receiver mouthing the words 'It's him', I knew there could be only one thing he was calling to ask. He wasn't getting away with it that easily; we were doing this face to face. I refused to take the call and was round his flat like a rat up a drainpipe. It was an out-of-breath, dishevelled and slightly chippy version of myself that now stood before him.

'Well,' I said. 'What have you got to say?'

Wordlessly, he passed over the ring. This was not going to cut it either. I was going to hear the words if I had to squeeze them from his throat with my bare hands. In a stand-off that lasted close to ten minutes I stubbornly refused to help him out. Just when I thought one or both of us might explode, he finally managed a reluctant, 'Will you spend the rest of your life with me?' Still not a proper fucking proposal frankly, but the ring was very nice. It would have to do. Technically the cat was in the bag but I knew from experience an angry cat in a flimsy bag could easily escape. The battle wasn't over. This was made abundantly clear when the first thing he asked me to do as his fiancée was not tell anyone about our engagement. I immediately called my sister and flatmate with the good news.

The Vetting Process

Word spread quickly and it wasn't long before it reached the ears of that gossipy old fishwife, Elton. By now Elton was one of my closest friends but I was still taken aback by his suggestion that he and then-manager John Reid vet Sten the following week over lunch. Elton had come to be a rather avuncular figure in my life and I knew he had my best interests at heart, but I believe a good 50 per cent of the reason he offered was plain nosiness. That and the fact he's a control freak. Elton is the mother-hen of all his friends and would always rather take charge of a situation than be left to be invited by someone else. If there was a celebration on the horizon or a lunch to be hosted, Elton would be the one to do it. On one of the very few occasions he and I attended a gathering he was not himself hosting, I found out what it was like to be stuck next to him all day because he refused to leave my side. It was fine, he was very entertaining but, like many of the greatest entertainers, Elton is happiest in his own comfort zone. Had it been my parents hosting, Elton would never have come. For him to feel comfortable it had to be on his terms and his turf but it was all the more special for it.

Asking for a daughter's hand in marriage is not something I imagine many men look forward to. In the event, my father barely looked up from his paper for the traditional query about Sten's prospects. It was over and done with in a flash and I think my father was probably glad to get me off the shelf and out of his hair. Elton was far more thorough and determined to put my fiancé through his paces. Sten had been to Harry's Bar plenty of times before, but not in the middle of the day and not with Elton John who, incidentally, he'd also never met before. Not only was he shamelessly poked and prodded but the examination took place under a gigantic spotlight. Elton's level of fame would cause a sensation in even the most diplomatic of crowds. If Sten had not attended this lunch in real life it would be exactly the kind of anxiety dream he'd have had the night before an exam. While he now purports to have been unfazed, I'm not convinced by his bravado. I happen to know the only other pop star he'd ever met was Olivia Newton-John. Nevertheless, he held his nerve and aced the audition. He was through to the next round.

I didn't invite Princess Margaret to the wedding because no bride wants to be upstaged by another woman. I still held her in great affection but, when David and I split for the final time in 1989, our paths ceased to cross. I'd never once spoken to her on the telephone in the whole time I'd known her so this wasn't an avenue for continued friendship either. The whole thing came to a shocking halt and, with David married to someone else, I felt too awkward to push things from my side. As the younger woman I also felt it wasn't my place to make the decision about whether we stayed in contact. I knew too that etiquette and loyalty to her son would prevent her from ever suggesting we might. It wasn't only David I lost in the break-up.

In all honesty, I can't say for sure how she came to hear about my engagement. Perhaps she read the announcement in *The Times* or the *Telegraph*. Whatever the case, her response was a dinner held in our honour. By this point I'd not seen her for nearly three years so the invite was totally out of the blue and staggeringly generous. Given my own mother's illness, Princess Margaret had been so much more to me than David's mother. I was deeply touched.

Princess Margaret was good friends with interior designer

Anouska Hempel, which was handy because Anouska owned Blake's Hotel in South Kensington. Blake's was well known for being discreet, which made it the perfect place for my ex-boyfriend's mother to host my engagement dinner without it getting into the press. Evidently she meant it to be a secret because, up until last week when I told him, David didn't even know about it. The private room was decorated in black silk and the result was ever so slightly 'den of iniquity'. Anouska and her husband, Mark Weinberg, were part of Princess Margaret's inner circle and I knew them well. Ned Ryan was there too, not just as my friend, but as Princess Margaret's as well. Ned was what's known as a 'walker', a term confined largely to the upper classes to denote a man, often gay, who'd accompany a single woman when she didn't have a date. Often they were much more than this. A confidant, advisor, protector and friend. Ned was all of these and much more to the princess. With someone like Ned there'd be no rumours about their dating; there'd be no social impact. Likewise, he'd be no threat to any man who might want to chat her up if the evening took that kind of a turn. I'm pretty sure it was Ned who took her to a Rolling Stones concert, and sometimes filled in as Joan Collins' walker when she was between husbands. Ned was a great friend to Princess Margaret. The only person I didn't know that evening was the photographer Mario Testino. Poor old Sten, on the other hand, didn't know any of them. Another baptism of fire for him.

Princess Margaret was a person with tremendous presence and this was not just down to her title. She sat herself with a great deal of purpose next to Sten and spent the next four hours telling him stories about how much in love and how well suited her son and I had been. She was an inherently mischievous person but I think there was more to it than that. Having people in her life over whom she felt a sense of ownership was quite a rarity. I think she felt territorial. She wanted to make sure Sten knew who she was to me. Human beings, however seemingly grand, are fairly basic creatures. We all want to feel loved and needed and be secure in our own little territories. I didn't mind at all; it was true. Given the role she'd played in my development in my twenties, I did feel like she had some sort of stake in me.

The evening was one I look back on with both affection and shame. If my father had been there he'd have said he wasn't cross with me; he was disappointed. I'd not long returned from my big ego massage with the gays in Santa Fe and was feeling particularly cocksure, which would prove my undoing. Mario Testino had just shot Amber Valletta's iconic campaign for Gucci so when he asked if he could photograph Sten and I together for our engagement, I should have been delighted. For reasons best known to no one, I told him there was no need. 'Herb Ritts is going to do it,' I said through a mouthful of prawn tempura, 'but thank you anyway, Mario.' Yes, I had the Fuji snaps and yes, Herb and I got on well, but at no point on the holiday did he ever turn to me and say 'Can I take your engagement photos when you get back if you do manage to bag that bloke?' I honestly don't know what possessed me. Herb is dead, thank God, so there's no chance of my lie finding its way back to him now but I still dread bumping into Mario at the airport.

So the deal was finally sealed. Or so I thought. I'm sure most brides experience some anxiety in the lead-up to their nuptials: will my hair look right; will this spot go down; will my alcoholic brother keep his mouth shut during the best man's speech? The list goes on. But from the moment Sten proposed, I lived on a knife edge. This was fuelled in no small part by his repeated use of the phrase '*If* we get married', in spite of the fact I was some long way into planning a three-course dinner and dance for 100 people. This tension was the undercurrent to the next six months and accompanied me everywhere I went. The upside was that I was never worried about fitting into my dress because my nerves kept my metabolism at an unhealthily high rate.

The Dress

My task was to choose a dress I wouldn't live to regret. I had timing on my side, having set a date in the '90s rather than the '80s when it was impossible to succeed in such a venture. I knew I wanted something simple, timeless and a bit covered up and I knew exactly the man to make it.

By this time Alistair was back in Paris but no longer working under his own name. He agreed to moonlight as my wedding-dress designer on evenings and weekends. I had a couturier in my back pocket and I was ready to roll. The cost of the dress, however, combined with my dad's rigid budget meant that, with the exception of my favourite cousin Toby, there was no room for any family on my side beyond siblings and parents at the wedding breakfast. It was a sacrifice I was very happy to make. I opted for quality over quantity. I ate up my part of the budget with handsewing and duchess satin and silk organza woven on an

Sadly, I have no idea where that dress or body have gone.

original nineteenth-century loom. Weekly fittings were carried out off Kensington High Street at the studio flat of Alistair's dear friends, Amy and Grace Lee. The fabric had been lovingly sourced by Spielberg's favourite costume designer and my son's godmother, Joanna Johnston. I can't remember how my dress was described when the pictures ran in *Vogue* but I'd have said something like 'The two layers of silk gave the illusion she was dressed in the water of a sunlit stream.' They should have; they cost a fortune. Hugh Green did my half-up half-down hair and the contents of my mother's jewellery box were pinned in lieu of the tiara we didn't own.

It was a miracle I reached the aisle at all. My friends told me repeatedly I was making a mistake. Initially they were excited for me but over time felt that if I was having to push this hard, perhaps it wasn't meant to be. I kept the worst of the truth away from my parents who were footing the bill but, as the day approached, Sten seemed to be getting less and less sure of his decision. An aggressive case of eczema ringed his neck as if his subconscious was trying to tell me how suffocated he felt. I ignored it all. In spite of the path being littered with red flags and having every legitimate reason to worry, I ploughed on regardless. It was my skipping past The Duchess again, whistling my happy tune. I'd invested three years in this thing and by God I was going to get there. I just had to hope it was stress rather than a lack of feeling for me that was causing him such torment.

I knew I had to find out whether he really wanted to get married but equally didn't want to see him face to face and give him the chance to tell me he'd changed his mind. I hate confrontation. Instead I sent out a smoke signal. With much understated ceremony, I cancelled my hen night, which was to be held at San Lorenzo the next day. I knew Sten would hear about this, that the signal would be passed from house to house, friend to friend, until it finally found its way to him and he could decide whether to escape through the open stable door or choose to stay. It was a case of bog-standard, plain old manipulation and all I had to do was hold my nerve. I never honestly had any doubt he wanted to marry me; I just needed to make him think he had a choice about it. He knew I'd be making all the decisions for the rest of our lives so this was really just a little parting gift to his autonomy.

Like a lot of women, it is in times of crisis that I find the strength and clarity to fight for what I believe in. I am someone who can be easily swayed by the views of the last person I've spoken to. Combined with the fact that I am also a professional people-pleaser, I often find myself saying what I think others want to hear rather than confront them with the truth. All that said, there are times when I am so convinced of my beliefs, I don't need advice from anyone. My marriage to Sten was one such occasion.

It Was Love at First Sight

My father had always been the kind of man who found it hard to empathise with anyone under the age of twenty-two – and this included his own children. We were a mystery to him. His passions were art and antique furniture: the acquisition of beautiful objects. As I got older I felt like he came to regard me like one of these pieces. He could admire me from afar but I never really became a comfortable, well-used part of his home. I heard through other people how proud he was of me but he never told me to my face. After his death I found hundreds of press cuttings he'd kept over the years under his bed. He was a collector. I would gradually come to find that I was one too. The only difference between us was that the valuable things I liked to collect were people.

It was 2006 when I first met Jake Shears – or Jason as I came to know him – and it was love at first sight. I was determined to have him and taken completely unawares by this surge of desire.

The Scissor Sisters had exploded from the US onto the

world's stage two years earlier – reanimating disco and glam rock for Millennials who wished they'd been around for Studio 54. They were entertainers who merged music with drag and stirred the whole thing up with a spoonful of sex. Jason was the secret ingredient that made the mixture rise. In spite of all this, their intoxicating perfume had so far wafted right over my head. At forty-four I'd long since stopped listening to the hit parade.

That summer we'd been invited to Elton and David's house in Nice – something Sten and I had been doing for the previous twenty years – and Jason was this year's newbie. The familiar drive to the Furnish-Johns' was short and windy and up a steep hill; their villa was hidden entirely from the road by a forest of pine trees. It was mid-morning by the time Sten and I walked out onto the terrace where Jason was sitting alone reading a copy of Haruki Murakami's *The Wind-Up Bird Chronicle*. I'm someone who's willing to write off a friend based on their book choices and Jason looks like the kind of person who only reads comics, so this was the first of Cupid's unexpected arrows. The list of books I find unacceptable include, but are not limited to: covers with photographs of people kissing; anything that's been a hit on TV first and found its way onto the bestseller list second; anything prominently displayed between June and September at the airport; adaptations with a still from the film on the cover; everything advertised as 'the perfect beach read', and anything by Andrew Morton. Never mind that millions of people have already read and enjoyed these books and that I myself have written two novels that fit at least part of these criteria. My recurring nightmare is Salman Rushdie finding me in

Sainsbury's and catching me red-handed with a copy of *Riders* by Jilly Cooper. I am the worst of all snobs. A literary one. Jason's holiday read threw me off step.

He got up immediately and came over to kiss us both hello. He leaned in with what I now know to be his signature Southern 'Hey, how's it going?' and I was floored. It was the only time I've ever met someone well known and not come out with a crass opening remark. I was tongue-tied. It was eighty degrees and he was fully dressed, his hair the white-blonde peroxide of a man with both huge sexual confidence and a complete lack of responsibility. There's a reason someone invented the word starstruck and I can only assume it was on the back of an encounter such as this.

A side note on sexual chemistry: Jason was gay. I knew it, he knew it, you couldn't pass him in the street without knowing it. It didn't matter. He exuded a raw, heat-seeking sexuality and was one of the most masculine people I'd ever met. It was like he'd distilled what it meant to be carnal and was actively secreting it through his pores – as if he was giving off pure pheromones. It's worth noting here that the definition of a pheromone is a behaviour-altering agent. Essentially a chemical an animal produces to change the conduct of another. It worked. Being around him made me feel like he'd unlocked something; that an adventure was about to happen. In that instant I'd have followed him anywhere. It was like being hit on the head with a frying pan. The only other time I'd felt this way was the evening I'd met Sten.

I don't for a second imagine I triggered similar feelings in Jason. He'd had only one sexual encounter with a woman in his life and it was nothing he was looking to repeat. He was sixteen years old and had thrown up in an empty packet of Cheetos before she'd had the chance to get to first base. The only kind of women he notices are drag queens and hookers. I, on the other hand, was the sort of lady his mother might know from her book group. I was invisible.

But falling for Jason wasn't about getting him into bed. It was much more innocent. He was the kind of boy that made teenagers want to pin his poster on their walls. A schoolgirl crush. You might have thought about kissing him but that was about as physical as it got. A crush is really nothing to do with sex. It's about proximity; wanting to be 'around' another. It's an amalgamation of feelings you can't quite put your finger on that manifests itself in a visceral, hollow pull in the front of your chest. It's amorphous. This feeling won't withstand close inspection; it's a mirage, dependent for its existence on distance. Pop stars go home at night and cut their toenails like everyone else but you don't need to know that about your crush. That's part of what sustains your desire. This is why no genuine relationship can compete.

For me, meeting Jason brought back all these sensations. I took the teenage crush he might once have been and added nostalgia for extra potency. He made me feel young again. After eight years of motherhood, he reactivated a part of me I'd put into storage. Possibility. Courage. The excitement of the unknown. By rights I'd already enjoyed that part of my life and filed it away under 'My Youth'. Here was an opportunity to experience some of it again but this time with more wisdom and a level of appreciation for the second chance it was. *That* was what was intoxicating. The fact he was gay meant I could enjoy these feelings with impunity. It would never be consummated, which made Jason the perfect, safe outlet for my mid-life crisis.

The only question on my mind now was how a middle-aged has-been might win over a rampant, peacocking, homosexual rock star? The odds were against me but I knew I must pursue him nonetheless. This was about desire in the truest sense of the word. He was an exotic object from a foreign land; the kind you'd once upon a time have collected on a Grand Tour. I wanted to wrap him up in the towel I knew I'd inevitably steal from Elton's guest bathroom and smuggle him home in my carry-on. But I was getting ahead of myself.

That first night we were taken to dinner at the incredibly grand home of local socialite Lily Safra. Villa Leopolda is well known for being the most opulent house on the Cote d'Azur and had rather distastefully once belonged to the teenage mistress of the Belgian pensioner King Leopold II. I did my best to put this out of my mind so as not to spoil the absolutely delicious canapés. Jason and I were seated together at what was clearly the children's end of the table. I was secretly delighted but, if I didn't know his music, he knew even less about Sloane Rangers, Littlewoods and Magic Knickers. I was on thin ice, but I persevered. Like a bitch on heat I couldn't help jumping up and putting my dirty paws on his nice clean top. Had I been a dog, at least he could have shut me in the garden until after dinner. I had very little to offer so I did what I always do and fell back on my upbringing. In a scene reminiscent of *Pretty Woman*, I pulled out everything I'd ever learned about charm: I put him at ease about the dos and don'ts of high-end cutlery, matching wine colour to food, and the importance of elbow etiquette amongst the well-to-do. I was the hotel manager to his Vivian Ward. I went full tilt doing my best to make myself indispensable. It was the most exhausting night of my life. I would go on to find out that what someone did or who they were was of absolutely no interest to Jason. I was projecting my own rules of people-collecting onto him. He was much less discerning and happy to take home any old bit of filth as long as he liked it. As it turned out, all I'd needed to be was myself. Stage one was now complete but the end goal was not just to get Jason to need me but to like me. And like me *best*. The road before me was a long one.

As a lifelong people-pleaser, my first question on meeting someone new is always 'Do they like me?' rather than 'Do I like them?' My decision about them will depend on their decision about me, which is clearly not the right way to go about making friends. Nevertheless, I launched myself at Jason and began a one-sided courtship. Maintaining a long-distance

Showing Jason off at Belvoir.

relationship with an international pop star is hard work but I excelled at it: I turned up backstage, invited him to Belvoir and anywhere else that might impress him, and rammed him and his music down the throats of my family. Having talked her down from a *High School Musical* theme, Esme's sixth birthday cake was in the shape of the Scissor Sisters' logo iced in pink fondant. I told everyone she'd asked for it but I knew the truth.

After three years of this, I finally wore him down.

I'm not proud of my behaviour but, in my defence, if it hadn't been for my crush we'd never have become such dear friends. The years I stalked him gave us just enough time to get to know one another properly. As it turned out, we really liked each other, so I'd been right to pursue him after all. When somebody really 'gets you' it's the most fabulous feeling in the world. When that someone is interesting, creative or stimulating you feel, by association, more interesting, creative and stimulating yourself. I've made a habit of gathering people like this around me and propped up my ego with their charisma.

What was Sten doing all this time? He was allowing me to make a fool of myself in the knowledge it would probably pass. Ours would have made a wonderful French marriage. One of the many reasons it has survived is that Sten has always allowed me the space to pursue my obsessions – whether that be a pop star twenty years my junior or a husky ride across the Arctic. Some come to nothing, but, in this instance, the story had a happy ending and I gained a friend beloved by not just me but by Sten and the children too.

Dencombe House

In 1922 my great-grandfather was the fifth wealthiest person in Britain. Unsurprisingly, my parents had been very wealthy too but managed to fritter most of it away before they both died. There was no family home to inherit and our holiday house in France was sold to pay for my mother's long-term care, Mrs A's dotage and my father's debts. Dencombe House was paid for by me and Sten.

We'd been looking to buy in Leicestershire for about five years. Then I got the call I'd been waiting for: 'Norman has died.' And so began a love affair I'm still enjoying now. Norman Burrows Has Died and his wife, Ann the Widow, had lived at Dencombe House in Sussex for over thirty years. The lime-green carpet and avocado bathroom suite were a love letter to the heyday of their life there. These were the things they'd put in place when their home was at its fullest and were still in situ as they carried Norman Burrows Has Died out on a stretcher.

I knew from a friend of Sten's parents that Norman had died and I called the widow the same day. Yes, as the words come out of my mouth now I hear how inappropriate this was but the property market is dog-eat-dog. He who dares, etc. When I arrived to view the house, Norman Has Died had been carried out only a few hours earlier. The bed was probably still warm. I was instantly besotted. It was home. There was no question we weren't going to live there. I just had no idea how we were going to pay for it. I knew I'd earned a lot of money over the previous five years, but not this much. True to form, I had the loosest grasp on my finances and was unaware Sten had been quietly investing my earnings. He'd turned my very nice nest egg into a small fortune – enough to buy Dencombe. Not enough to run or renovate it though. There was absolutely no surplus cash so we had to effectively start all over again, albeit in the most beautiful surroundings. I didn't care. It was worth it.

But we had another problem. Unfortunately Ann the Widow had not yet found somewhere else to live so part of the deal was that we let her stay in the house until she did. Our children needed to start school that September and we'd already sold our house in London so we moved into the three-bedroom flat above Ann the Widow's garage for six months. Sten, me, three kids and two Labrador puppies. I'd never been more content.

Cece, Esme and Joe with Sten and I at my brother-in-law's wedding, *c*.2007.

My first instinct once we were in the house was to change everything. Eight years later we were no further forward. Fifteen and we finally got round to that renovation but the lime-green carpet survived. What I realised was that you have to really live in a house to know what kind of a home you want it to be. It is gradual. It adapts around you and in this way becomes an extension of your family. I'm secretly glad that we have the kind of house other people's children like to come to because it means I get to see my own children more than I might. I know this is more to do with the fact we have a swimming pool and I offer my services like a servant than wanting to see me per se, but I'll take what I can get.

Just like everyone else in our family, the house has to work hard for its keep. It's not something we can afford to take for granted. It would be disingenuous of me to pretend I don't know what a luxury it is to live somewhere like Dencombe. It is an exceptional place. It is also one we have to work hard to hold on to. Buying the house was just the first hurdle. Maintaining it is quite another thing and one I had not considered properly when we moved in. Dencombe sits on 127 acres of land, 70 of which are protected woodland. That's quite different from just having a really big back garden. My time at Dencombe has been a steep learning curve. I was lucky to have grown up in the countryside and I pride myself on having a good understanding of the land around me, but caring for Dencombe has been a step further again. This has really fallen to my husband. Our unspoken division of labour is that I take care of the inside of the house and he takes care of the outside.

Like any family home, there are a million things that need

doing and a mother's job is never done. Sten works staggeringly hard. It requires intense focus for nine or ten hours a day. Like all working mums, my days are the same but the work I do outside office hours is unpaid and never-ending – cooking, cleaning, washing, animal husbandry. When I get resentful – which I often do – I remember the time and effort my husband invests as custodian of the woods. Dencombe Woods aren't just any old woods. They are classed as an Area of Outstanding Natural Beauty, an ancient woodland filled with native species that have been here for hundreds of years, and a Site of Special Scientific Interest (SSSI) due to the rare species of flora and fauna. Lucky us. But with this comes a big responsibility that is laid squarely at Sten's feet. They need managing. Coppicing, clearing, replanting, chopping and chain-sawing for our biomass boiler which runs off woodchip. When I run through the woods, I think *How beautiful*. When Sten does the same he has the satisfaction of knowing it's thanks to his hard work they are healthy and disease-free.

We are only the third family to have lived here. The gardens were laid for the first. I get huge pleasure from knowing we're carrying that on, taking care of it for the next family. I had no idea I would come to feel this way about Dencombe when I first saw it; all I knew was I had to have it. It was exactly the feeling I'd had about Jason except Dencombe has been a lot more reliable in the long run. Even now I can't believe we live here. After many detours, I'd finally ended up back where I started. In the country. I'd come full circle.

Penny for the Guy

It was 2007 and Mika had just gone to number 1 with 'Grace Kelly'. In light of my love affair with Jason, I was furious. It was clearly a rip-off of the Scissor Sisters and, annoyingly, a very good one. Jason and his bandmate Scott Hoffman – aka Babydaddy – were on their way to stay for Bonfire Night and so, in the spirit of solidarity, the children and I built a life-size effigy of Mika to burn alive. We dressed him in his signature stripy trousers and tight white t-shirt and I printed out a picture of his face and stuck it on the head, which I'd fashioned from an old pair of Magic Knickers. We topped it off with an Edwina Currie wig last worn at our 1997 Election Night party. It doubled very nicely as the luxurious curls of a young, effeminate Lebanese man. The overall likeness was really quite uncanny. I waited until Scott and Jason were already on their way to tell them Mika would be joining us for lunch, knowing this would make it impossible for them to cancel. Like a pair of polite American tourists, they accepted the bad news with good grace. The children propped the mannequin up in prime position in their father's seat at the head of the table to await our guests. I was rather pleased with the quality of my craftsmanship; from a great distance it was really quite convincing. If only we'd had time to push him round the village in an old pram before he met his death. A particularly cocky Jason entered through the back door and came into the kitchen, puffed up in anticipation of a meeting with his nemesis. A momentary pause was followed by relieved laughter. I had not in fact made friends with the dreaded Mika. Balance was restored.

By his own admission, there is nothing Jason likes better than a good roasting by his friends so this was one up to me.

When it came to country life, both Jason and Scott were laughably unprepared. It was like Thatcher's visit to Balmoral all over again. Neither had 'outdoor' shoes. Nine times out of ten Jason can be found in denim cut-offs and wife-beater, irrespective of outside temperature. He famously never makes any provision for the inclemencies of the British weather. Like a six-year-old packing for holiday, he'd only chuck in whatever was right under his nose. Plastic dinosaur, string of fairy lights, alarm clock but no pants or socks. In spite of the fact he's spent years touring the world, he arrives religiously unprepared for anything other than seventy degrees and sunny. Neither he nor Scott were ready for a November walk through the woods. I would need to kit them out myself.

Jason was easy; he's the same size as a teenage girl so my daughter's clothes were perfect. Scott is the classic, wide, gay bear but, in spite of his barrel-chested presence, he has incongruously small feet so was at least able to fit into my wellingtons. Too broad for any of Joe's or Sten's coats though, a horse blanket was the best we could come up with at short notice.

In the field at the edge of the woods we'd built a bonfire ten foot high, so a ladder was needed to reach the top. With the help of Scott, Jason climbed this precarious construction with the life-sized effigy of his rival stuffed under his arm. Once at the top, Mika was successfully impaled on the summit. The wood was enthusiastically doused in petrol by Sten and the match lit excitedly by Esme, who was fairly obviously as much in love with Jason as I was. Like a loyal groupie, she

288

set fire to this glorious monstrosity and we sat and watched the fire lick up the branches. Poor old Mika was engulfed in flames quicker than his career would be.

Years later Scott did a workshop with him only to find he was not the dreadful person we'd all hoped he would be but actually a very nice boy from Beirut called Michael.

Babydaddy

Scott dressed like a man who was just about to sink into a La-Z-Boy with a beer in his basement. If you don't know who he is, look at a photo of the band and he'll be the one standing side-on looking like the stylist ran out of steam. When I was with Trinny I'd be the one to stand at the back too so she could cover half my body with hers. Scott was a kindred spirit.

Scott was Jason's bandmate and co-writer, but as people they were nothing alike. For someone in an ensemble that's bordering on burlesque, Scott was surprisingly conservative. Traditional, even. Where Jason bowled through life picking up waifs and strays, Scott was much more discerning. The first time we met, one night on tour with their second album, he found me backstage in their communal dressing room. I was in the middle of a brash, critical analysis of their wardrobe. I tore through it as it hung from the rails, dismissing each piece with a 'Jesus, you must be joking' or just a simple 'No.' This was my MO. I believed Jason liked me because of my ballsy, uninhibited shock factor and I felt this was my currency in their world. Knowing what was expected I took on the role of performing monkey or court jester. I was Jason's latest find, his newest shiny toy, and I didn't want to be replaced. Their costume designer, Zaldy Goco, was also in the room that night and must have been enormously offended. He wasn't some back-room seamstress. As well as creating the on-stage visuals for the Scissor Sisters, he'd been costume designer for Michael Jackson, Lady Gaga and Britney Spears. He's designed for Cirque du Soleil and has three Emmys for his work on *RuPaul's Drag Race*. A critique by the woman off *What Not to Wear* was really quite unnecessary. Scott and I have joked about this episode many times since, but only in researching this book was he more candid. 'I was very put off by you. I didn't like your energy. I didn't like you coming into our home and making fun of us.' I must have seemed like a vile, precocious child, especially since he'd had no say over my sudden appearance in his private life. I was performing for Jason, earning my keep. I was also doing my best to show I wasn't intimidated, that I could hold my own. I didn't appreciate that I was being incredibly insensitive and intrusive. I'm mortified to think of it now. It took a long time for Scott and I to become friends because, in truth, he didn't like me at first. He kept me at arm's length. He was a considered person; he didn't leap onto any old bandwagon. Had it been down to him, he would happily have written me off. As it was, he found me repeatedly thrust into his orbit. I wasn't going away. I suppose gradually he saw that I wasn't just brash: I was very loyal and stuck with the people I liked. Over the years he came to see a side of me he preferred. Scott didn't need to be wowed; he just needed you to be the most honest version of yourself.

Scott's conservatism played a big part in his attitude to my drinking. By his own admission, the 'Oops, I've had a bit too much' culture in the UK does not sit well with him. He calls a spade a spade. I had an alcohol problem and he didn't like it. While he was never judgemental, I know he disapproved – which seems a funny thing to say of a guy in a group like the Scissor Sisters. He was level-headed about my drinking and didn't like the way I treated him when I was drunk. I'd call him and be unforgivably obnoxious until, in the end, he finally said 'Enough.' I mustn't call him any more in that state. He didn't want to be abused by a drunken lush. He wasn't a put-your-foot-down type, it was more of a 'This isn't working for me' scenario. For Scott it was a significant watershed. For me, my drinking was so bad I barely heard his request. This is a truly horrible thing to acknowledge about myself. It's also quite destabilising to suddenly see things differently after so many years of thinking I'd handled it all very well. That my drinking had only affected me. I'm sure Scott can't be the only friend who felt these things, but he was one of the few brave enough to confront me.

Closure

My mother's drinking stopped overnight when I was around twenty-five. I've questioned since whether she was a true alcoholic, but now believe it was self-medication covering depression and crippling shyness. Like me, she always drank in secret. Grapefruit juice, bitter lemon or ginger ale would be half emptied and refilled with spirits. I marked her bottles with faint lines, which she got round by watering down the vodka. There was no question of her going to AA; she was in and out of hospital so frequently with her bi-polar disorder this overshadowed any problems that might have stemmed from alcohol abuse. When she started taking heavier medication for her depression she'd become hopelessly lethargic and would often nod off. If she fell asleep watching television it would be another *'Pull yourself together, Mary-Rose!'* from my father. For those few seconds, it was out in the open that he knew about her drinking. A bolt of anxiety would shoot through me and I'd hold my breath hoping the genie would quietly slip back into the bottle and we could all pretend it hadn't happened. This was absurd. Of course he knew about her drinking but because it seemed like he didn't, it made me feel I was the only one who *did*. This put me in a position where I felt responsible for what was going on between them. As if it was my job to hide it from him. I filled in the gaps of his silence with my own conclusions.

As a teenager and young woman I'd felt responsible for my mother. Once I'd made my own life – married and had children – I somehow felt better able to cope. The main reason for this was my husband. When Sten and I married I gained a family, and their backing gave me strength to cope with my mother in a way I'd been avoiding in the years prior. I was no longer expected to cope alone. This was what I'd been looking for in a relationship all those years. With David I'd found a first love and with Imran I'd had the thrill of the chase. With Sten I was able to be my whole self; nothing was held back.

They say when you marry a woman you marry her mother but Sten didn't leave when he saw what his future might hold. We joined forces and were stronger for it. This is what I'd been unwittingly looking for in my 'prince'. Contrary to what

I'd expected, the fairytale was finding someone who could be stronger than me when I was at my most vulnerable.

Throughout my childhood I'd never had the security to fall apart in times of emotional stress, but now here was Sten to catch me. Had it not been for him I would not have been as present as I was at the end of my mother's life. I didn't properly understand the meaning of family until we married. He didn't push me to see my mum, but he was so generous towards her, giving her time and treating her as an equal, I learned a new way to be around her. I learned to accept her.

I didn't want to hide her or her illness from my children. I felt it was important for them to see that this was real life. I was also proud of them and wanted my mum to know her grandchildren. Every Sunday I'd collect her to come and spend the day with us at home. By this time, her mania had subsided. The dementia had superseded her depression and she was now just silent; still. Even so, she'd always manage to muster a smile around the children. In this smallest of gestures, somehow she was able to access her maternal core and show a glimmer of the parent she'd long stopped being. She knew to make the effort, which implied something in her knew she was the grown-up. The mother. Something deep down in her was still working.

When my father died of an aneurysm at sixty-nine, she'd deteriorated very quickly. It was dreadful to see her decline, and worse that she survived in this reduced manner for over a decade. In the end she fell and broke her hip. She was recovering from the operation when her heart finally gave up. I was living in London but had visited with Esme only two days before. This was more luck than judgement but it changed everything for me.

On my visits, my mother always seemed to know me but could equally confuse time and place and the connection between us. By this stage, she barely spoke. Life slowly but surely trickled away as I stood holding her hand. I stroked her hair to comfort us both. Unprompted, Esme clambered onto the bed and lay on top of her as only a small child can do. She was four years old and looked exactly as I had at that age. I watched as my mum put her arms around my daughter and whispered '*I'm sorry.*' It didn't matter who Esme was or who my mother thought she was talking to; it was something she needed to say. Unfazed, Esme lay still. To see them together I understood my poor mother was not responsible for what she'd done or the way she'd behaved. Watching her with my child, I was able to put myself in her shoes and I saw her as the mother she'd always wanted to be.

When I found out she'd died two days later, there was an overwhelming sense of relief, for both of us. That she died knowing, or believing, she'd said sorry was a blessing. It was like she had a moment of clarity. She'd looked at Esme with such love. She must have felt the need for forgiveness, but at that point I suddenly felt she'd done nothing to be sorry for. My greatest sadness is I wasn't able to tell her she had no reason to ask. You didn't need to say sorry, Mum.

Just as with the gothic novels of my childhood, the ghosts of the past had haunted my mother until her death. I didn't want them to determine the patterns of the future – for myself or my children – but for over a decade I failed to stop it happening. I do sometimes wonder whether the ten years that followed her passing and the alcoholism I succumbed to were, in part, a prolonged form of mourning and an adjustment to all that had happened in the lead-up. A delayed response to things I'd not been able to process as a child. I came from a long line of female drinkers but it is impossible to know for certain how much of my own addiction was nature and how much was nurture. The only thing I can say for sure is that my name is Susannah and I'm an alcoholic.

My father's death was a much lighter-hearted affair. Following his aneurysm he'd had a week in the Leicester Infirmary. He was in his element: a hypochondriac surrounded by pretty nurses not even having to bother to do his own breathing. I think he'd have been quite pleased with the set-up had he known what was going on. It was quite a fitting end. After much discussion about ethics and the meaning of life, the ventilator was eventually turned off and Nits and I hovered around not really knowing what to do next. A nurse approached us tentatively with a 'I'm sorry for your loss' look on her face. She obviously needed to discuss something urgently. It was a press release, and the need to get one out quite quickly. I embarrassed myself, immediately thinking it must be on account of my fledgling television career. In fact, for the entire duration of his stay, staff at the hospital had believed my father to be King Constantine of Greece. It was a mix-up that provided a fitting end for a man who'd always secretly wanted to be an aristocrat. It couldn't have gone better.

In the spring of 2014, with some of the biggest hurdles of motherhood under my belt, I was finally ready to take a gap year. Although I thought a week would probably suffice. I didn't want to fuck with my Ocado delivery slot.

It was my first time in Berlin. Indeed, my first trip to Germany, if you discount a drive-by en route to the Alps in a Vauxhall Corsa stuffed with three kids, a husband and five enormous hard suitcases. Now I was completely unencumbered. Three t-shirts, one sequined top, five pairs of knickers and an Egyptian cotton sheet I'd stitched into a sleeping bag made up the bulk of my luggage. Jason had invited me to stay with the caveat that his current rental was pretty basic. I interpreted 'basic' as clean lines with a smattering of abstract artwork. I had not anticipated the Communist bolthole that stood before me now. The apartment – if it could be legally marketed as such – was big enough for an average-sized pigeon, similar to the one that cooed and shat relentlessly on the windowsill outside. A makeshift bed had been fashioned from four vegetable crates and a naked piece of yellow foam. The 'carpet' was an explosion of fishnet tops and discarded pants. The silver trunk from which they'd originated now doubled as a bedside/kitchen/coffee table. Molecule, Jason's perfume of choice, disguised the aroma of sex and Singapore noodles. It was the kind of room in which you'd expect to keep a hostage.

There was never a question that Jason might meet me at the airport, even though we'd not seen each other for more than a year. Having buzzed me in, he pounced with all the brainless enthusiasm of an inbred pedigree dog.

'Waddya think?'

I scanned the room.

'It's a shit hole, Jason.'

I could tell I'd misjudged the situation because he stopped panting and jumping around. 'It's a dump,' I back-peddled, 'but I love it.'

Berlin had taken to Jason and Jason had taken to Berlin. But, while a squalid bedsit in the Turkish Quarter might have worked for Dostoyevsky, the experimental lifestyle Jason was enjoying had clearly expanded beyond the confines of his current space. It was time, I told him, to look for somewhere new. Mainly I was interested in nosing around other people's homes and flat-hunting with Jason seemed like the perfect opportunity.

We let ourselves into a run-down house converted into apartments, owned by a friend of a friend looking to make some cash on the side. Without the irritation of an estate agent breathing down our necks, we could snoop at our leisure. Snooping was one of my top ten pastimes and I'd learned from the best: Princess Margaret. Jason was untrained in such pursuits and spoiled the moment immediately by needing to go for a poo. I left him to carry on my investigations alone. I quickly found the owner had removed anything of interest and the apartment was annoyingly devoid of diaries and dildos.

'There's no fucking toilet roll!' came a shout from the bathroom. My initial once-round-the-flat had already told me he was unlikely to find any, but I went through the motions of looking for some nonetheless. The gradually rising pitch of Jason's pleas implied panic was beginning to set in. After a cursory rifle through the kitchen cupboards I returned to find him with his pants around his ankles and presented him with my range of suggested alternatives.

Rather than the used Vileda kitchen mop or mint teabag on offer, he resorted instead to the sanitary towel he'd already found in the bathroom drawer. He made the right choice. We both agreed the mint would smart and the mop was a hygiene bridge too far even for him.

This was a work trip for Jason. His creative mojo had gone AWOL during the production of their last album and he'd come to East Berlin to try and find it again. But you can't go to Berlin without sampling the nightlife, and by this point he'd absorbed enough of it to work as an 18–30s holiday rep. It went without saying we'd be going out that evening and 'Muscle Night' was the first stop on the agenda. Muscle Night sounded quite fun until I learned I would either need to pass as a man or, at the very least, a convincing pan-sexual. This was a men-only night and the only thing I had in my favour, Jason told me, was that I 'walked like someone who'd just got off a horse'.

In the space of an hour our work was done. A borrowed vest emblazoned with the face of an unidentified anime character, stone-washed jeans and Birkenstocks was the final accepted look. Make-up was forbidden and my drop earrings swapped for studs. Apparently, keeping my mouth shut in the queue was the final, most important, part of the equation. I felt buoyed by the fact that I'd won over the female bouncer at Vauxhall's Horse Meat Disco on another of our outings. A few flattering tweaks to her unforgiving uniform and an ear for her life story (heroic single mum of three kids and two jobs) and we were in. But if Vauxhall were Brooke Shields, Berghain was Mother Teresa. It was going to take more than a wedding ring to gain entry.

The door policies for Berlin's nightclubs are some of the most talked about in the world. Online forums detail the clothing and behaviour most likely to get you in. Ultimately, bouncers at Berghain are there to curate the clientele based on who will and won't handle what they might find inside. Who might gawk or puke is the key to their decision-making process. They are the original stewards of safe spaces with a responsibility to protect the freedom of expression of their guests. For a club to thrive, the bouncer must create an environment in which no one feels threatened by their sexual orientation or disposition. It's all about tolerance. With people selected to fit perfectly together, the results can be euphoric.

Berghain's infamous doorman, Sven Marquardt, was a striking specimen, all bar a few inches of his face inked and pierced, his grey hair groomed and his beard manicured. Marquardt was a man who looked like he'd never broken into a smile in his life. At well over six foot, he may well have wandered straight off the set of *Mad Max*. His expert eye was the aesthetic filter for the Berghain and his word was law in the world of underground sexual hedonism.

Every weekend, as dawn breaks over Berlin, a line of people can be seen snaking back from the hulking shell of East Germany's decommissioned power plant. From midnight on Saturday till noon on Monday, this is Berghain, a club as famous for its techno as its round-the-clock debauchery.

From the outside it looked like a Brutalist take on an art deco telephone exchange. Inside, its gutless interior made the perfect dance floor. There was no bottle service, no guest list and queues of up to three hours.

After a heated debate with Sven – which it looked very much like Jason was losing – the only thing left in his arsenal was name-dropping. 'She's just had dinner with DJ Boris!' he shrieked. 'They shared a dessert!' Evidently Mr Boris Dolinski was a person of some note in this town. The rope was pulled back and we were inside. Jason shoved me from behind down a narrow, dark corridor. I was met immediately with swags of kitchen roll hanging from the walls. Pink and yellow Marigolds sat ready in empty buckets and a selection of Tupperware was on display for anyone who might want a container. All bases had been covered. These people evidently meant business. I did my best not to let my bare arms touch anything wet or sticky.

The corridor gave way to the floor of an immense warehouse. Twenty-foot ceilings dwarfed the sea of sweaty men below and the room was dominated by a nose-bleed-inducing bass. I felt it reverberate through my chest. The only way of communicating now was sign language or lip-reading. Wall-to-wall singlets evaluated one another for sexual potential. Language was not the way these men communicated; how you stood or what you wore was enough to tell someone whether you gave or received. The atmosphere wasn't aggressive but there was an underlying tension that said things could turn very dirty very quickly, probably as soon as the MDMA kicked in. There was something pure and animalistic in the air, like an electric charge. There were strict rules to get in but you had the feeling that once you were, it was lawless, like the Wild West. Had this been a straight club, the volume of testosterone in the atmosphere would have ended in a fist fight. There wasn't another woman in sight. For the first time in the company of gay men, I felt vaguely uneasy. I reached for Jason's hand. He was nowhere to be seen.

The first rule of an emergency is not to panic and don't call the police if you don't have to. Yes, I felt out of my depth, but equally I was invisible to these people. Free to explore. Four shots of Dutch courage and what was the worst that could happen? I did what my children often did when they were small. I went for a wander.

The lower levels of Berghain house 'dark rooms' where club-goers are free to engage in their hearts' desires, unfettered by morals or etiquette. Jason had assured me this wasn't a scat night so that was something of a relief. Still, I was surprised by the sight of a gentleman pissing over a grille into the mouth of a man below. *'It's OK. I'm still dry. Don't panic, Captain Mainwaring.'* With the vodka starting to do its job, I decided to brave the basement but was barred for having a vagina. I tried another door.

Berghain wasn't an S&M club so there were no whips or cat-o'-nine-tails, but gimp masks, strap-ons and all manner of rough riding equipment were artfully arranged on the rendered wall. A very comfortable-looking hammock hung from the ceiling in one of the grottos, tempting and unoccupied. I hoisted myself into it and let my legs dangle either side, swinging myself to the beat. Two harnessed men arrived, opened their flies and began stroking themselves behind me. They weren't embarrassed and strangely nor was I – just grateful to rest my tired feet for a minute or two. When their grunts rose above the music, I politely excused myself and moved on.

It's funny how the human mind can process the extreme and make it palatable; normal, even. Here I was in the outer galaxy of sexual expression but, after the initial shock and awe, it was just as if the goings on inside Berghain were part of the very fabric of mainstream living. I was interrupted from my reverie by an uncharacteristically worried Jason: 'Where the hell have you been?!' His entourage of string vests looked on inquisitively. 'I've been resting in that hammock,' I said, pointing to the sex sling now obviously being used for its true purpose by the men who'd been so happily masturbating behind me. Ah, so *that's* why it's made of rubber. The penny finally dropped. I realised that, like everybody in the playground, they'd just been waiting for their turn on the swing.

Jason thought my faux pas was hilarious – a fact about which I was surprisingly cross. I was therefore very pleased to be spotted by a group of German autograph hunters at the bar. 'Hey, you are Susannah from Susannah and Trinny, no?!' I always knew we had a large gay following but had not imagined it would be bigger than Jason's or that it might have reached the sex dungeons of Berlin. Maybe it was just that I stood out as the only person with a proper pair of boobs, but I enjoyed my moment in the sun nonetheless and it certainly shut Jason up.

The Low Point

This sounds like great fun but the truth was, by August of that year, I was a mess. The career I'd had for the past fourteen years with Trinny was over. In its place was an empty vortex. I was a wine-drinker and, by this point, would happily polish off a bottle or two a night. A lot of people do this and don't think anything of it and certainly wouldn't regard themselves as having a problem with alcohol. I knew I had one because I couldn't and wouldn't go anywhere socially without a drink first. And when I say socially, I include interaction with my family in that definition.

Six o'clock was the arbitrary time I'd set myself to begin the night and my eyes were on the clock for a full hour in the lead-up. I would never, ever put myself in a situation where this time arrived and I didn't have an easily accessible, full bottle of wine to hand. It was a thing I never left to chance. Should that situation ever have presented itself, it would not have meant going without. I'd have sniffed out something. We never drink spirits in my house as a rule but I'd have found some ancient bottle of port or cooking sherry tucked away from Christmases past and satisfied myself with that.

Was six o'clock really arbitrary? For my parents and their friends it was always the hour for pre-dinner drinks. In my twenties, it was the time we were expected to congregate in the drawing room or study in whoever's home I was a guest. Sometimes those drinks were taken back up to bedrooms to sit on the dressing table as you put on your face for dinner. It was all part of the dance. In the corporate world, six o'clock drinks are a full stop to the working day. A way to diffuse. An appropriate time and place to offload the cares of your day. For the man going to his club, it was still early enough to unwind with his peers before making sure he was home in time for his wife and the meal she'd made him. Maybe even kiss the children goodnight. Six o'clock had an acceptable ring to it. There was nothing arbitrary about it.

By 2012, drinking had become a completely solitary activity for me. Something done explicitly away from company. If we were entertaining, it was pre pre-dinner drinks alone, anywhere I could separate myself from the crowd. If the kitchen was empty I'd do it there, straight from the bottle. Alternatively, I'd find somewhere quiet where I wouldn't get caught and take the bottle with me. I never used a glass. By the time our guests arrived I'd be half a bottle down. By dinner, I'd be six glasses ahead of the next biggest drinker. I managed this by having two drinks on the go at all times – one from the bottle somewhere out of sight, the other from a glass which I drank with everyone else. A dual existence. It would have made a great farce had it not been so pathetic.

Even now I don't know the root of it. Is it just that I'm an alcoholic? What does that even mean?

Whether I was with people I did or didn't like, it didn't matter. Alcohol made every social interaction – good, bad or indifferent – fun. Not exciting. Just more fun. I never consciously thought of a reason to drink at the time, I just wanted to. It started out as a way to combat shyness, which was a very big thing for me when I was younger. But boredom too. The prospect of enlivening a situation. But then the alcohol became more exciting than any event in itself. It gave me permission to be the person I believed I was. I thought I was funnier, more interesting and more interested. Who knows whether I was. I don't even want to ask.

My brain has always been very busy. I find it difficult to enjoy the moment over the sound of my thoughts. Alcohol helped quiet this noise and I looked forward to the 'clarity' of mind it brought me. I felt focused. It made me not want to be anywhere other than the place I was in at that moment. To focus on the food I was eating, the person at my table or the voice on the end of the phone.

But another way of defining that 'clarity' would be that I had tuned out everything I didn't want to hear. Alcohol helped me remain in denial and prevented me from addressing some very unhappy thoughts. Though I didn't recognise it explicitly at the time, I think I hated myself so much I poured my energies into getting others to like me instead. I wanted to set myself apart; be unique; be special; but there is nothing unique or special about alcoholism. It just helped me gloss over the top of my sadness with an upbeat performance. That's the way I do things. Fighting anxiety with lightheartedness and flippancy. I may as well be skipping past The Duchess with my fingers in my ears – *La, la, la. I can't hear you, I can't hear you.* My approach to stress or unhappiness has not changed since childhood. Emotional development, frozen in time. Arrested. If I can pull the bed covers over my head in the hope the monsters will go away, I will. I won't confront them until they're staring me in the face and I can reach out and touch their clammy skin with my fingertips. Even then, if I can distract them with food or music, I'll take it; however temporary the fix.

Now I'm sober and the truth is out, I see it was glaringly obvious to everyone when I'd been drinking because I became an exaggerated version of my happy self. Cece knew, because she was the watcher, just as I had been with my mother. Interestingly, my husband said to me recently that he doesn't consider me to be an alcoholic. I suppose this comes down to how you define one. It doesn't really matter what you call it though; you know in yourself when something is wrong.

I wasn't a violent, angry or depressive drunk so you could argue it didn't matter. The reason it did was because, while everyone else was being their true selves, I was impersonating someone else and my friends and family were having a relationship with that person rather than me. Looking at it from the outside I see that, in creating this 'other' persona, I was inadvertently absenting myself from life. From my friendships, family, home and my responsibilities. I was there physically, but not emotionally.

This is a hideous thing to write. As I do, it brings back the emotional memories of what life was like when I was drinking. The lies I told. The people I hurt. My drinking was the worst of me.

I knew what I'd done to my family, but until now I'd felt I'd covered my tracks professionally and never let my drinking interfere with my career. Today I learned of an incident where this was not the case. I can remember it vividly now I am reminded of it. I was presenting with Trinny on QVC, which fell into a dangerous area for me because it was on late at night. This gave me plenty of time to be drinking before our slot. The studio was a large, well-lit, harsh environment which moved at pace because it was live. You needed to be on your A-game. I was well below par and couldn't find the light for my camera which, unbeknown to me, was obvious to everyone in the studio. With QVC you're in people's homes, in real time. Falling apart for the housewives of the world to see, minute by minute; second by second. For my peers too, my performance was a source of chatter. They watched, open-mouthed, to see how this would pan out. Eventually I stood back and Trinny took the wheel – as I'm now realising she must have done on more than one occasion. I don't imagine this was an isolated event. Hearing about it now is like I walked through the Met Gala with my skirts tucked into my knickers, having spent the past ten years thinking I looked fantastic on the night. It is humiliating beyond measure and I am sorry I put Trinny and the production team in that position. I've spent a long time trying to ignore the quiet rumblings from the background of my past, hoping I'd never have to address what those voices might say. Today I actually feel relieved to have heard them.

But this isn't a confessional. The only way you can forgive yourself is by staying sober. The same is true for making amends. This is not a unique story.

When and why did I decide enough was enough? That's easy. We were staying with our fun-loving Australian cousins in Cornwall. Their social drinking allowed me to normalise my own. I always found an excuse to socialise at the houses of people I knew to be big social drinkers – to be able to do it legitimately. My husband is not teetotal but equally not a person who needs a drink to enjoy life. I can only guess how boring he found these evenings with me. He must have felt he was there alone, no doubt preparing for every one in the knowledge it would end with him taking home an undignified mess. Actually, it must have been worse than this. You get used to manhandling a drunk into a car at the end of the night. The stress comes from the psychological dread and anticipation of what the evening ahead might hold. Knowing you will have to sit by and watch as someone you love gradually unravels and embarrasses herself and you have to defend her to others and yourself. Sten never tried to stop me but I think his strategy was to pray I'd hit rock bottom and come up from there. He had the wisdom to know it was something I'd have to do alone.

Sten and I were staying in a small coach-house attached to the main building. Everyone was pissed, but evidently not as much as I was. We walked back to our rooms in the dark and somewhere along that path I blacked out and fell. The next thing I knew I was being helped up by my brother-in-law and Sten and carried into our bedroom. It was only when I started to undress that I realised I'd wet myself. Wetting yourself without realising is a fairly degrading wake-up call.

It was the perfect storm. In the past I'd made a habit of trying to excuse my behaviour but the only person these excuses convinced was me. The physicality of this particular situation was hard to swerve. To not be able to remember or recount what's just happened to you is a pretty eye-opening predicament to find yourself in. I was mortified but felt worse for Sten, who was humiliated in front of his brother. It was an undeniable state of affairs. I was a fucking drunk. I had also fractured two ribs.

The morning after I got on my knees by the side of the

bed as I had done as a child and put my hands together and prayed for help to stop. I was exhausted from the lies and deceit that were required to keep this charade going. I went into the kitchen and called Sten and the kids together and told them that things were out of control. That I knew I needed help. I asked each of them how it was affecting them. My two eldest children brushed it off as 'a bit embarrassing'. Cece went very quiet, but finally said 'You do need help, Mum.' Sten said nothing at all. I knew he must be angry and scared and even now I am too afraid to ask how he felt for fear of bringing it all back.

That day I called John Barrett, a friend in America. I knew he knew of a recovering alcoholic in Brighton and, as soon as I got back to Sussex, I went to see her and she took me to my first meeting. I was now on the start of a long journey to get sober, regain some dignity and make amends to my family.

What I feel now, with some distance, is not humiliation but shame. These two are quite different. I will never get over what I put my children through. Especially Cece. Especially after I'd been through the same myself with my mother. It was inexcusable but I was as helpless as her. I don't know if my mother's drinking had any bearing on my own and feel reluctant to lay any responsibility at her door. I don't blame her. She couldn't help it. But I do think that even though I hated her drinking as a child, I was also used to it. To having it in my home. To seeing my own mother fall over; lose control; try to kill herself. There was a level on which it was normal for me. It was not such a huge jump to make. I thought I'd do it 'better'. That it wouldn't be the same for me – but of course it was; an alcoholic is an alcoholic. There is no such thing as a special one.

There's an Old Joke . . .

Two men are walking through the jungle when they see a tiger in the distance. The first guy panics and starts running. The second crouches down, calmly takes a pair of trainers from his bag and casually starts putting them on. 'What the hell are you doing?!' says the first guy. 'You'll never outrun a fucking tiger!' 'I don't have to,' says the second guy. 'I just need to outrun you.' Whenever I think about Oprah Winfrey this is the joke that comes to mind. In the five times Trinny and I worked together on her show, it was always me Oprah sat next to because it looked more flattering that way. I didn't need to be fatter than Oprah, I just needed to be fatter than Trinny. Which I always, always was. I think she may have been a bit frightened by Trinny too; even though she doesn't mean it, Trinny's clipped tones can make even the most powerful, self-assured person feel like she's telling them off. Trinny, on the other hand, always thought Oprah had a little schoolgirl-crush on me but I still think it was the weight thing that really drove the seating plan.

I never had the luxury of a buffer to sit in between Trinny and me. I was always just 'fatter than Trinny' and this was typically abbreviated further by the tabloid press to simply 'the fat one'. In real life, one of the most common comments I get is something along the lines of 'You're not as fat as I thought you'd be', which manages to be both complimentary and offensive at the same time, but I'm OK with that. I'm 5'8" and just shy of eleven stone. At sixty I've been through enough iterations of myself to feel this is a pretty good shape to be in. The villain of the piece is, and always was, my boobs. Conservatively, I'd say each one weighs more than my head. I'm a 36G and require reinforced scaffolding at all times. Including in bed. Any woman with huge boobs will tell you they're a responsibility and mine have gained momentum with age. I've never been the kind of girl who could look simply sporty or lithe because they were always there whispering '*sex*' to the casual observer. I didn't tell them to say that, but they have a mind of their own and I am unable to control the statements they make about themselves.

The beautiful girl with the fat friend is a textbook set-up – even if the first girl is not that beautiful and the second not that fat. Comparisons will always exist: it just depends on the context. For the majority of my working life, I was the fat friend. I made a career as the dumpy one standing next to the rangy, languid-limbed Trinny. To sweeten the pill, I hung on to the fact she had short legs. Ironically she'd always say 'People fancy you and not me,' and, as beautiful as she was, I think she may have been right. I'm slightly grubby so men could picture throwing me in the hay and having their way with me. Giving me a good hiding. I don't think they felt that way about Trinny. She's more the girl you'd take to meet your parents. I'd be the sort they'd want waiting outside the bedroom window on the flat roof as a 'digestif'. I might have looked that way but, ironically, my nickname for years was Concrete Knickers. In the event, I didn't even live up to the hype.

Being a young woman is an odd state to be in. Going out into the world is like walking onto the decks of a pinball table and hoping the person in charge of the levers is a sluggish ten-year-old boy rather than Roger Daltrey. Buffeted from every angle, you just have to cross your fingers you'll make it to the other side without going down one of the holes.

As a young woman I took my youthful state entirely for granted. I wouldn't even describe it as confidence, more the absence of awareness. In my early twenties I'd been introduced to the son of a Greek shipping magnate (remember . . . the Greek coke addict).* He was 5'5" in his stockinged feet and, objectively, madly in love with me. 'Susannah, your skin is like porcelain,' was his constant, lisping refrain. I mention this not out of vanity but precisely because I set no store by it at the time. It wasn't that I thought this sort of thing would go on for ever – I never thought about it at all. At my age I'd be quite glad of someone bothering me with their unprompted compliments, but in my twenties it was more like an irritation; a fly that kept reappearing over the afternoon cakes and jam to be swatted away with my prep book. The arrogance of youth can be really quite mind-blowing but it's also what propels young people forward, giving them enough blind courage to go out into a world that would otherwise be overwhelming. If you're going to step into the abyss, you might as well do it with confidence.

Possibly the best example of my youthful conceit was the night I turned down Mario Testino's offer to take my

* He later married Daphne Guinness, so I imagine he'd sorted himself out by that point.

engagement photos. My lack of humility is still something that haunts me now. I could blame it on youth, but truthfully it is one of the few times in my life I've behaved arrogantly. I was very comfortable with the assembled group and Testino was a new interloper. I'm sorry to say, but I'd had too much to drink and, just like Teddy Robinson, was a little bit ex-and-shoff.*

Eventually, moments like this stopped happening. Let's face it, no matter who or how lovely you are in your youth, no one ever stays 'that girl' for ever. If you're lucky, you get better with age but youth is ephemeral. The make-up goes on, an awareness comes over you and, in a puff of smoke, it's gone. You can never get it back.

That girl is still in there somewhere, I think, but now she's hidden under a 7-tog layer of quilting. People talk about middle-age spread as if it's the second coming – it will definitely come to pass but you're never entirely sure when. I secretly thought of it as something that only affected lazy women or ones who purposely let themselves go to avoid their husband's sexual advances. My late forties, however, were like an initiation to a middle-aged version of Fight Club – all sorts of horrible dark secrets were revealed to me. The day my pubic hair was obscured by my stomach was the day I knew we were approaching the point of no return. I'd reconciled myself to a muffin top some years before but I drew the line at a FUPA.

The writing was very definitely on the wall:

Flagging career – tick.

* Excited and showing off.

313

Back fat – tick.

Stomach I could cradle like a baby while watching TV – tick.

When the call came from Sport Relief, I answered on the first ring.

I wish I could tell you I went into Sport Relief with honourable intentions but my decision was motivated entirely by vanity. It was 2017 and not long before I'd had a series of press photos taken. Whilst I'd been very happy with my look at the time, the prints revealed a tired, middle-aged woman hiding in the body of a sixty-five-year-old sedentary office worker. If you've ever tried to roll up a sleeping bag and secure it with a piece of string you'll know what I looked like in a belt.

I had no idea things had reached this point. It was as if my mind and body colluded behind my back to present me with a horrible fait accompli. *'Ta-dah!!! You're two stone overweight.'* We'd arrived at Defcon 1 without my having noticed we'd missed the slip roads for levels 5, 4, 3 and 2. In my defence, it had happened incrementally. It began with the digging-in-of-the-jeans-waistband phase before I eventually relented and moved into elasticated items where possible. From there it was a seamless transition into prairie dresses which, on reflection, was a dreadful schoolboy error. Even when I turned to the side, my width was still broader than my front view had been five years earlier. It didn't help that my head – already quite small in comparison to my body – had stayed the same size while my torso had scaled up to twice its original volume. A pigeon roosting on top of a bell tent would be the most accurate comparison.

I'd stopped drinking a few years earlier but reallocated that calorie allowance into the chocolate column. I'd slipped into the demographic stationers target with cards that say things like 'Who says I don't have a balanced diet?! I have just as much wine as I do chocolate!' The portmanteau 'chocoholic' seems to be the backbone of at least 50 per cent of greetings cards sold to women and around 70 per cent of those bought by men who want to make a joke about their wives' weight without confronting them head on. It's a marketing-friendly, catch-all slur that allows manufacturers to target the broadest possible audience with the least amount of thought. I imagine the marketing man who invented the word got a small, celebratory erection and, no doubt, a promotion.

For the first time in my life I was living up to my moniker 'the fat one' and knew I needed to do something about it. This was a Code Red situation that required an urgent and drastic response.

There's not much I can tell you about the altruistic aspects of Sport Aid that haven't already been said so I'll just jump straight to the nitty-gritty. We started at a very low bar with the producers' suggestion our section be called 'From Fat to Fit'. This went down well with no one and in the end they modified it to 'Famously Unfit' as a small sop to our egos. Miles Jupp, Les Dennis, Tameka Empson and I were apparently going to 'embark on a muscle-grinding mission to regain fitness while trying to inspire the British public to do the same'. A cursory glance round the room at our first meeting at a leisure centre in Stratford was enough to convince me this was an incredibly ambitious statement. We were a shoddy, mismatched bunch with nothing to mark us out as athletes or indeed a team. Les has the overall look and feel of a man recovering from a heart attack and Miles that of a public-school boy who's just emerged from the woods after a surreptitious fag during a cross-country run. At face-value Tameka seemed to hold more promise but after she cried throughout our initial go at the assault course and revealed she had a genuine phobia of mud, I realised this was nothing more than a pipe dream. I wasn't convinced we'd be inspiring anyone.

I'd never previously met any of my teammates but was relieved to find none of them were wankers. That didn't mitigate the fact I was determined to beat them all.* This was a brutal exposition of just how competitive I really am but, to their credit, they each managed to put my bare-faced ambition aside for the greater good of the team and we began a friendship under the WhatsApp group heading Guff Ties.

Before embarking on the event, I'd enlisted the help of ex-SAS Captain Name-Must-Be-Redacted-For-Reasons-of-National-Security, who advised me to face my fears head on with the mantra 'Bring it on!' Every time you're confronted with something you don't think you can handle, rather than turn and try to outrun it, ask the bastard for more. In order to get into the right mind-set for this, he advised me to think of someone famously angry as a model for my rage – 'like Zeus or Ross Kemp'. I didn't need to look far. My old agent Michael Foster was the most incensed man I knew.

* I beat them all by twenty minutes.

When Trinny and I landed *What Not to Wear* in 1992 we'd also bagged Michael. Hugh Grant had recommended him with the caveat 'He probably won't take you.' HG, however, had underestimated the buying power of women. With Trinny and me he knew he had not just one golden goose in his bag, but two.

Michael Foster was an agent with the reputation of being absolutely ruthless; a thoroughbred, supersonic, intergalactic cunt. Not to his clients – who all worshipped him – but anyone they worked for or with was fair game. If he could catch it, he'd kill it. It is a measure of his cuntishness that this is not even something he'd mind my saying. He took wholesale

The other *dynamic* duo.

ownership of it, wearing it like a more morally sensitive person might a CND button badge. Even standing on the sidelines of one of his outbursts was a stressful experience and something I witnessed on more than one occasion. Most memorable was the day Trinny and I arrived on his birthday to present him with a cake.

We cupped the candles protectively as we hovered outside his door, assured by Sweet Pea, his long-suffering secretary, that he was just finishing up a call. We waited excitedly for our moment. He was going to love this. Chocolate ganache was his favourite. We'd got extra cream. From inside his office we heard his voice get gradually louder. One of the candles puttered out and had to be relit from its neighbour. The 'conversation' turned fairly quickly into an all-out rant. Wax was beginning to drip down onto the chocolate. It would seem someone had done something they shouldn't have and Michael was making it abundantly clear what he thought about this situation. Evidently the loudness of his voice alone wasn't working, though, and he introduced an audible-from-where-we-were-standing-outside-the-closed-door smashing of the finger onto the desk to reinforce his point. He combined this with an unfettered screaming of insults. So forceful was the jabbing he didn't realise – or didn't care – that the finger was now broken. He carried on regardless. All that mattered was the situation was now resolved and it was extremely unlikely whoever it was who'd done it would ever be doing something like that again. All the candles were now wilted stumps, their wax obscuring our heartfelt 'Fearsome, Fabulous & Fifty' iced onto the cake's smooth, mirrored surface. I was beginning to feel decidedly uncomfortable and sensed our surprise had lost something of its potential magic. Michael, however, was utterly unfazed by the episode and ushered us into his office like two girl scouts selling cookies – as if butter wouldn't melt in his mouth. This was the moment I realised he would move heaven and earth for those he represented but woe betide anyone who found themselves on the receiving end of his wrath.

One of Michael's greatest assets was that, like Thatcher, he was not afraid to be disliked and he became hugely powerful for it. He was a straight-talker who shot from the hip – although, at 5'5", that meant his arrows only reached the shins of his adversaries. Known to me as LJ – or Little Jew – and by others as the Tripod (for reasons best known to his lovers and his tailor), Michael was a fusion of Napoleon and Lew Grade with a touch of Dirk Diggler on the side. He'd learned the ropes in the US from legendary Hollywood agent Ed Limato at CAA. Ed's lack of empathy extended to the naming protocol used for his assistants, known to him simply as 1, 2, 3 and 4. Under Ed's tutelage, Michael became a businessman, negotiator and, crucially, a salesman. For many, his combative approach was extremely unpalatable. When you walked into his office you certainly had to keep a firm hold of your bowels.

To the unassuming observer, he looked like a veteran of the rag trade, as if he'd be at home with a tape measure draped around his shoulders. He had a nose for the really fine things in life – wine, cigars, clients – though never anything to excess; he was too much of a control freak for that. Every time he negotiated a deal for Trinny and me, we bought him a new tailor-made Richard James suit to add to his wardrobe. If Michael ever had a moment of self-doubt, I never saw it in the twenty years we worked together. He was the most supremely confident human being I've ever come across. And I include Janet Street-Porter in this statement. But it was rage that powered his engine and he was full to the brim with it. While I had enjoyed every moment of the ride, I was relieved when his adrenalin and anger finally meant he burned himself out and we could just be friends. He remains a trusted advisor and one of my nearest and dearest.

As with so many big, powerful figures I've encountered in my life, Michael was as charismatic and intoxicating as he was frightening. The awe-inspiring drive he possessed meant that seeing him in action was like watching a fireball tear through a street of wooden houses. You either followed in his wake or got out of his way. You knew you had to be either with him or against him. There were no grey areas with Michael, which could make dealing with him impossible for people just trying to do their jobs and speak their minds. There's no question he made things happen but you either made the decision you weren't happy with his MO or held on for dear life. He operated in his own microclimate. For him to succeed now – in a way that would be deemed acceptable – would mean a clipping of his wings, and I imagine he'd rather die than be stifled in that way. Instead he's become a silent partner in many of his old clients' careers – mine included. He can say and do whatever he pleases and you can either take it or leave it. I still choose Michael every time.

Fast forward ten years and his rage has now dissipated, leaving what is a very kind, philanthropic gentleman, but it was the '90s version of Michael I used to inspire me in my hour of need.

A Little Sporting Relief

Our digs for the Tough Guy endurance challenge were the 2.5-star Norwich Travelodge, where we rubbed shoulders with a swathe of athletic Norwegians who'd also come to compete. On the morning of the race they arrived bare-chested, banging drums in the spirit of their Viking forefathers. Add to that a higher than average incidence of dreadlocks and dogs on strings, and the overall effect was how I imagined Greenham Common must have been in the 1980s. The Vikings must have assumed we were family members come to egg on our loved ones rather than contestants, given our combined list of comorbidities, which ranged from red-flag levels of blood sugar to semi-functional hip flexors. Ours was very much the *Dad's Army* team of this particular equation. Nevertheless, we walked the course like everyone else to prepare ourselves mentally for the task ahead. Tameka cried (again) throughout, while Miles and Les were determined but also, I thought, completely deluded.

The start of the race was nothing less than terrifying. There were so many people, and at such a high level of fitness, it was genuinely overwhelming. Our race numbers were daubed across our foreheads in permanent marker like cattle heading for the slaughter – which is a very accurate appraisal of how the whole thing felt. But then something kicked in. I felt invincible. Like a warrior. Anyone who's run a marathon will tell you you push past the pain and embrace it to propel yourself forward. The adrenalin rush is all-encompassing and I'm sure the reason why so many people become addicted to extreme sports. Wild, cold-water swimming is the same. The feeling of invincibility it brings is intoxicating and something we struggle to find in the relative ease of modern living. In the twenty-first century, certainly in the developed world, we are presented with very few natural opportunities to get this kind of high. Hence the creation of manufactured scenarios such as Tough Guy or Ayahuasca retreats. One of the greatest lessons I took from the experience was that your ability to complete the course is in no small part down to strength of mind, although I never tired of telling my husband I was physically fitter than him for the first time in my life.

I'm not sure if our part of the show was even watched by anyone else and, if it were, whether it motivated them but, to my great surprise, it had inspired me and this was something of a turning point.

Eva Peron's Dead Body

Three years after Eva Peron's death her embalmed corpse was stolen in the middle of the night by the Argentinian military and went missing for over twenty years. There are multiple accounts of what happened to it on its grand tour, ranging from a stint in the back of a bakery van to plain old necrophilia.* In any event, when she finally turned up again she was in chronic need of a blow-dry, and missing a finger; things had evidently got a bit Hunter S. Thompson somewhere along the way. Sadly, there is no surviving footage of this jaunt so our imaginations must fill in the gaps. If, however, you'd care to watch my opening number in the 2018 season of *Strictly Come Dancing*, you will see a fairly close approximation of what I think she must have looked like five or ten years into her adventure.

I already knew *Strictly*'s 'celebrity coordinator' Stefania Aleksander when she floated the idea of my going on the show after we'd worked together on another project. My first reaction was a hard no. *Strictly* was not something on my radar. Ironically, I'd always loved Hollywood for its fantastic choreography – Cyd Charisse, Fred and Ginger, Gene Kelly – but I'd not really realised that this is what I would be getting with *Strictly*. I just thought it was another reality TV show. Coinciding as it did with our Saturday night family dinners, I had never watched an episode – a fact I would quickly come to regret.

The potential traumas of *I'm a Celebrity* are well known; will you or will you not be able to eat an animal penis without being sick in a bin is the question anyone considering participating must ultimately ask themselves. Having now done both, I can say with confidence that the fears – real and perceived – of the jungle pale in comparison with the terrors of *Strictly*.

---

* Interestingly, when questioned about the motivation for their attraction, 5 per cent of necrophiliacs cited 'not interested in conversation' as their primary driver.

Though I've never considered myself to be a good dancer I do have a recurring dream in which I am an absolutely *outstanding* one. It's so vivid I'd never been quite sure the incident hadn't happened sometime in the past and I'd just been too drunk to remember. Watching the first thirty seconds of myself in the couples dance was enough to confirm once and for all it absolutely had not. I should have known better. Thirteen years earlier, when Elton and David got engaged, Elizabeth Hurley came up with the brainwave she and I should choreograph a dance to 'West End Girls' to perform at their stag night. I was hesitant but she was brimming with confidence. 'I'll be the Fosse to your Minnelli,' she said – or words to that effect. I imagined myself in a bowler hat and short shorts. My bottom has always been my strong point. I was in. We rehearsed for what seemed like weeks at her offices in Chelsea. The secrecy was intoxicating. I daydreamed about our surprise entrance onto the stage to the opening violins; laughter would turn to cheers as the high-hat built to the bassline; the crowd oohing and ahhing as we hooked our stockinged legs around our bentwood chairs and tipped our hats over our kohl-rimmed eyes. Kiki Dee would start the wolf whistles and Tim Rice would probably throw some pants onto the stage. In my mind things were progressing very nicely until Elizabeth broke the news that I was going to be 'let go'. I was being asked to leave the band on account of creative differences. I later learned these differences were that she could dance and I could not. This was a red flag and one I should have recalled before agreeing to dance in front of a possible 13 million people.

Anton

When it came to partners, I didn't realise it at the time but I struck gold. Anton Du Beke. The consummate professional and a true gentleman, he put me instantly at ease. He was generous, warm and supportive in the face of my obvious nervousness. Buoyed by his signature enthusiasm, my nerves turned slowly to confidence and my reticence faded away. He would have made a wonderful double-glazing salesman because by close of play, I'd bought into the whole thing. I even suggested we do a showy end; something with a bit of pizazz. 'Why not spin me on the floor,' I suggested, 'to finish the whole thing off?' By now the adrenalin was coursing through me and my inhibitions were left crumpled in a bag under my new leotard. I felt like the Girl from Ipanema. As I left the dance studio and got the train home that evening I couldn't switch off. I began fantasising about an inaugural performance in which I combined the surprise wow of Susan Boyle with the raw sexuality of Jennifer Beals. Audiences, I believed, would be discussing my innate rhythm on daytime television for weeks to come.

The first time my feet touched the ballroom floor was on the day of the live rehearsal. In my high heels and leggings I looked like a middle-aged woman arriving for a keep-fit class but I felt like a cast member from *Fame*. This was *Strictly Come* Fucking *Dancing* and I was about to make my debut.

Anton and I had been training three to four hours a day, so I breezed in, a whiff of smugness trailing in my wake. I always feel better when I know there's someone worse than me in any given situation, and on this occasion I believed that person to be Katie Piper. She was absolutely lovely but cripplingly nervous. So far so good. I covertly did the rounds, sizing up the competition. Faye Tozer was a potential obstacle. Skill-wise I knew she'd have me over a barrel – she'd spent most of the '90s in a wraparound cardigan – but also rationalised that *What Not to Wear* would trump *Steps* amongst menopausal voters. Another point to me. Joe Sugg had only ever listened to grime and garage, and Sean Walsh looked like a plodder – no threat from that direction. I was rapidly gaining momentum. When Ashley Roberts told me they were regularly clocking up fourteen hours a day in rehearsal I felt the first thread of the tapestry I'd woven come loose. A swift straw poll confirmed that, even taking my low numbers into account, the daily hourly average was well over ten. It was only a matter of time before things began to unravel.

Anton says he knows very quickly whether someone will be able to dance, and with me this point was 'The moment we started moving.' To his credit he managed to keep this to himself until after I'd left the show. There was no sense in us both being awake all night.

We changed together and were dressed and ready five hours before showtime. I was already exhausted. Anton's trousers were so tight I expected he'd either have to go commando or don a thong but, ever the best and most expensively dressed gentleman, his clothes whoring included a fine pair of Smedley jockey shorts. Once sewn into our costumes he said I looked 'marvellous' and I said he looked 'ridiculous' as we posed together in the mirror. One of Anton's greatest gifts is the ability to laugh heartily at himself.

*

To really pull off Latin American choreography, it comes down to sex and the ability to exude it in high volumes. It's all about heat, passion, seduction and joy. While I don't consider myself to be uptight in everyday life, the dawning of how ill-prepared we clearly were had knocked me off my perch. I was also about twice the size and age of every other woman there and was beginning to feel positively frigid – and that, let me tell you, is no way to embark on ninety seconds of rhythmic gyration.

I want you now to think of the most humiliating thing that could possibly happen to you and then imagine it happens live, in front of 10 million people. To put that into perspective, that's the population of Azerbaijan. Five million more than Norway, if we're restricting ourselves to Continental Europe.

The playback of our inaugural dance shows a man in fringed trousers lobbing an orange sack of potatoes across a

Eva and Anton.

barn floor. Our attempts at a samba roll are more 'man wind-ing a stiff clock' than 'about to seduce a lover'. As a viewer you'd be forgiven for thinking the worst aspect of all this was my performance. As the protagonist, I can tell you that was just the tip of a really large, horrifying iceberg. On one level, it's not quite as bad as it seemed in real time. On another, deeper, psychological note, it's much, much worse. The indignity of it all is breathtaking. If we're really going to start laying souls bare, the crux of my shame is that, until the first live rehearsal, I had considered myself to be doing rather well. Let's not understate things; I genuinely believed I might win. When friends had excitedly called to catch up on the gossip I'd tell them it was going great; 'I can really do this!' I'd say, 'I'm looking forward to opening night.' I'd even told my husband, 'I really think I've found something I'm good at.' It is unlikely there will ever be a time I can say that out loud without feeling crippled with embarrassment. Even writing it down sends a small shudder down my spine. I can honestly say my cameo on the show was one of the lowest, most shame-filled moments of my life, and, let's not forget, I was rejected by Dolph Lundgren.

There's a breathless moment at the end of every dance when the dancers are expected to hold for applause. When you know the performance you've just delivered is suffi-ciently dire, the last thing you want to do is stand, unoccupied, holding a pose while the audience is obliged to clap. The anxiety in that moment is enough to make those four or five seconds feel like *just* enough time for your entire life to flash before you. As Anton and I came to our moment, there was of course applause, but it was sympathetic rather than jubilant. There is an unspoken ballroom etiquette that says no matter how woeful the performance, it is your duty to support the dancers. Alongside *Gardeners' Question Time*, *Strictly* is one of the last remaining bastions of good manners. This is why they're obliged to have a baddie on the judging panel so that they can say what the audience will not.

And so, this final indignity was a close-up of my face and a mouth full of what, inexplicably, looked like black teeth, which the cameras lingered on quite a bit longer than necessary. Craig Revel Horwood lovingly tried to rescue the situation afterwards, telling me that by getting such low marks we'd had the biggest favour handed to us. 'You'll get the sympathy vote,' he said. Claudia told me not to worry, Anton's popularity would keep me safe, like a force field. I felt a little encouraged by all this but in the end it gave me false hope. If you're a passenger in the Popemobile it's very unlikely you *will* be assassinated but ultimately it *could* happen. And it very quickly did. We surpassed ourselves the following week with lower marks than we'd garnered in the first. Even my most supportive friends could not see a way to spin things.

After this, there was no getting the cat back into the bag. I was dreadful. Anton had known it for some time and now so did I, but the show, as they never tire of saying, must go on. Fortunately, my 'emergencies-only' London doctor is the type who can still be persuaded to prescribe the sorts of medicine that were largely outlawed in the 1970s, albeit reluctantly. Xanax in hand, I felt marginally better able to face the music.

Strictly selects its celebrities from people who can perform.

Everyone is well versed in the art of entertainment. Politicians, sports personalities, presenters, actors – they're all able to play to an audience and there is a very good reason they are selected: live television is terrifying.

I've often wondered why people sentenced to death never just made a break for it as they're led up the hangman's steps. Why walk dutifully to the chopping block and obligingly place your head right where the axe will fall? Why not take your chances trying to escape even if that means being shot in the back with an arrow? Statistically there must be a sliver of a chance you'd be the one that gets away. Standing in the wings waiting to descend the *Strictly* staircase, it certainly felt very much like lining up for our own crucifixion – 'Out of the door. Line on the left. One cross each.' I knew I was preparing for my own, slow death, and yet I willingly walked to the scaffold. We all did. Like lemmings on the brink of the cliff we jumped into the abyss. If you'd promised a friend you'd kill yourself, but in the moment changed your mind, I think it unlikely you'd go ahead purely on the basis that you 'didn't want to let anyone down'. Yet that is the situation we found ourselves in. United by fear, we trod the path to our inevitable deaths with leaden feet. The only exception to all this was Graeme Swann, who is the human equivalent of a Teflon pan and the only person I've ever met with fewer inhibitions than me. Much of his backstage time was spent socialising in his standard-issue spray-tan paper pants. He was gloriously unburdened by these stresses.

There is a body of kind, wonderful, loyal middle-aged women who I know supported me – 'There but for the grace of God' and all that – but even they were not enough to hold back the tide of reality. Under the listing for Anton Du Beke, Wikipedia catalogues a long line of 'duds' he's been obliged to partner over the years. When it comes to me, they really don't sugarcoat the pill. 'In 2018 Anton was partnered with Fashion Journalist Susannah Constantine. They finished last (the first time Du Beke had ever done this) with an average of 12.00 (Du Beke's lowest).' We all have issues that wake us in the night; things we must reconcile with if we are to move on unfettered by bitterness or fear. Mine is that Ann Widdecombe got to week ten. Let that sink in. I have had to.

There were good and bad dancers in my cohort – Ashley and Faye were notably outstanding and Joe and Stacey's transformations were brilliant to watch. What they all brought to the table – that I did not – was a sense of humour. The competitor in me refused to approach it with anything other than winning in mind and therein lay the problem. Had I bothered to watch a series beforehand I'd have seen *Strictly* is as much about camaraderie and entertainment as it is about dancing. I didn't realise there was room for another type of person in the show – the clown. I never mind making a fool of myself so why I didn't grab this by the horns I don't know. I can only think it was because if I can't be the best, I fall apart. Much of the joy of *Strictly* is learning to let yourself go and understanding someone will be there to catch you. It's a journey, and one I've watched religiously ever since. I, however, didn't even get on the train. Women all over the UK would have sold a child for the chance to partner with Anton and I'm so sad to have wasted it.

After the first show my confidence had turned back to nerves, segued immediately into stress, before graduating to outright panic and for some reason I felt I had to hide this from everyone – including Anton. We'd made such a connection but now I had to put on a performance – even around him – which was very isolating. I'd loved being myself and, ironically, felt completely relaxed when we were dancing.

Katie Piper turned out *not* to be the person worse than everyone else; that was me. If I can salvage the smallest morsel of dignity from the ashes, at least I can say my patent lack of flair must have provided some comfort to the rest of my cohort as they lay in their beds at night rhythmically chanting, 'I'm not as bad as Susannah, I'm not as bad as Susannah . . .'

In the end, as Anton very graciously put it, 'We lunched better than we danced so we decided to focus on lunch.' When you get to see the show from the vantage point I had, you realise *Strictly* is the nearest thing we have to the old Hollywood studio system in which hordes of creative people get to showcase their talents. Wardrobe, make-up, choreography, set design, props – the list goes on. From the ladies who sew you into your costume to the people who source everything from umbrellas to candy canes for Musical Week, *Strictly* is its own living, breathing ecosystem. Like a garden lying fallow for the winter, once a year the water system springs on and the whole thing comes back to life and it's wonderful to see. I watch *Strictly* every year now. I just wish I'd started earlier so I knew the opportunity I was being given.

The Ostrich

If you've ever had a particularly intense, realistic dream, it's not uncommon to wake feeling you could relay it to someone in minute detail, only to find that when you try to articulate it, the words fall away. There are gaps in your story that suddenly make no sense. This is how I feel about trying to piece together the path towards my own alcoholism as it wound around my mother and father and the environment in which I grew up. I don't have a full story, I cannot fill in the gaps, but I feel like I'm getting towards something like a convincing storyline.

My descent into the disease was a gradual one. When we moved out of London and bought Dencombe, it was everything I'd ever wanted but I still felt as if I'd lost something. When I confided in Jason he told me, 'You've lost your dream. You've got to find a new one.' It was true. I had nothing more to work for. Like my mother, I needed purpose. For a time, this lack of a goal created a void I slowly filled with white wine.

While I believed myself to be managing my alcoholism in a way that had little effect on my children, I was kidding myself it was only in evidence when I was actually drunk. The wider effects of alcoholism stretch beyond the hours you are drinking. There's the constant anxiety of hiding a secret; the stress of maintaining a career and a marriage. It was my childhood all over again. Children can sniff these things out – they see right into your solar plexus. Mine may not remember seeing these things in me – they may not even have realised that's what they were looking at – but to live around a person who is depressed or anxious is stressful and confusing. It damages the trust between you and your sense of security. I know this to be true because it's how I felt around my own mother.

In trying to untangle my past I am left with a complicated mixture of feelings about how well I've succeeded in my own attempts at marriage and motherhood. There has never been a question mark over the way I feel about my children. My world revolves around them. But when I was drinking I created a situation similar to the one I'd experienced as a child myself. I was not wholly emotionally available to them (or my husband) even though they were right under my nose. I don't have an excuse for this or even a satisfactory answer as to why I let it happen. I don't believe I will ever reconcile myself to what I did. All I can do now is make amends by staying sober.

Where I differed from my parents is that when I wasn't drinking my children were in no doubt about what they meant to me. I believe that the grounding we had as a family went some way to minimising the effects of my drinking. I hope my children might look back at me with more sympathy than I did my own mother and see me for what I was: a woman who needed help. At least I can say I owned it and went on to do something about it instead of letting it fester and poison our family from within. I didn't brush it under the carpet or deny it. Thank goodness that's not the way we deal with things in *my* family.

An Education

An education is a broad thing to define. I suppose it's designed to prepare you for life, or at least the life you think you're likely to lead. My expensive but threadbare academic instruction was no accident. It was a strategic part of the plan. I'd never ever had a conversation about my career or financial future with my parents; I didn't need to. I was training to be a wife, no more, no less. To marry and to marry well would bring quality of life and the luxury not to work – or so I was told. I wouldn't need an academic education for that.

I wasn't a debutante or presented at court, but I still went to the right kinds of parties with the right kinds of people because those were the places, it was hoped, I'd find a husband. It was an impossibly old-fashioned set-up, not far from the strategic, arranged marriages of the past. As girls we were expected to stay in our lane and were promised we'd be rewarded if we did. But what would a 'good' marriage bring us? Money? A title? A nice house? Yes, all of that potentially but no real autonomy. What I now realise is, there were serious consequences to a comfortable life. The Duchess and my mother showed me this. They had the financial freedom to enjoy their lives without work but this came at a price and that price was their independence. When my mother and father watched television, it was his programmes they watched. When there were decisions to be made about their children's upbringing, it was my father who'd make them. Even the etiquette around what my mother and her friends wore was subliminally dictated by their husbands. And this is a very glib summary of what were, at times, quite dangerously suffocating relationships. The wives I knew were an extension of their husbands. My mother lived bang in the centre of a patriarchy with little hope of ever escaping, and I was involuntarily set on the same path. Was it honestly something I wanted? While I would never suggest these women endured any real hardship, theirs were shockingly empty lives. A depressing waste. Why was so little made of so much? It was a pattern repeated over and over in the circles I mixed in. Women were so often left to rot away, unheard, unused and unhappy; trapped inside the traditions and social mores of their class. There was nothing in any of the marriages I'd seen that I wanted for myself. There was a high price for everything those women had, and it was not one I was prepared to pay.

But What Next?

For someone who'd been getting ready for absolutely nothing else, at thirty-two I married relatively late. When it finally happened, my greatest feeling was one of relief. *Thank God*, I thought, *I'm free*. The weight of expectation had been lifted. For the first time in my life I was able to think about something other than my fucking wedding. To think about what I wanted out of life. What I was capable of. But what *was* that?

To my surprise I found out marriage wasn't all about laying the table. Being a wife didn't just mean making dinners and putting the washing on. Successful marriage was about strategy and compromise; identifying your strengths and weaknesses and those of your partner and marrying these up to best effect. It was about anticipating the needs of others and balancing them with your own. About learning how to accommodate a broad spectrum of opinions. I had no blueprint for a marriage like this. Sten and I would just have to wing it. Like everyone else, we'd have to learn as we went. Were we ready? Of course not. Who is? Training for marriage is done exclusively on the job.

The night after our wedding I felt like Sten and I had accidentally veered onto the motorway without either of us ever having had a driving lesson. The plates were off. No dual control. No pedantic instructor making sure no one pulled into a blocked box junction. It was terrifying. It was all suddenly very real. Just the two of us. Alone at home. Together for ever. I panicked and began to second guess my new husband. He seemed cold and distant, which I interpreted as him thinking he'd made a mistake. That he had regrets. Personally I had none but was scared I'd pushed him too far. I did what I always did when I was frightened and retreated into my shell. For six months we went through the motions of being married. We talked and had sex and steak and chips for dinner, but there was absolutely no emotional connection between us. In all the years thinking about this day, I'd never expected to feel so alone. I'd bulldozed my way into the marriage despite the reservations of friends and family, and consequently didn't feel there was anyone I could turn to for reassurance. Then one morning, completely out of the blue, we both woke at dawn. I have no idea where it came from but, as we lay silently next to one another, I turned to Sten and said 'We're going to be OK,' and the veil lifted between us. I meant it. I was completely confident we would be. The feeling was profound. There was a palpable shift in the dynamic. There was no need to discuss it further.

I'm not sure Sten actually played any part in this existential crisis. I projected my insecurities onto him. It was another example of my filling in the gaps with my own convoluted conclusions. My guilt at having 'trapped' him made me interpret any silence between us as my fault. I was dealing with my husband like I'd dealt with my father when I thought he was cross with me. I panicked and shut down, not wanting to be told off. But Sten was not my father. He was – and is – a very different kind of man. He wasn't asking me to shoulder our marriage alone. He wasn't cross. Why would he be? I'd hurried him along a little too fast for his liking but he was no fool. He didn't agree to marry me because he was afraid to say no. He was an adult. And an independent one. It was me who was still behaving like a child. Me who wasn't ready to grow up. My marriage was the first truly adult situation I'd ever been in

The greatest of Danes.

338

and it was a huge shock to the system. I'd also brought my own emotional baggage to the table and I hadn't travelled light. Now I needed to unpack it and start all over again. Thankfully, Sten proved the perfect person to help me.

The Wrong Kind of Training

It gradually became clear that, while I'd trained all my life to be a wife, what I really wanted to be was my own woman. Fortunately, that's what Sten wanted too and he made it quite clear he had no intention of paying for everything anyway so I had no choice but to get on with it.

It turned out I was ready for much more than I'd realised; it was just that the strengths I had were undervalued by the world I grew up in. I'd wasted so many years hanging around waiting for someone to rescue me, I didn't realise I could do the job just as well myself. It might be a truth universally acknowledged that a man in possession of a good fortune will be in want of a wife, but I was coming to see that what that woman wanted was just as important.

My father had spent a lifetime trying to paper over his mercantile roots rather than seeing there might be merit in conveying such skills to us, his female children. What was so attractive about people who didn't have to work? What values did he see in them that were better than the values of those setting and striving for their own goals? My father was a skilled, successful businessman but at no point did he ever sit Nits and I down and suggest we become the same. I was brought up to believe that marriage was the end goal. That an education was not only *not* sought-after, it was bordering on a disadvantage. Instead, we were expected to model ourselves on our purposeless mothers. The reason for this was that there was only room for one decision-maker in the marriages of my parents' day. Encouraging us to follow our mothers was a form of coercive control. An opinionated wife was not an ideal one and, if she had her own income too, that was a disaster waiting to happen. A free-thinking, determined, independent woman is not so easy to manipulate. What I gradually came to realise was that I didn't want what my mum had. I wanted what the boys had. I wanted a modern marriage but Sten and I were going to have to work out how to make one.

The rules of my social class said I shouldn't have amounted to anything. I'd grown up as a two-dimensional individual. A mannequin. When I'd met Alistair Blair I was put to good use and I excelled – it was just like being in the stables with Mick. I loved the feeling of being needed and working towards a goal. Of being a valued part of a team. Of striving for something more. And I was also bloody good at it. I actually had no reason to assume I wouldn't be. Whenever I'd been given something I cared about as a child, I was devoted to it, no matter how hard I had to work for it. Dandy was a silly old pony but he took hundreds of hours to care for, which I did with passion and vigour. The rewards were huge. A sense of achievement, satisfaction and feeling like I mattered to someone. In the end it was this feeling I followed rather than the signposts I'd been given by my parents. I forged my own path even when it meant going against the social mores of my class. It's only since writing this book and putting the words on paper that I've really seen this for what it is. I've always assumed that because so much was handed to me on a plate in my childhood, my career was given to me as well. It's been very gratifying to unravel my life and see that, actually, whatever career I had, I earned myself.

When I met my husband, I knew I didn't want to replicate the role my mother played in her marriage. There was no way I was going to fall in line behind my husband as the bread-winner and have the direction of our entire lives dictated by his goals. His were important, but only as important as mine. When I was presented with the opportunities afforded me by my career, there was no question in my mind – or his – I had to take them, any more than there were questions he should be allowed to take his. At the height of my career Sten sacri-ficed a huge amount for me. There aren't many men who'd

Not a bad pay-off for a few nights' work.

do what he did. Had I married a man like my father, my career would never have been possible but I married someone who gave me the freedom to pursue the things that made me happy and I count that as one of the greatest gifts of our relationship. Marriage wasn't the conclusion to my story; it was the beginning of a completely new one.

Peaceful Protest

But a marriage is not a straight-out-of-the-tin type of meal. It's more a slow-cooker recipe which, if you're lucky, gets better the longer it's in the pot. It also takes a bit of time to get the ingredients right. Little tweaks based on previous disasters are the key to a perfect recipe. I'm not sure there's really a secret to a good marriage but learning to accept compromise is probably one of the bigger hurdles. However bad things get, there's no sense puncturing the raft if you're going to go down with it, no matter how much you might hate your partner in that particular moment. Marriage *is* a form of incarceration. There's no point dressing it up. Yes, you've volunteered to do the time but the shortcomings are no less aggravating. When things get really bad in prison, inmates resort to a dirty protest to express their anger. In a marriage, since you'd invariably be the one to have to clean that up, passive aggression is a much more practical form of rebellion. My most sensational low came when I purposely peed in the bath before Sten got in after an especially infuriating row. The knowledge I'd done it saw me happily through the irritations of the next few days. It's the little highs that have kept my marriage alive.

I'm sure there are key points I've missed in this book but I put that down to the menopause. What I have remembered with absolute clarity is all the food I've eaten over the years, which I can pin down to time and place with startling precision. Of all the conclusions I've come to there is none bigger than the fact that I live to eat. If I ever go into a coma, I have no doubt that the best way to revive me will be to waft a plate of sausages under my nose. Preferably from Mr Taylor, the butcher in Bottesford.

Meet the parents.

Acknowledgements

Let's be clear. I didn't want to write this book. Never considered my life that interesting. It took the foresight of my agent, Caroline Michel at PFD, and the passion and enthusiasm of Louise Moore at Michael Joseph to lift this thing off the ground. With their combined glamour, ball-breaking expertise and unwavering support they have held my hand from beginning to end.

Ready For Absolutely Nothing would never have been written without my partner in prose, Charlotte Sones. For nine months we spoke daily – for hours – unravelling my past and unearthing the true meaning of memories I'd glossed over. She has been the curator of my life, a true representative for the reader in highlighting moments I considered mundane, but she found jaw-dropping. Without her the writing process would have been torturous. But I have never laughed as much as we did, or got those tingling flashes when we realised we'd hit a rich seam for me to expand upon. I cannot thank you enough, Char.

Strangely but fortuitously the crew at Penguin/Michael Joseph are all girls. This has without question been a team effort. Clare Parker and Ellie Hughes. Is there a media outlet you can't sweet talk into coming on side? You have worked to the bone, travelled the country and nearly died at the hands of a particularly erratic driver. At least we would have pegged it together. The ghostly powerhouse that is Vicky

Photiou. Thank you for your subtle but massively effective hand in marketing. Aggie Russell and Emma Henderson. There have been times when I've wanted to punch you both in the face for toning down extracts during the editing process. Annoyingly, and despite being young enough to be my daughters, you have always been right. Helen Eka I'm sure you were egging them on! Lee Motley what a cover you have designed. Stand out brilliant. Every photograph had to be cleared and this was down to the tireless work of Alice Chandler. You found photographs that I thought had been lost for life. All of you are the real powers behind this throne. You have kept multiple plates spinning and it has been a privilege to watch you all turn my scribblings into a piece of work I am truly proud of.

One of the reasons MJ were keen to publish *Ready For Absolutely Nothing* was the level of loyal engagement I have on my Instagram (never thought I'd write these words). With the help and guidance of Antonia Ralph my followers have grown from a measly 15,000 to 90,000. I'm praying that some of these followers might want to read a little more about a ropey life they can all identify with, even if on occasion it includes Her Majesty the Queen.

My family have taken absolutely no interest in this book but the writing of it has impacted their lives, be it no food in the fridge or ever-growing mounds of dirty laundry. Sten (aka Smell), Joe, Esme and Cece thank you for your patience and keeping my feet firmly on the ground. There aren't enough words to express my love for you.

Big thanks must go to Staines Magistrate Court for a six-month driving ban for totting up speeding points. If I hadn't been grounded, I believe delivery of the first manuscript would have been severely delayed. Unfortunately, this had a negative impact on Sten who had to take on the role of my taxi driver. No mean feat for someone who works ten hours a day and, unlike me, he didn't complain once. I couldn't consider life without you.

Without Nits' forensic memory so much would never have made it onto these pages. You are my protector, advisor and the best sister in the world.

Michael Foster, ever cautious, advised me not to write anything I wouldn't say to someone's face. That I call him a c**t in the book is testament to our abiding friendship. Foster, you are and will always be my barometer on how far I can push the envelope.

To my wise friends who gave their time to read early drafts – Trinny Woodall, David Furnish, Toby Constantine, Robbie Campbell, Prue Bertelsen, Dave Karger, Terry Clarke, Scott Hoffman, Victoria Cator, Helen, Ali McGougan, Sharon Combe, Alice Wingfield Digby, Kate Bush, Emma Rutland, Johnny Bergius, Beth and Georgia. Thank you for your critiques and observations.

And finally, despite Trinny Woodall and David Furnish being my two other husbands, your impact in my world could never have been given the justice it deserves. Our time together is too precious and too private to share.

Picture Credits

Every effort has been made to trace copyright holders and obtain their permission for use of copyright material. The publisher apologises for any errors or omissions and would be grateful to be notified of any corrections that should be incorporated in future editions of this book.

Endpapers © Terry O'Neill/Iconic Images

Integrated pictures 1, 3, 5, 6, 7, 8, 10, 11, 12, 16, 18, 19, 23, 29, 33, 34, 38, 44, 46, 48, 49, 50, 51, 54, 55, 56, 57 belong to Susannah Constantine.

Colour inset pictures 1, 2, 5, 6, 7, 8, 9, 10, 11, 12, 13, 14, 15, 16, 17, 18, 19, 20, 21, 22, 25, 28, 29, 31, 36, 37, 42, 43, 44, 47, 48, 49, 50, 51, 54, 55, 56, 57, 58, 59, 60, 63, 64, 65, 66, 67, 68, 69, 70, 71, 72 belong to Susannah Constantine.

Integrated pictures:

2. © Terry O'Neill/Iconic Images
4. © Colin Davey/Getty Images
9. © William Hustler and Georgina Hustler/National Portrait Gallery, London
13. © Tim Mercer
14. © TopFoto

15. © Desmond O'Neill
17. © Alan Davidson/Shutterstock
20. © Alan Davidson/Shutterstock
21. © Richard Young/Shutterstock
22. © Joan Williams/Shutterstock
24. © Lichfield/Getty
25. © Lichfield/Getty
26. © Lichfield/Getty
27. © Lichfield/Getty
28. © Tim Graham/Getty
31. © Anwar Hussein/Shutterstock
32. © Roxanne Lowit
35. © Yasmin Le Bon
36. © Shutterstock
37. © Slim Aarons/Stringer/Getty
39. © Richard Young/Shutterstock
40. © Alan Davidson/Shutterstock
41. © Alan Davidson/Shutterstock
42. © Alan Davidson/Shutterstock
43. © Terry O'Neill/Iconic Images
45. © David Munden/Popperfoto/Getty
47. © Terry O'Neill/Iconic Images
52. © Evan Hurd Photography/Getty
53. © Guy Levy/BBC Photo Archive

Colour inset pictures:

3. © AP/Shutterstock
4. © David Crump/Daily Mail/Shutterstock
23. © Capital Pictures

He just wanted a decent book to read ...

Not too much to ask, is it? It was in 1935 when Allen Lane, Managing Director of Bodley Head Publishers, stood on a platform at Exeter railway station looking for something good to read on his journey back to London. His choice was limited to popular magazines and poor-quality paperbacks – the same choice faced every day by the vast majority of readers, few of whom could afford hardbacks. Lane's disappointment and subsequent anger at the range of books generally available led him to found a company – and change the world.

'We believed in the existence in this country of a vast reading public for intelligent books at a low price, and staked everything on it'
Sir Allen Lane, 1902–1970, founder of Penguin Books

The quality paperback had arrived – and not just in bookshops. Lane was adamant that his Penguins should appear in chain stores and tobacconists, and should cost no more than a packet of cigarettes.

Reading habits (and cigarette prices) have changed since 1935, but Penguin still believes in publishing the best books for everybody to enjoy. We still believe that good design costs no more than bad design, and we still believe that quality books published passionately and responsibly make the world a better place.

So wherever you see the little bird – whether it's on a piece of prize-winning literary fiction or a celebrity autobiography, political tour de force or historical masterpiece, a serial-killer thriller, reference book, world classic or a piece of pure escapism – you can bet that it represents the very best that the genre has to offer.

Whatever you like to read – trust Penguin.